D1431705

Corporate and Investment Banking

Fidelio Tata

Corporate and Investment Banking

Preparing for a Career in Sales, Trading, and Research in Global Markets

Fidelio Tata
Berlin School of Economics and Law
Berlin, Germany

ISBN 978-3-030-44340-5   ISBN 978-3-030-44341-2   (eBook)
https://doi.org/10.1007/978-3-030-44341-2

This Palgrave Macmillan imprint is published by the registered company Springer Nature Switzerland AG
The registered company address is: Gewerbestrasse 11, 6330 Cham, Switzerland

Foreword

I am delighted to write the Foreword for this book by Fidelio Tata, my friend and colleague for some twenty-five years. This book is special for a number of reasons. First, Fidelio is uniquely placed to write it, as I have known and respected his ability as a finance professional while working with him on Wall Street. Second, the importance of this book arises from the fact that, to my knowledge, nothing quite like it has ever been written. I feel confident in this assessment, as I have been a finance professional myself, with over 35 years of experience across a wide range of business lines and activities, including positions as CIO at the World Bank, portfolio manager and proprietary trader at Caxton Associates, Goldman Sachs, Credit Suisse and JPMorgan, Chief Investment Advisor at Deutsche Bank, Partner at Brevan Howard and Head of Global Trading Strategies at UBS. Even with this background, I am surprised to see how much new material Fidelio's book covers, how much material that I had forgotten gets refreshed and how many useful details the book provides where my grasp was less than perfect and got reinforced. Books like this can be dry and hard to plough through, but this one is different. It will stay by my side for many, many years. I believe it is of great value to young students seeking a career in finance, to professionals curious about other parts of the business, to academicians who lack direct experience of the business, to policymakers and perhaps even to the general reader who is curious about what finance professionals do.

Fidelio has targeted young students and early career professionals, in particular, when writing this book. I still recall going to Wharton for my M.B.A. in 1983 (from a prior career in Real Estate) and being totally confused about the vast array of opportunities available across the finance industry. This book addresses such a need quite directly, and also the needs of young professionals looking to switch from one financial sector to another. I have been a portfolio manager, hedge fund/proprietary trader and have advised institutional and private clients and was delighted to see how accurately, and in simple language, Fidelio has described and explained all these functions. Like Fidelio, I have also been a teacher of economics and still recall how handicapped I felt not having experience in finance at the time to explain how policy actually transmits to the economy via the plumbing of the industry. Fidelio addresses this need too. During the Great Financial Crisis, and again during this COVID-19 pandemic, I noticed that policymakers, economists in particular, struggled to make policy tools more effective because they were not familiar with practical aspects of the business. Fidelio addresses this need as well. He has also brought to bear the perspective of several seasoned finance professionals, some of whom I have known for many years. Finally, by keeping the presentation jargon and acronym free, and providing useful exercises to check your knowledge, Fidelio has addressed the need of students and young professionals as well as the need of seasoned financial advisors who need to explain complex concepts (including dreaded Derivatives!) to their clients. Whether your perspective is that of a salesperson, portfolio manager or trader, researcher, or a student, Fidelio has addressed your need accurately and efficiently here.

I have kept this Foreword short for a very good reason; I don't want it to stand between you and this book. So dive in and enjoy reading it, and learning from it, as I did over the last several days.

Greenwich, CT, USA   Vinay Pande

Preface

The purpose of this book is threefold. First, the book helps aspiring Global Market employees to decide which part of the markets area is *best suited* for them. Some candidates are in the favorable position of been admitted to a graduate training program of a large, global bank during which all bank areas are covered; a job selection can be postponed until afterwards. However, only few banks are still offering such comprehensive (and expensive) training and instead expect job applicants to already know where their interest lies. In fact, one of the standard questions during a job interview is whether you view yourself more as a trader or as a salesperson. Answering "both," or "I don't know" does not sound particularly smart. Also, you may be expected to know roughly what each business unit is all about. A trader may ask you whether you have an idea what he or she is doing for a living. Answering "buying low and selling high" would be funny, but even better would be a reply including some specific aspects like electronic trading, market making or proprietary trading. Apart from helping you to look good (i.e., competent) during the interview process, this book supports you to identify areas where you can add most value, given your current interests and skills. Mid-career switches between, say, sales and trading are possible, and I have seen them, but they are actually quite rare. If you don't excel in one area, it is more likely that you get fired than that another opportunity is extended to you somewhere else within the organization. Thus, it is better to start right away where you have the most competitive advantages. But how can you make that decision without knowing all major aspects of the job? This book provides some guidance.

The second goal of this book is to provide some *desk-readiness*. Not all banks offer a practitioner-run training program that teaches the ins and outs on the trading floor, the market lingo, the market conventions and the basic understanding of used tools. You may just get placed next to an experienced Global Markets employee and asked to pick things up by observing. "Watch and learn"! This is a tough method of acquiring knowledge. The teacher, i.e., the senior market expert, may not be motivated, may have little didactic skills or simply not enough time to babysit you. Once you are put in the position to act based on what you have learned (or not), a seemingly small mistake may have huge financial consequences and could even cut your career short. This book also gives you some insights about which academic concepts and theories can be useful for your career in Global Markets. The ones discussed in this book have certainly helped me on an almost daily basis. You will eventually create your own, highly individual bag of tricks, but it does not hurt to start with a set of concepts that served other candidates in a similar position well.

The third purpose of this book is to help academic scholars identify *real-world applications* of financial market theory. For example, reference is provided to behavioral finance and to principal-agent theory throughout the book. A bachelor, master or Ph.D. student looking for empirical research topics will find plenty of ideas. Some of the largest financial market failures in recent history can be linked to conceptual misunderstandings about how the Global Markets business is conducted in the real world. Enhancing existing theoretical frameworks to better reflect the reality will hopefully lead to a better understanding, better regulation and better risk management in financial markets overall.

Berlin, Germany   Fidelio Tata

Acknowledgments

I like to acknowledge the critical comments and detailed subject matter suggestions by many former colleagues of mine I had the privilege and pleasure to work with, including Barry Cohen, Howard Corb, Alec Crawford, Brian Jones, Deep Kumar, Richard Leibovitch, Michael O'Leary, Peter Mullany, Jorge Portugal, Jérôme Sabah, Stella Stoyanova, Werner Weingraber and Paul Younes. Of course, all remaining errors are mine.

I am grateful to Peter Joel, Fabrice Pilato and Vincent Chaigneau for adding their perspective as seasoned practitioners to the sales, trading and research chapters.

While not directly contributing to the book, many additional former colleagues of mine at JPMorgan, Credit Suisse, HSBC, RBS Greenwich Capital and Societe General helped me understand financial markets and their products. It is impossible to list them all. I am particularly grateful having worked with David Ader, Ralph Axel, Alexandre Babadjamian, John Bates, Chad Brandt, Philippe Buhannic, Michael Cloherty, Neil Cooper, Bruce Cook, Vikram Dongre, Ken Ford, Tim Graf, Dominic Konstam, Mikko Koskinen, Avi Kwalwasser, Herman Laret, Michael Lyublinsky, Jason Manske, Craig Martone, James Mather, George Oomman, Robert Rakich, David Scicolone, Gagan Singh, Neil Smith, Ken Sullivan, Zsolt Szollosi, Andreas Thommen, Eric Workman, Albert Yu and Kashif Zafar.

Many thanks to my editors at Palgrave Macmillan, Tula Weis and Lucy Kidwell, and the production team, headed by Shukkanthy Siva.

I like to thank the following for permission to reproduce copyright material: Fig. 4.1 from Douglas Healey/Polaris; Fig. 6.1 from Orbital Insight; Table 3.3 adapted from SWF Institute. Every effort has been made to trace copyright holders, but if any have been overlooked, I will be pleased to make the necessary corrections at the first opportunity.

The work was partly supported by the Berlin School of Economics and Law.

About This Book

The origin of this book can be traced to material I collected when running JPMorgan's derivative training program in 1996–1997. Over time, it developed into a broader set of training material that I used while working as a derivative marketer, fixed income salesperson and interest rate strategist on Wall Street. It is also partially based on the *Investment Banking* and *Capital Markets* courses I have been teaching at Berlin School of Economics and Law for the past years.

Other books cover various aspects discussed in this book, and the goal is not to replace them, rather than to develop a framework within which they can be used to supplement and enhance the analysis. There are excellent books that give an overview about financial markets and their market participants. *Financial Markets and Institutions* by de Haan et al. (2015), *Financial Institutions, Markets, and Money* by Kidwell et al. (2017), *Financial Markets and Institutions* by Mishkin and Eakins (2018) and *Global Banking* by Smith et al. (2012) belong to this class of literature. However, those books typically lack the trading floor-specific aspects of conducting sales, trading and research business in a client-specific situation. Then there are books dedicated to particular financial instruments, especially their modeling, pricing and risk management. *Options, Futures, and Other Derivatives* by Hull (2018) is probably the most famous one when it comes to derivative theory. For trading, *Algorithmic Trading* and *Quantitative Trading* by Chan (2009 and 2013, respectively) and *Algorithmic Trading & DMA* by Johnson (2010) may serve as examples. Those books, however, do not span the entire spectrum of Global Market business and better serve for a deep dive into a specific topic. Finally, there are some very good books by academic-turned-practitioners or practitioner-turned-academics that combine theory and practice, similarly to what this book is aiming to do. Those books include *Interest Rate Swaps and Other Derivatives* by Corb (2012) and *Fixed Income Securities* by Tuckman (2012). What those books don't do, though, is treating sales, trading and research as three distinct business areas that require an individual treatment.

The distinction between sales, trading and research is still widely underrated in academic circles. When global market employees introduce themselves to each other, pretty much the first thing they mention after their name is which of those three business areas they belong to. "Hi. I'm Peter Miller. *Rates Sales* at JPMorgan." Yet, most textbooks are agnostic about whether the discussed products or concepts are applied to a sales, trading or research environment. This book takes a different approach. It views products, markets, market participants and finance theory differently from a sales, trading and research point of view. As a consequence, you will read multiple times about the same product throughout the book. Take repo as an example. A repo transaction can have a very different meaning to a salesperson (e.g., an indicator for suggesting bond switches to real money investors), to a trader (e.g., specifying the funding levels for the trading book) and to a research analyst (e.g., help predicting CTD switches in the deliverable basket of a futures contract).

A career in Global Markets begins with a rapid acquisition of knowledge about products, markets, market participants and financial theory. Because those four dimensions are interconnected, there is no obvious order in the process. In academic circles, there is often the focus on one single dimension (say, a graduate course on financial markets, a textbook for derivative products, or an article about hedge funds). On the trading floor, however, one picks up knowledge "en passant," constantly jumping between markets, products, market participants and theoretical concepts. This is actually not a bad way to learn. It ensures that the most needed skills (depending on the specific job position) are developed first. It also creates a quick overview, so that there is less of a risk of missing the forest for the trees. This book applies the same piecemeal approach to picking up knowledge. A particular client situation is given. Now you need to learn about the products involved. Do you use this opportunity to learn about *all* products? No, because there is not enough time. That's why product knowledge is sprinkled throughout the book, introduced only when needed.

Sometimes the book does not explain a technical topic or a financial product in detail until after it had been mentioned a few times before. This is by design. It would unnecessarily bog down the flow if every single financial market term needed to be detailed the very first time it gets mentioned. Also, after making mention of not-yet properly explained terms in the context of concrete sales, trading or research settings, the awareness of their relevance is boosted, and the anticipated explanation is later on absorbed more easily. This also reflects to some degree the learning process in the financial markets. You won't run into the library to look up "repo" the first time someone mentions that term, but after it had come up a couple of times in your day-to-day dealings, you will surely seek to understand it.

The book is organized as follows. After a brief introduction in Chapter 1, Chapter 2 provides a broad overview about the banking business, including the main areas of global banking. Chapter 3 then discusses the financial markets' main markets participants, as well as selected fundamental academic concepts in finance. Chapters 4–6 take a deep dive into the three distinct areas of Global Markets: *Sales*, *trading* and *research*. Chapter 7 covers *derivatives* separately, because they are part of all three Global Markets segments and deserve an individual look. The book ends with a list of exercises in Chapter 8.

References

Chan, Ernest P. 2009. *Quantitative Trading: How to Build Your Own Algorithmic Trading Business*. Hoboken, NJ: Wiley.

Chan, Ernest P. 2013. *Algorithmic Trading: Winning Strategies and Their Rationale*. Hoboken, NJ: Wiley.

Corb, Howard. 2012. *Interest Rate Swaps and Other Derivatives*. New York, Chichester: Columbia University Press.

de Haan, Jakob, Dirk Schoenmaker, and Sander Oosterloo. 2015. *Financial Markets and Institutions: A European Perspective*. Cambridge, UK: Cambridge University Press.

Hull, John C. 2018. *Options, Futures, and Other Derivatives*. Boston, MA: Pearson Prentice Hall.

Johnson, Barry. 2010. *Algorithmic Trading & DMA: An Introduction to Direct Access Trading Strategies*. London, UK: 4Myeloma Press.

Kidwell, David S., David W. Blackwell, David A. Whidbee, and Richard W. Sias. 2017. *Financial Institutions, Markets, and Money*. Hoboken, NJ: Wiley.

Mishkin, Frederic S., and Stanley G. Eakins. 2018. *Financial Markets and Institutions*. Boston, MA: Pearson Prentice Hall.

Smith, Roy C., Ingo Walter, and Gayle DeLong. 2012. *Global Banking*. Oxford, UK: Oxford University Press.

Tuckman, Bruce. 2012. *Fixed Income Securities : Tools for Today's Markets*. Hoboken, NJ: Wiley.

Contents

About the Author

Fidelio Tata is a senior market structure specialist with deep understanding of global financial markets. He has over 25 years of executive experience in derivatives marketing, institutional sales, risk management and global fixed income research. During 17 years on Wall Street, he developed an in-depth familiarity with a US and European client base consisting of hedge funds, real money and sovereign investors, with a strong appreciation of the many nuances of client requirements.

Fidelio has broad teaching experience that includes the development of J. P. Morgan's global derivatives training program, acting as frequent guest-speaker at conferences and trainer in asset and liability management to central banks, as well as 5 years of academic teaching at the Berlin School of Economics and Law (HWR). He received his own academic education at the University of St. Gallen, the London School of Economics and Political Science, the New York University Stern School of Business and the Harvard University.

Fidelio demonstrated leadership and management responsibilities as a managing director on Wall Street and as a senior market expert at a management consulting company.

Fidelio lives in Berlin and has one daughter.

List of Contributors

Vincent Chaigneau

Head of Research and Group Investment Strategy at Generali

Vincent Chaigneau is an experienced strategist with over 25 years of experience in both, sell-side and buy-side research. He spent some 24 years between Paris, New York and London, serving as the co-head of global fixed income research and global head of rates & FX strategy at a major European universal bank. Since 2017, he assumes the position of head of research at a global asset manager. Vincent holds a Master's and a postgraduate degree in Economics and Finance from the University of Bordeaux. He lives in Paris and has four children.

Peter Joel

Director at BNY Mellon

Peter Joel is a seasoned sales professional with 25 years of experience in marketing interest rate and derivative products to institutional clients at various top-tier universal banks in New York, including JPMorgan and Credit Suisse. He holds an M.B.A. from Wharton, lives in New Jersey and has five children.

Fabrice Pilato

Managing Director at Morgan Stanley

Fabrice Pilato is an experienced trading professional with over 25 years of experience in trading interest rate and derivative products, both in the capacity as a flow and as a proprietary trader and is global head of xVA. He holds an M.B.A. from Cornell, lives in New York and has two children.

Abbreviations

APM	Arbitrage pricing model
ATM	At-the-money
AUM	Assets under management
bn	Billion
bp	Basis point (0.01%), or basis points
CAPM	Capital asset pricing model
CIB	Corporate and investment bank(ing)
CIR	Cost income ratio
CRM	Corporate risk management
CSA	Credit support annex
DCF	Discounted cash flow
DCM	Debt capital markets
DV01	Dollar value of a basis point (pronounced dee-vee-ohh-one)
e.g.	Exempli gratia (for example)
ECM	Equity capital markets
EMH	Efficient-market hypothesis
et al.	Et alii (and others)
ETF	Exchange-traded fund
EUR	Euro
Fed	Federal reserve
FHLB	Federal home loan bank
FICC	Fixed income, currencies and commodities
FOMC	Federal open market committee
fwd	Forward
FX	Foreign exchange
G10	Group of Ten
GSE	Government-sponsored enterprise

HNW	High net worth
i.e.	Id est (in other words)
IBD	Investment banking division
IPO	Initial public offering
ISDA	International swaps and derivatives association
LIBOR	London interbank offered rate
LR	leverage ratio
M&A	Mergers and acquisitions
mm	Million
NPV	Net present value
OTC	Over the counter
P&L	Profit and loss
prop	Proprietary (as in "proprietary trading")
PV	Present value
SEC	Securities and exchange commission
UHNW	Ultra-high net worth
USD	US dollar
VaR	Value at risk
vol	Volatility

List of Figures

List of Tables

1

Introduction

The Global Market business is huge in almost every dimension. It intermediates an estimated $250 trillion in global funds.[1] An approximate one-quarter of a million employees work on trading floors (some populated by around 5000 traders) in financial centers around the world.[2] Bonus payments, the variable part of employees' compensation, on Wall Street alone are in excess of $30 billion in 2017,[3] of which Global Markets accounts for a significant part. Earnings (or net income), globally, are probably to the tune of $50–60 billion, exceeding that of the (as of 2019) most-valued (i.e., capitalized) publicly traded company in the world, Microsoft.

Global Markets units of major universal banks service large corporations and financial institutions with respect to traded assets, derivatives and structured products. Financial institutions are institutional investors that include governments, asset managers, pension funds and hedge funds. Traded assets are pretty much anything that can be bought and sold in the financial markets, including stocks, bonds, currencies, credit products and commodities. Derivatives and structured products are contractual agreements that synthetically create financial claims. To better serve financial institution, Global Markets is divided into sales, trading and research. Sales has the client-facing function of identifying and serving institutional clients' needs, trading creates a marketplace for assets by standing ready to buy and sell, and research aims at providing analysis and insight that facilitates the clients' investment process.[4]

Starting a career in Global Markets can be challenging because of the breadth and depth of knowledge required. Ironically, it is often easier to

© The Author(s) 2020
F. Tata, *Corporate and Investment Banking*,
https://doi.org/10.1007/978-3-030-44341-2_1

get away with a gap of knowledge when you are already a seasoned, highly specialized market participant than when you are about to start your career. It is perfectly acceptable for a senior bond trader to know near to nothing about options. But when a job candidate does not know the difference between a call option and a put option in an entry-level interview, it looks bad.

Expertise in the context of Global Market business is often a combination of market knowledge, understanding of market participants, product knowledge and financial market theories or techniques. For example, a client conversation with a hedge fund about swaption-implied distribution assumptions requires some knowledge about the over the counter (OTC) swap and swaption market,[5] about how hedge funds use derivatives, about options and about option theory (see Fig. 1.1).

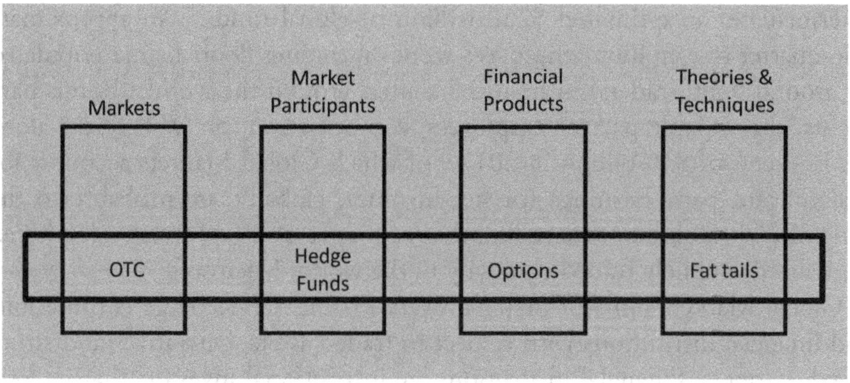

Markets	Market Participants	Financial Products	Theories & Techniques
OTC	Hedge Funds	Options	Fat tails

Fig. 1.1   Combination of Global Market knowledge areas

The Global Markets business is very transaction oriented. Motivating examples, anecdotes, case studies and exercises will be used extensively throughout the book. They help applying conceptional knowledge to specific trades and client interactions.

Financial theory not only allows to better understand the interaction of market participants in financial markets but can also be a useful tool when conducting business in Global Markets. A few key concepts of financial theory will be introduced and applied to specific job-related situations in sales, trading and research throughout the book.

Notes

1. Source: McKinsey & Company (2018).
2. Estimating the total number of employees in Global Markets is not easy because banks typically do not provide an employee breakdown for individual business areas. The one-quarter of a million estimate is established as follows: JPMorgan reports in its 2018 annual report a CIB headcount of 54,480. CIB includes investment banking, and it is assumed that the Global Markets area accounts for roughly 30,000 employees. According to *Dealogic* (as of January 1, 2019), JPMorgan has a market share of 11.6% in Global Markets. Thus, the total number of Markets employees of all banks is roughly 30,000/0.116, or 258,620.
3. Source: Office of the New York State Comptroller (2018).
4. Not part of Global Markets is investment banking, which is mostly advisory with respect to mergers and acquisitions (M&A), capital-raising activities (such as initial public offerings, or IPOs) and corporate finance risk solutions. Not part of Global Markets either is anything targeted to non-institutional investors, such as retail customers or ultra-high net worth individuals.
5. Swaps are derivative products in which two parties exchange cash flows based on some variables. Swaptions are derivative products that give the holder the right, but not the obligation, to enter into an agreed-upon swap transaction.

References

McKinsey & Company. 2018. Banks in the Changing World of Financial Intermediation. November 2018 Report. https://www.mckinsey.com/industries/financial-services/our-insights/banks-in-the-changing-world-of-financial-inter-mediation. Accessed on January 20, 2020.

Office of the New York State Comptroller. 2018. NYS Comptroller DiNapoli: Wall Street Profits and Bonuses Up Sharply in 2017. News from the office of the New York State Comptroller, March 26, 2017. https://www.osc.state.ny.us/press/releases/mar18/032618.htm. Accessed on January 20, 2020.

2

A Taxonomy of the Banking Business

Before starting a career in Global Markets, it is advisable to look left and right to see what else is going on in a universal bank. Maybe you find something more interesting, such as mergers and acquisitions, in which case you may as well put down this book now. But even if you end up sticking with sales, trading and research, you'll find that similar functions are also provided in other areas of the bank, e.g., in wealth management. This is important to know because not only do those areas create potential career transition opportunities in the future but knowing your "counterparts" in other areas of the bank will help you to network and to exchange ideas.

Universal banks do offer a wide spectrum of services, and their organizational setup reflects that. We will see later that the catalyst for today's banking giants is the repeal of the Glass-Steagall legislation in the USA. Between 1933 and 1999, commercial and investment banks were artificial separated by law, but afterward banks were no longer restricted from offering their clients any type of banking service. In banking, like in most other industries, it is important to "follow your customer" and to become a one-stop shop for all services required.

There are a number of reasons why formally specialized banks eventually turned into giant flow monsters that are engaged in the whole spectrum of banking services: First, some banking activities are natural offsets, or hedges, to each other. Corporate customers may be interested in buying protection against an increase in interest rates (e.g., interest rate caps[1]), while retail customers may buy structured products that include selling protection against higher interest rates as a mean to create some sort of yield pickup. In this

© The Author(s) 2020
F. Tata, *Corporate and Investment Banking*,
https://doi.org/10.1007/978-3-030-44341-2_2

case, there is a two-way flow between retail and institutional banking that allows the bank as an intermediary to earn a commission without assuming much risk on their own book. Second, clients have become somewhat spoiled in the sense that they expect from their bank relationship manager to provide a solution to all of their banking problems, rather than having to shop around. Institutional bank clients typically limit their banking relationships to few hand-selected financial services providers.[2] Third, there is always the risk to lose customer business if one has to direct the customer to a competitor for those areas where no service is provided. The competitor will likely pressure the customer to do the whole package with them. Sometimes it is better to offer all financial services, even if some of them are not profitable for the bank, to avoid this kind of situation.

Since the financial crisis of 2007–2008, *some* banks have reversed course and chose to become niche players again (e.g., in asset and wealth management). But the majority of banks engaged in Global Markets activities are still offering services in other areas of banking, so it is worthwhile to look at the entire playing field of banking.

Each universal bank has a slightly different organizational setup, but the overall structure is very similar. Figure 2.1 illustrates the organization of an archetypical universal bank.

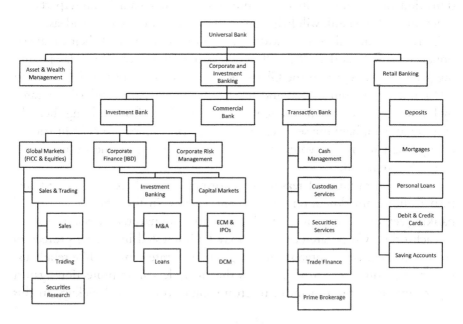

Fig. 2.1 Illustrative organization of an archetypical universal bank

2.1   Asset and Wealth Management

Asset and wealth management is one of the growth areas of universal banking and many banks have been trying to grow this area since the financial crisis of 2007–2008. Wealth management services benefit from a consistent growth of global wealth (see Fig. 2.2). Measured in current US dollars, total global wealth rose from $117 trillion in 2000 to over $360 trillion in mid-2019,[3] a rise of $243 trillion, equivalent to roughly three times global GDP. The USA accounts for roughly half of the global wealth creation, followed by Europe with roughly one-quarter. What makes asset and wealth management so attractive for banks is that it is a relatively stable source of income (less cyclical than other parts of banking) and is less balance sheet intensive than, say, trading.

Asset and wealth management not only focuses on institutional investors, but also on so-called ultra-high net worth (UHNW) individuals, typically defined as individuals with a net worth of $50 million or more (while high net worth, or HNW, individuals have "only" a net wealth between $1 mm and $50 mm). The number of UHNW individuals increased by more than 100,000 since the financial crisis of 2007–2008. The USA leads the ranking of the richest people in the world, followed by China, Germany, the UK, France and Australia. However, a lot of the *new* ultra-rich people are from lower-income countries. Emerging nations are now home to 22% of

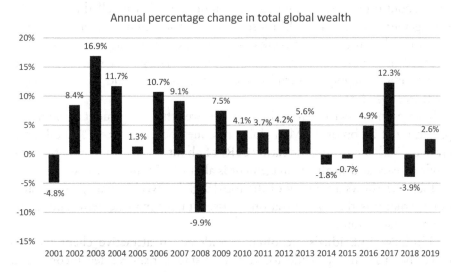

Fig. 2.2 Global wealth keeps increasing (Data based on: Hechler-Fayd'herbe 2019, 135)

the world's UHNW population. According to Forbes, China is home to 324 billionaires, more than half the 607 billionaires living in the USA.[4]

There is now a widespread recognition of the high concentration of wealth in the world. As of 2019, the richest 1% of the world's population control roughly 45% of the world's total global wealth, while the bottom half own less than 1% of the total global wealth.[5] What is less known, however, is that even within the exclusive group of UHNW individuals, there is a massive concentration of wealth. As of mid-2019, there are roughly 168,000 UHNW individuals; of these, almost 56,000 are worth at least $100 million, and about 4800 have assets above $500 million.[6] What this implies for the asset and wealth management business is that there is a massive competition for covering the richest of the UHNW individuals, multi-billionaires essentially, making it a winner-takes-all industry.

It is worth looking at what *kind* of wealth is managed by wealth managers. For example, a wide definition of wealth includes human capital. Human capital, however, is typically not managed by a bank's asset and wealth management group.[7] According to estimates by the World Bank, global wealth equates to some $1143 trillion[8] (i.e., more than one quadrillion dollars!). However, besides produced capital, this includes natural capital (e.g., forests, agricultural land or energy resources), human capital and net foreign assets. Produced capital is only about 27% of that, some $303.5 trillion.[9] But even that amount is not the basis for asset management because roughly two-thirds of it are assets that are not actively managed. Only about one-third, or some $100 trillion, are what is called assets under management, or AUM.[10] Off those roughly $100 trillion AUM, some 20% are owned by customers of bank's asset and wealth management units, i.e., so-called mass affluent, high net worth and ultra-high net worth investors. This creates a roughly $20 trillion basis for global asset and wealth management (see Fig. 2.3).

If we estimate net revenues in asset and wealth management to be in the proximity of 25 bp of AUM, a global revenue pocket of about $50 billion is created. With a cost income ratio (CIR) of about 66%,[11] the estimated total profit of asset and wealth management is about $17 billion annually.

Table 2.1 shows a ranking of the top-10 global wealth managers. What is quite striking is the concentration of assets under management among the top 3–5 institutions.

(U)HNW individuals are often considered an attractive client base to banks because they provide for relatively stable, risk-free fee income and are less price sensitive and competitive compared to institutional investors. Perceived benefits of dealing with (U)HNW individuals include:

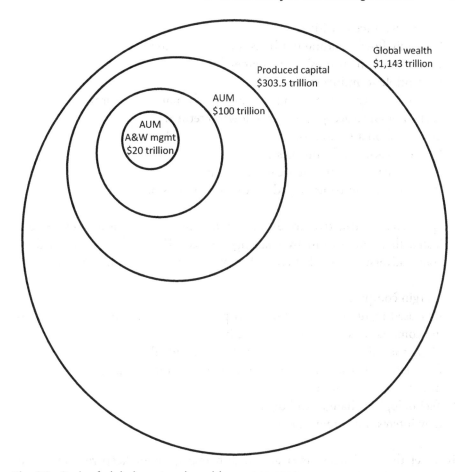

Fig. 2.3 Basis of global asset and wealth management

Table 2.1 Global ranking of wealth managers

Ranking 2019	Institution	AUM 2019 ($ billion)
1	UBS Global Wealth Management	2432
2	Bank of America GWIM	1126
3	Morgan Stanley Wealth Management	1116
4	Credit Suisse	790
5	JPMorgan Private Bank	597
6	Goldman Sachs	482
7	Citi Private Bank	460
8	BNP Paribas Wealth Management	423
9	Julius Baer	429
10	HSBC Private Bank	335

Source Szmigiera (2019)

- Often less price sensitive;
- "Friendly flow" (trading not based on superior knowledge);
- Can be sold on "stories" and "themes"[12];
- Susceptible to inducements;
- Tax- and safety-arguments may trump performance measures;
- Rich enough to accept periods of low/no return;
- Tend to shop around less;
- Mostly (risk-free) fee business;
- Less restricted in what they can invest in;
- Relationship can be leveraged for other bank businesses.

Despite overall attractive conditions in the asset and wealth management industry, there are also many challenges ahead. The business is plagued by the same adverse factors that create headwinds for banking in general:

- Margin compression;
- Increased regulation (e.g., MiFID II preventing asset managers from paying commissions to incentivize distributors);
- Higher sophistication among (U)HNW individuals;
- Economies of scale in the asset and wealth management industry causes further concentration;
- Technological changes and digitalization;
- Low interest rate environment.

To meet the challenges, asset and wealth management keep relying on an increasing IT infrastructure that creates significant fixed cost and creates scale economies for large market participants.

Since one of the most difficult parts in developing an asset and wealth management franchise is to get the (U)HNW clients' mandate to manage their assets, asset and wealth managements units tend to collocate close to their customer base. And because rich individuals have the means to establish their home base in the most pleasant places in the world, offices of asset and wealth management groups can be found at exotic places like Palm Beach (Florida), Dubai (UAE) or in St. Moritz (Swiss ski resort).[13]

2.2   Corporate and Investment Banking

Corporate and investment banking brings together investment banking, commercial banking, and transaction banking expertise under one common corporate division. CIB advises and executes on the multiple financial requirements of corporate clients and institutional investors. CIB units are large and complex divisions within a universal bank that, for operational reasons, still consist of individual subdivisions specializing on a narrow mandate.

2.2.1 Investment Bank

Unlike asset and wealth management that is targeted to wealthy *individuals*, the investment banking area is set up to serve the needs of large *corporate* customers and financial *institutions*. Financial institutions are institutional investors that include governments, asset managers, pension funds and hedge funds. Because there is less of a need to be in close proximity to institutional investors' corporate headquarters and their financial units,[14] investment banks tend to set up their tent in financial market centers (New York, London, Frankfurt, etc.) to benefit from nearby financial market infrastructure (stock exchanges, law firms, IT services, etc.). Also, many institutional investors have set up their financial business unit in a financial market center to be better covered by financial service providers (including banks).

Table 2.2 shows a ranking of the top-10 investment banks. The top five spots are occupied by the biggest US investment banks.

The investment bank can be further broken into three parts: Global Markets, corporate finance and corporate risk management (CRM). The *Global Markets* area deals with financial markets' products that are already trading in the market. *Corporate Finance* deals with transactions not executed in the financial markets or those leading to the creation of new financial products. *Corporate Risk Management* deals with techniques and strategies to measure and to reduce various risks.

Table 2.2 Global ranking of investment banks

Global ranking 2018	Institution
1	JPMorgan
2	Goldman Sachs
3	Citi
4	Morgan Stanley
5	Bank of America Merrill Lynch
6	Deutsche Bank
7	Barclays
8	Credit Suisse
9	HSBC
10	UBS

Source Damyanova (2019)

2.2.1.1 Global Markets

The Global Markets area deals with financial markets' products that are already trading in the market. It combines (institutional) sales, trading and (investment) research across bonds, equities and equity-linked products, exchange-traded and over the counter derivatives, foreign exchange, money market instruments, and structured products. Research provides analysis of markets, products and trading strategies for institutional investors.

Global markets typically comprise of two distinct areas: FICC and Equity. FICC stands for Fixed Income, Currencies and Commodities and includes credit (investment and sub-investment grade bonds, loans, emerging markets, exotic and structured debt), developed market (or, "G10") rates (e.g., government and municipal bonds, swaps, short term interest rates, money markets, repo), G10 foreign exchange (FX), commodities, emerging markets and securitized products.[15] Equities include cash equities and equity derivatives.

In Global Markets units, three key competencies are combined. First, Global Markets, as the name already implies, has to provide market knowledge. This includes an intimate understanding of different market channels (exchange-traded, over the counter, electronic vs. voice execution, etc.) as well as global market locations. Second, a thorough understanding of the particular needs of various client groups must be demonstrated. And finally, there needs to be significant knowledge about all relevant financial market products.

2.2.1.2 Corporate Finance

Corporate finance, also called Investment Banking Division (IBD), deals with transactions not executed in the financial markets or those leading to the creation of new financial products. Unlike the Global Markets area, analysis is primarily based on cash-flow analysis and other corporate finance techniques, rather than on observable market prices. It concerns itself mostly with the client's liability side of the balance sheet, i.e., the amount of and ratio between equity and debt capital.

The corporate finance area can be divided into two sub-areas. First, there is investment banking in the narrow sense, which assists in mergers, acquisitions and sales of business units or entire corporation (often referred to summarily as mergers and acquisitions, or M&A), as well as the restructuring of (typically high-yield) loans. Second, there is a capital markets group, performing capital origination services, including issuance of equity capital in Equity Capital Markets (ECM) and issuance of debt capital in Debt Capital Markets (DCM). If publicly traded equity capital is created for the first time, it is called an Initial Public Offering (IPO).

2.2.1.3 Corporate Risk Management

Corporate risk management (CRM) deals with techniques and strategies to measure and to reduce various risks. Arguably the most famous CRM group was JPMorgan's unit which developed in the late 1980s a firm-wide *Value at risk* (VaR) system that became the so-called 4-15 ("four-fifteen") report submitted to the CEO Dennis Weatherstone at 4:15 p.m. every day.

CRM services are applied internally to manage a bank's risk exposure (which is also required by regulators), and also utilized in client relationships to help manage a customer's risk exposure (often with the purpose of conducting the resulting risk mitigation trades for the client afterward). There are multiple sources of risk, including interest rate risk, exchange rate risk, default risk and liquidity risk that need to be addressed as part of a comprehensive risk management process.

2.2.2 Commercial Bank

Commercial banking provides services to of businesses, from small enterprises and mid-market companies to large multinationals.[16] Banking services include trade and receivables finance, global liquidity and cash management, multi-currency accounts, commercial cards, overdrafts, working capital finance, insurance, term loans and syndicated, leveraged, acquisition, project finance, real estate business and international banking. Commercial banking focuses on so-called relationship lending; long-term ongoing relationships between the bank and its clients are the basis for building a loan book. Sometimes, loan book-business is not profitable by itself and rather the basis to offer additional banking services (e.g., derivative hedges) on top of the lending business. In contrast, investment banking often focuses on so-called transaction lending. Here, the ability to price a deal and to have the distribution power are the main selling points.[17]

There is some overlap between investment and commercial banking; large corporate customers may fall in either category.[18] Unlike in investment banking, commercial banking is typically provided in regional networks to better adapt to the regional specifics and to be close to the clients.

The separation between commercial and investment banking is an artificial one, triggered by law. Responsible is the Glass–Steagall legislation that describes four provisions of the US Banking Act of 1933. The 1999 Gramm–Leach–Bliley Act repealed the provisions restricting affiliations between banks and securities firms.

After the repeal of the Glass-Steagall Act in 1999, there was little reason to keep the artificial separation between investment and commercial banking alive. Most former (pure) investment banks merged with commercial banks or, if they already have been the investment banking arm of a commercial bank, adopted the commercial bank's branding. Former investment banks often had the know-how (derivative expertise, etc.), while commercial banks had the "balance sheet" (i.e., capital), making a combination attractive.

Many pure investment banks failed or needed to be bailed out in the wake of the financial crisis of 2007–2008; talent quickly found a new home in commercial banks seeking to enhance their investment banking footprint The last two remaining large investment banks, Goldman Sachs and Morgan Stanley, became bank holding companies in 2008[19] (see Fig. 2.4).

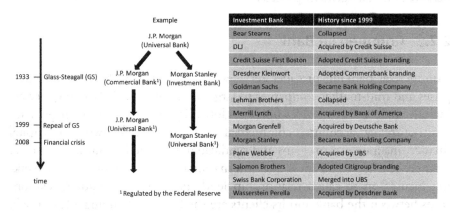

Fig. 2.4 Impact of Glass-Steagall Act and developments since its repeal

2.2.3 Transaction Bank

Transaction banking supports the safe and efficient movement of cash and securities around the global financial system. This includes cash management (support of clients' treasury functions like liquidity management, payment and collections), custodian services (safekeeping of assets for clients in multiple jurisdictions, settlement and tax services), security services (payment and administration services), trade finance (international, cross-border trade financing and risk management services) and prime brokerage (bundled package of services for hedge funds that need the ability to borrow securities and cash).

2.3   Retail Banking

Retail banking (also known as consumer banking or community banking) offers its (retail) customers standardized banking and financial service products designed to meet all basic financial needs. Its core products are deposits (taking customer deposits for short contractual maturities, i.e., sight or overnight deposits), saving accounts, mortgage loans (collateralized lending), personal loans (uncollateralized consumer loans) and debit/credit cards. The product range is sometimes completed by standardized investment products (especially investment funds) and insurance products.

Retail banking has turned into a multi-channel business, including branches, self-service terminals, call centers, online and mobile banking.

Historically, retail banking generated term-transformation results (borrowing at a low interest rate and lending out at a high rate).

Notes

1. An interest rate cap is a derivative instrument in which the holder receives periodic payments if interest rates exceed an agreed-upon level.
2. For example, dealing with a contract partner in over the counter (OTC) derivatives typically requires to put agreements in place first, a process that is time-consuming and costly. Those agreements are based on templates provided by the International Swaps and Derivatives Association (ISDA) and include the ISDA Master Agreement and the Credit support annex (CSA).
3. Credit Suisse (2019, 5).
4. Forbes (2019).
5. Credit Suisse (2019, 2).
6. Credit Suisse (2019, 12).
7. There could be exceptions, though. For example, a Chinese UHNW individual may ask the wealth manager to invest into certain assets in the USA that qualify for the federal EB-5 investment visa program, making his or her children eligible for a green card and ultimately citizenship that allows them to attend college in the USA.

8. Lange et al. (2018, 44).
9. Lange et al. (2018, 47).
10. Calculations based on PwC (2017), Shub et al. (2016) and author's own data and approximations. The fact that about half of global assets are not under management yet provides for further growth opportunities of asset and wealth management (increasing the penetration rate).
11. Carrubba et al. (2019, 4).
12. However, over time (U)HNW individuals have become increasingly more professional and demand to be treated just like institutional investors. It simply no longer suffices to "wine and dine" them.
13. Some rich individuals also live in London (e.g., Russian oligarchs), Zurich or New York, i.e., places where Global Markets units of the bank are also located.
14. Personal contact with institutional decision makers is still important, but a great deal of interaction takes place via email or telephone, and for the remaining contact needs a visit can be scheduled.
15. Including Asset Backed Securities (ABS), Commercial Mortgage Backed Securities (CMBS), Residential Mortgage Backed Securities (RMBS) and Collateralized Debt Obligations (CDO).
16. See also Kidwell et al. (2017, 363–420).
17. Commercial banks are often "balance sheet-monsters" and can take down large deals/loans; investment banks tend to be nimbler and aim at off-loading risks in the market quickly. Commercial banks profit from owning an asset and wealth management business, into which deals can be placed (especially those that don't sell well in the market); investment banks, on the other hand, have deep derivative, structuring and advisory expertise. Because both commercial banking and investment banking expertise are needed, universal banks combine commercial and investment banking expertise under one roof.
18. It is not unusual that bank customers' transition from one client segment into another and that there is competition between bank units for the same client. A client may start out as a retail customer, develops a business and receives commercial banking services, experiences an increase in wealth and becomes a client of asset and wealth management and ultimately grows the business to a multinational organization, to be covered by investment banking.
19. Being a bank holding company, regulated by the Federal Reserve, has the strategic advantage of creating access to the emergency discount window open only to commercial banks.

References

Carrubba, Joe, Renaud Fages, Dean Frankle, Benoît Macé, George Rudolph, Thomas Schulte, and Qin Xu. 2019. How Asset Managers Can Win in a Winner-Takes-All World. Boston Consulting Group, May. http://image-src. bcg.com/Images/BCG-How-Asset-Managers-Can-Win-in-a-Winner-Takes-All-World-May-2019-R_tcm9-219356.pdf. Accessed on January 20, 2020.

Credit Suisse. 2019. Credit Suisse Global Wealth Report 2019. https://www.credit-suisse.com/media/assets/corporate/docs/about-us/research/publications/global-wealth-report-2019-en.pdf. Accessed on January 20, 2020.

Damyanova, Vanya. 2019. JPMorgan Tops 2018 Global i-Bank Ranking; Deutsche Stable: Credit Suisse Down. S&P Global Market Intelligence, March 20, 2019. https://www.spglobal.com/marketintelligence/en/news-insights/latest-news-headlines/50672572. Accessed on January 20, 2020.

Forbes. 2019. Billionaires: The Richest People in the World. https://www.forbes.com/billionaires/list. Accessed on January 20, 2020.

Hechler-Fayd'herbe, Nannette. 2019. Credit Suisse Global Wealth Databook 2019. https://www.credit-suisse.com/media/assets/corporate/docs/about-us/research/publications/global-wealth-databook-2019.pdf. Accessed on January 20, 2020.

Kidwell, David S., David W. Blackwell, David A. Whidbee, and Richard W. Sias. 2017. *Financial Institutions, Markets, and Money*. Hoboken, NJ: Wiley.

Lange, Glenn-Marie, Esther Naikal, and Quentin Wodon. 2018. Richer or Poorer? Global and Regional Trends in Wealth from 1995 to 2014. In *The Changing Wealth of Nations 2018: Building a Sustainable Future*, ed. Glenn-Marie Lange, Quentin Wodon, and Kevin Carey, 43–68. Washington, DC: World Bank.

PwC. 2017. Asset & Wealth Management Revolution: Embracing Exponential Change. https://www.pwc.com/gx/en/asset-management/asset-management-insights/assets/awm-revolution-full-report-final.pdf. Accessed on January 20, 2020.

Shub, Gary, Brent Beardsley, Hélène Donnadieu, Benoît Macé, Zubin Mogul, Achim Schwetlick, Benjamin Sheridan, Kenneth Wee, Qin Xu, and Yasuhiro Yamai. 2016. Global Asset Management 2016: Doubling Down on Data. Boston Consulting Group. https://www.bcg.com/publications/2016/financial-institutions-global-asset-management-2016-doubling-down-on-data.aspx. Accessed on January 20, 2020.

Szmigiera, M. 2019. Leading Wealth Managers Worldwide in 2019, by Assets Under Management. Statista, October 23. https://www.statista.com/statistics/329685/leading-wealth-managers-by-assets-under-management-usa. Accessed on January 20, 2020.

3

Fundamentals of the Banking Business

3.1 Global Market's Ecosystem

Institutional investors' behavior is bound by rules and constraints; knowing and understanding them is essential in the Global Market business. For example, a money market fund will only buy money market instruments and trying to sell them stocks is a waste of everyone's time. Or a particular mutual fund may have a weekly internal meeting during which portfolio reallocations are being coordinated, and knowing the precise timing of the decision-making process is valuable knowledge to any salesperson covering this client. Successful sales, trading and research employees are able to "put on the hat" of each of their clients and are able to anticipate their very next move. One of the biggest compliments you can get from your client, after proposing an idea or sharing an observation, is that this is something they just now planned on focusing on next and that your input is timely and relevant.

3.1.1 Buy-Side vs. Sell-Side

The *buy-side* refers to market participants that put capital at work, often on behalf of their own end-customers. This typically involves purchasing securities, although part of the management of portfolios may also involve the occasional selling of securities. The *sell-side* consists of firms that issue, sell or trade securities. Examples for buy-side firms are investment managers,

© The Author(s) 2020
F. Tata, *Corporate and Investment Banking*,
https://doi.org/10.1007/978-3-030-44341-2_3

pension funds and hedge funds; examples for sell-side firms are investment banks, broker-dealers[1] and advisory firms.[2]

Although the buy-side and the sell-side work very closely with each other on a daily basis, there is no denying that there are often conflicts of interest.[3] The agent acting on behalf of the buy-side firm, say a portfolio manager of a mutual fund, is tasked to make investment decisions that generate the best risk-adjusted return on capital within the specific portfolio management mandate. The agent acting on behalf of the sell-side firm, say a broker-dealer, is expected to *monetize* the client relationship in such a way that the benefits of the sell-side firm is maximized in the long run. This may include earning high fees and trading commissions, or to gain insight into the trading flows of the buy-side that, in turn, helps their own trading desk to enter into profitable trading positions. If, for example, the agent of the buy-side and the agent of the sell-side are discussing a potential trade that generates a high commission income for the sell-side firm, but creates an inappropriately high-risk position to the buy-side firm, the agent of the sell-side firm may feel compelled to "push" the trade anyway. Proclaiming "this is not a good trade for you" does not get the sell-side agent paid, although it may help develop a more trusting long-term relationship that creates a more profitable relationship in the long run.

Many agents of the buy-side have started their career on the sell-side. The buy-side likes hiring from the sell-side because those hires not only bring valuable product and market knowledge but are also less susceptible to potential sell-side pressure. More than once a client (from the buy-side) had told me that he or she was in my position some years back, which felt like receiving a friendly warning not to try some sell-side "tricks."

The role of buy-side agents extends beyond "just" executing trades. A buy-side agent is often required to perform in-house research, present views on markets, products and investment opportunities within his or her organization or its clients, perform financial modeling and valuation, or to grow AUM. From a sell-side agent it is de facto required to assist the buy-side counterparts as much as possible in those tasks, even though this does not immediately lead to trading revenues. Smart buy-side agents will try to offload as much of their daily workload to the sell-side as a prerequisite for "doing business" with them.

It is often debated whether it is more advantageous to work on the buy-side or on the sell-side. The benefit of being on the sell-side is that one has little, or no, responsibility for the performance of the financial market instruments sold to the buy-side. Buy-side agents, on the other hand, are typically measured against the risk-adjusted returns resulting from their investment decisions. For example, many sell-side employees that were, at least in part, responsible for the dissemination of US mortgage products that ultimately created tremendous losses to the buyers were able to hold on to their job, while many of their buy-side counterparts got laid off in the wake of the mortgage market crisis. In fact, the career on the buy-side, e.g., as a trader for a hedge fund, can be rather short (only a few years, although remuneration is typically attractive during that period), while there are many employees working on the sell-side for ten to twenty years, or even longer than that.

One (perceived) advantage of being on the buy-side is to be in the stronger position during a buy-side-sell-side negotiation. As a customer, the buy-side agent can expect to be treated with courtesy and respect, while the sell-side agent is often beaten up and abused by demanding and, at times, rude buy-side representatives. An illustrative way in which to dramatize the difference between being on the buy-side and on the sell-side is captured in the following adage:

> On the buy-side, you say, "F*** you!" and hang up the phone.
> On the sell-side, you hang up the phone and only then say, "F*** you!"

3.1.2 Banks

Banks are *depository institutions* that have a *banking license* required to accept deposits from retail customers. The original business model of banks is often jokingly portrayed in the following way:

> "Once upon a time, there were bankers whose lives were
> marked by three numbers.
> Do you know those numbers?
> They were 3, 6 and 3.
> Bankers paid 3% interest on deposits,
> earned 6% on loans,
> and at 3 in the afternoon they drove to the golf course."[4]

Following the banking crisis of 2008 and with more FinTechs offering bank-like services, banks are no longer trusted to be the sole providers of banking services. With or without banks, banking remains necessary. For now, most banking services are still provided by classical banks. Typically, a banking license is required to provide certain banking services. For all intents and purposes, a provider of banking services has to either become a bank or partner up with a bank.

Banks play two major roles in the financial markets. First, they act as advisers, earning fee income for businesses such as mergers and acquisition services. Second, they act as intermediaries between lenders/savers and borrowers/spenders, typically earning a spread. For the latter, they use their balance sheet to conduct what is called financial transformation. An example for financial transformation would be to accept short-term consumer deposits and to use that money to give a construction loan. The deposit would go onto the liability side of the bank's balance sheet, while the loan makes it onto the asset side. Thus, financial transformation increases a bank's balance sheet. Providing balance sheet, however, is expensive because for regulatory reasons a part needs to be covered by equity, thus requiring the generation of a proper return on equity (RoE) or return on risk-adjusted capital (RORAC).

Financial transformation, capitalizing on mismatches between the asset and liability side of a bank's balance sheet, can take several forms. The most important ones are *size transformation, maturity transformation, credit transformation, liquidity transformation* and *risk transformation*.

Size Transformation makes the size of assets and liabilities most appealing to supply and demand in the financial markets. Banks typically cover both, small-size and large-scale market participants and bundle/split otherwise offsetting financial flows to fulfill the need for a particular size. See upper-left box in Fig. 3.1. *Maturity transformation* is the business model of borrowing money on shorter time frames and to lend it out for a longer time. If the yield curve is upward-sloped, this results in a positive margin. See lower-left box in Fig. 3.1. *Credit transformation* is the process of enhancing credit quality (often by means of securitization). This is done by *pooling* assets, and then *tranching* them into separate sets of claims with different priorities. Due to institutional supply-demand imbalances,[5] credit transformation allows higher-yielding credit pools to be financed at a lower average yield. See upper-right box in Fig. 3.1. *Liquidity transformation* is the funding of illiquid assets with liquid liabilities. Because illiquid assets command a liquidity premium, liquidity transformation results in a yield pickup. See lower-right box in Fig. 3.1. Finally, *risk transformation* is the process of mitigating risks by applying risk-reduction techniques such as diversification, pooling, screening and monitoring of assets, or formation of reserves.

For the Global Markets area of a universal bank, other banks can be clients or competitors. If another bank requests a quote on, say, an interest rate swap, this could be to take advantage of a mispricing of your own trading

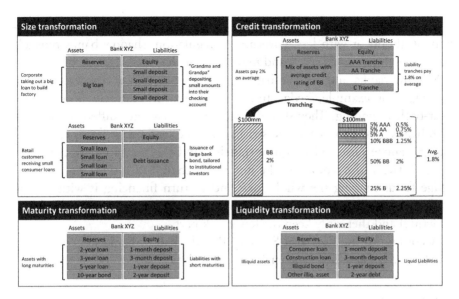

Fig. 3.1 Size, maturity, credit and liquidity transformation

desk (i.e., acting as a competitor), or to reduce the maturity gap on their balance sheet (i.e., acting as a client of yours).

3.1.3 Shadow Banks

Shadow banks[6] are market participants providing banking services outside the scope of regulatory supervision. They include hedge funds, insurance companies, pension funds and money market funds. Because they don't have a banking license that is required to accept retail deposits they are also called *nondepository institutions*. Lacking the ability to fund themselves through deposits, shadow banks tend to use *wholesale* funding, including repo[7] (see Fig. 3.2).

Fig. 3.2 Depository vs. nondepository institutions

Like "regular" banks, shadow banks also engage in financial transformation. Without, or with less, government regulation, shadow banks typically hold less equity and reserves, and may use more leverage.

Shadow banks and regular banks are not always in a competitive relationship. For example, hedge funds and banks increasingly team up for asset-backed lending. They slice the securitized loan into different tranches, with banks taking the senior (less-risky) tranche, and hedge funds taking the junior tranche (also called equity tranche) and the mezzanine tranche (the trance between the senior and the junior tranche). This is done either by the hedge funds making the whole loan and in turn financing it with a bank lending line, or banks advance two loans simultaneously (in a so-called A/B structure) and then only keep the lower risk part.

According to the Financial Stability Board, shadow banks are controlling roughly half of all global financial assets and their share keeps increasing.[8]

3.1.4 Exchanges

Exchanges are physical or virtual locations where buyers and sellers (or their agents) meet at to trade standardized products (fungible goods) according to set rules. Nowadays, most financial market exchanges allow for electronic order submissions (as opposed to floor trading) where orders are matched according to algorisms on the exchange's computer server. Thus, they are virtual locations, similarly to ebay.

Exchanges compete with each other in the sense that they try to become the most liquid market, attracting most of the order flow. From a global market participant's perspective, selecting the most appropriate exchange place is a crucial part of the trade execution decision-making process. A hedge fund engaged in high-frequency trading and statistical arbitrage trading may have completely different preferences than, say, a mutual fund executing a large block of securities.

Exchanges differentiate themselves from each other is by having differing trading models. They include:

- Quote-driven markets, where some (dedicated) participants stand ready to transact at given prices;
- Order-driven markets, where buy and sell orders are collected and matched in auctions;
- Hybrid markets with combinations thereof.

3.1.5 Pension Funds

Pension funds collect, pool and invest funds contributed by sponsors (employers) and beneficiaries (employees and their family members) to provide for the future pension entitlements of beneficiaries. Pension funds are, after mutual funds, the most dominating private investors with some $28 trillion in aggregated assets under managements in the OECD area.[9] More than 90% of that coming from just seven countries,[10] with the lion share of almost 60% coming from the USA alone. This means that if you end up covering pension funds as your client base, they most likely consist of mostly US and UK pension funds. For example, Swedish pension funds have less than 0.2% in assets under management than the USA.

Pension funds operate with different business models:

- Pay-as-you-go;
- Defined benefit;
- Defined contribution;
- Hybrid types.

The business model is important because it dictates to a large degree the pension funds' market behavior. A defined-benefit model guarantees future pensioners a certain pension. In order to grow contributions to that target amount, a specific return on investment is needed. That target return can be higher than what low-risk investments yield during a low-yield environment, which incentivizes those pension funds to become less risk averse and to move more money into risky assets. *Reaching for yield* becomes a popular strategy in this environment and your job covering pension funds will likely center around identifying investment opportunities with an expected return close to the funds yield target. A pension funds running a defined contribution scheme makes no promises regarding the investment performance and will likely continue a conservative investment strategy even in a low-yield environment.

The investment behavior of a pension fund also depends on whether the plan is growing (i.e., increasing premia are collected from additional plan participants) or declining (i.e., outflow payments to pensioners exceed inflows). If the plan is growing, the pension fund manager can still invest in long-dated assets that typically yield more than low-duration assets; if the plan is in decline, the fund manager must shorten the duration of portfolio assets, which further reduces the expected yield.

3.1.6 Insurance Companies

Insurance companies are in the business of assuming risk on behalf of their customers in exchange for a premium. Typically, premium payments are collected prior to payouts expected to occur, so that a significant portion of premium income needs to be invested in the market. As of 2017, assets held by insurance companies worldwide are to the tune of $33 trillion globally.[11]

The protracted low-yield environment is eroding life insurers' capital positions, particularly for companies offering products with long-term guaranteed rates and big duration mismatches between assets and liabilities. As a result, many insurance companies, just like pension funds, are allocating an increasing portion of their financial assets into more risky asset classes in an attempt to boost investment returns. According to a survey conducted in 2019, asset managers of 360 global insurance companies intend to increase asset allocations into private equity by 24% on average, into real estate by 21% and into hedge funds by 14% over the following 12–24 months.[12]

3.1.7 Mutual Funds

With roughly $40 trillion in assets under management, mutual funds are the largest group of real money investors, accounting for about 40% of global assets under management. Mutual funds are investment vehicles whose underlying assets are identifiable and are marked to market on a regular basis.

Advantages of mutual funds include

- Liquidity/convenience;
- Size transformation;
- Diversification;
- Transaction cost reduction;
- Managerial experience.

Table 3.1 shows a ranking of the top-10 mutual funds as of January 2020. The top eight spots are occupied by US institutions.

Due to the intense competition between mutual funds, minimizing transaction costs has become a major issue in the industry. As a result, mutual funds are investing a lot of energy in developing trading platforms tailored toward cost-efficient and market impact minimizing portfolio trading. An example for such a platform is Aladdin®, an operating system developed by

Table 3.1 Global ranking of mutual funds as of January 2020 by AUM

Global ranking	Institution	AUM in $ bn
1	BlackRock	6964
2	Vanguard	4530
3	Charles Schwab	3940
4	State Street	2810
5	Fidelity Investments	2459
6	J.P. Morgan	2200
7	BNY Mellon	1900
8	PIMCO	1880
9	Capital Group	1860
10	Amundi	1750

Source Mutual Fund Directory (2020)

BlackRock for investment managers that provides risk analytics and tools for portfolio management, trading and operations. To some degree, this leads to a disintermediation of broker-dealers, reducing their ability to earn commissions and fees from mutual fund flows.

3.1.8 Index Funds

Index funds are special types of a mutual funds or exchange-traded funds (ETFs) with a unique investment style. Instead of *actively* managing the asset composition, index funds aim at *passively* replicating an existing market index.

Finance theory typically assumes efficient markets, including the notion of minimal transaction cost. There are indeed some very liquid markets, such as the institutional market for plain-vanilla swaps or institutional foreign exchange (FX) transactions. Fees charged by actively managed funds, however, are large enough to hurt performance (see Table 3.2), and over the last ten years or so, an increasing publicity was given to the empirical observation that the majority of mutual funds fail in providing above-market returns on an after-fee basis.[13] As a result, an ever-increasing percentage of fund money is going into index funds that provide diversification benefits at much lower fees. For US equity funds, already more than 50% is invested in passives.[14]

Among the index funds with the lowest expense ratio in the world is the Vanguard 500 Index Fund, replicating the S&P 500 stock market index. Its expense ratio (for investments of $3000 or more) is merely 0.04%, or 4 bp p.a.[15] There is virtually no difference in performance between the

Table 3.2 Illustration of transaction cost

Transaction	Typical fee	Fee per $1 mm
Liquid swap transaction with institutional investor	¼ bp	$25
Vanguard S&P 500 index fund	4 bp p.a.	$400
Schwab Emerging Markets Equity ETF	13 bp p.a.	$1300
Average stock purchase with non-online broker	1%	$10,000
Retail structured product	1.5%[a]	$15,000
Hedge fund	2%[b] p.a.	$20,000
Playing one round of roulette in a casino	2.7%	$27,000

[a]For example, Deutscher Derivate Verband (2018)
[b]Calculated by assuming a 2% management fee (ignoring the profit fee typically 20%, that is charged additionally when performances exceed a certain threshold)

replicated index and the index fund: Since inception in November 2000 and December 2019, the index had a performance of 6.73% p.a., and the index one of 6.75% p.a.[16]

From a broker-dealer's perspective, index funds are quite unattractive customers. They execute (often algorithm-based) buy and sell orders proportional to security compositions within an index, have little or no discretion for security selection, are not inclined to pay for securities research, aim for the most cost-efficient way to transact and need little, if any, advise.

3.1.9 Hedge Funds

Hedge funds are part of a group of non-traditional investment funds called *alternative* investment funds.[17] The term goes back to 1949, when Alfred Winslow Jones founded one of the first hedge funds with a capital of $100,000.[18]

Initially, hedge funds aimed to deliver positive returns under all market conditions (so-called alpha) by *hedging out* all types of market risk (the "beta"). Soon after, hedge funds engaged in risky investment behavior, moving away from pure (risk-free) arbitrage, to "relative value," to "informed bets" or market-directional trading.

Hedge funds can be classified according to their self-described *investment style*. However, often hedge funds give themselves so much latitude that they can do whatever they want, no matter how they market themselves to investors. *Long-Short funds* are taking long and short positions in stocks to limit their exposures to the stock market. *Event-driven funds* take positions on corporate events (corporate bankruptcies and reorganizations; merger arbitrage). *Fixed income arbitrage* involves trading of price or yield along the yield curve. *Global Macro funds* rely on macroeconomic analysis to take bets on the major risk factors, such as currencies, interest rates, stock indices and commodities. *Multi-Strategy funds* don't limit themselves to any strategy.

Hedge funds employ a wide range of *trading strategies*. These trading techniques are not unique to hedge funds. Many of them are used by university endowments, pension funds, wealthy family portfolios and proprietary trading desks of commercial and investment banks (where a number of hedge fund managers came from). Wall Street firms also regularly employ highly leveraged positions, especially when they use short treasury positions to hedge the corporate bonds and mortgage bonds in their inventory. Some wealthy families reportedly run their own trading operations much like those of hedge funds. More details about hedge fund trading will be discussed in Sect. 5.5 within the chapter on trading.

Some hedge funds, called *quantitative hedge funds*, focus on mathematical relationships among prices in what is called *statistical arbitrage* and have been founded by computer scientists, mathematicians and engineers. Two of the most successful quantitative hedge funds are *Renaissance Technologies LLC* and *Two Sigma Investments LP*. *Renaissance* is a $84 billion quantitative investment firm founded in 1982 by former military code-breaker Jim Simons. It is considered to be one of the most profitable hedge funds, returning an estimate 39.1% annualized (after fees) over a 30-year period from 1988 to 2018.[19] It is a pioneer in quantitative trading, strictly adhering to mathematical and statistical methods. It employs mathematicians, statisticians, pure and experimental physicists, astronomers, and computer scientists; about a third of its about 300 employees are believed to hold a PhD. *Two Sigma* is a roughly $60 billion quantitative investment firm founded in 2001 by former mathematician and statistician John Overdeck.[20] Its annualized return 2014–2017 is about 17%. Two Sigma is applying artificial intelligence, machine learning and a supercomputer-sized distributed computing platform to their trading strategies, utilizing some 42+ petabytes of data, more than 10 thousand public and proprietary data sources and almost 100 thousand CPUs providing 100 teraflops of computing power.[21]

Hedge funds are known for the exorbitant salaries they pay to their best-performing traders. The *Institutional Investor* magazine publishes an annual list of the highest earning hedge fund managers, called "The Rich List."[22] According to the 2019 list, Ray Dalio from the hedge fund *Bridgewater Associates* earned $2 billion, James Simons from *Renaissance Technologies* $1.5 billion, Kenneth Griffin from *Citadel* $870 million, John Overdeck and David Siegel from *Two Sigma* $820 million each and Israel

Englander from *Millennium Management* $750 million. Some hedge fund managers have so much money that they buy themselves sport teams: In 2019, Steve Cohen (Point72 Asset Management, formerly SAC Capital) brought himself the New York Mets (baseball team) and David Tepper of Appaloosa Management is a minority owner of the Pittsburgh Steelers (football team) and bought the Carolina Panthers (football team) for $2.275 billion.

It is both a privilege and a challenge to cover hedge funds. A *privilege* because hedge funds are among the most sophisticated market participants in the market (although the failure of the one-famous hedge fund Long Term Capital Management, LTCM, has tarnished the reputation of hedge funds). They tend to hire only seasoned and exceptional staff and rigidly weed out underperformers. Hedge fund traders and strategists will likely refuse to talk to you unless you can demonstrate some ability to add value to them. They simply don't have the patience and time to deal with someone they don't consider being at their eye level. Once you established a line of communication, you can learn a lot of things you won't find in textbooks or research publications. For example, as a salesperson or a research strategist, you may be able to interfere from the hedge fund's reaction to a proposed trade idea, whether there are some conceptual flaws, errors in the trade construction (e.g., assumed weightings of the legs[23] of the trade), market imbalances or structural changes that prevent the trade to perform the way anticipated (e.g., if it is some sort of mean-reverting trade) or other issues you have not considered yet. If you have a really good relationship with the hedge fund, you may even get direct feedback; often, however, the hedge fund will simply not react to your proposal and it is up to you to read between the lines. Hedge funds are notoriously tight-lipped because they don't want to give away any of their advanced knowledge that sets them apart from the average investor. For traders it can be advantageous to deal with hedge funds as well, as they may learn about better ways to calibrate their pricing models or about other pricing-related issues. However, when it comes to hedge funds, traders often have to learn those things the hard way. This is because hedge funds will likely try to exploit any pricing and evaluation divergence by trading, causing a trading loss to the trader on the broker-dealer side. That's why broker-dealer flow traders will make sure to transact only in rather small size (although hedge funds often pressure to do big-size trades). Refusing to trade with hedge funds is typically a short-sighted strategy, because then there is no more potential to improve modeling, pricing and calibration by interfering information from the hedge fund relationship, which often causes even worse trading losses in the long run.

Covering hedge funds can be quite a *challenge*. As already mentioned, hedge funds are often ruthless when it comes to exploiting any kind of mispricing they identify.[24] For a trader, winning a trade with a hedge fund is a double-edged sword. On the one hand, there are many benefits to a confirmed transaction: The trader may have earned some commission, the trader may have offset some risk position for the trading book and the trade may have given some valuable insight into the hedge fund's thinking process and market knowledge. On the other hand, the trade will likely suffer from the so-called *winner's curse*, a phenomenon describing the doubt of a winning bidder in an auction that he/she may have had put in a too aggressive bid. Since hedge funds often request price quotes of instruments that need to be priced to model, being identified as the (from the hedge fund's perspective) most attractive price quote among a group of broker-dealers with presumably excellent modeling skills raises the possibility that there was some error been made in the pricing process.[25]

3.1.10 Sovereign Wealth Funds

Sovereign wealth funds are state-owned entities that own and invest a country's pool of assets. For example, Norway's sovereign wealth fund manages money in excess of $1 trillion originating from oil drilling revenues. The China Investment Corporation (CIC), also managing close to $1 trillion in investments, is in charge of investing a portion of China's foreign currency reserves.

Table 3.3 shows a ranking of the top-10 sovereign wealth funds as of January 2020.

Table 3.3 Global ranking of sovereign wealth funds as of January 2020 by AUM

Global ranking	Institution	AUM in $ bn
1	Norway Government Pension Fund Global	1099
2	China Investment Corporation	941
3	Abu Dhabi Investment Authority	697
4	Kuwait Investment Authority	592
5	Hong Kong Monetary Authority Investment Portfolio	509
6	GIC Private Limited	440
7	SAFE Investment Company	418
8	Temasek Holding	375
9	Qatar Investment Authority	328
10	National Council for Social Security Fund	325

Source Sovereign Wealth Fund Institute (2020)

Sovereign wealth funds differ from other investment funds in a number of ways. First, they do not merely follow *economic* objectives, such as capital preservation or risk-return optimization, but also have *strategic* and *social* goals. Second, they often delegate asset management to external asset managers. And third, because they view themselves as long-term investors, a significant part of their assets is held in less liquid private market instruments and alternative investments, such as private equity or real estate.

3.1.11 Central Banks

Among the most important market participants in the financial markets are central banks. Central banks are each country's government authority in change of monetary policy. Although central banks are technically part of the government, they often benefit from a large degree of independence and can be treated at separate decision makers.

The most important central banks in the global financial markets are the US Federal Reserve Bank (Fed), the European Central Bank (ECB), the Bank of England (BoE), the Bank of Japan (BoJ) and the Bank of Canada. Central banks perform many functions, whereas their monetary policy has the biggest impact on the financial markets.[26] Monetary policy is actions taken by central banks to influence the cost and availability of money in an economy. To achieve this, a number of tools and measures are at a central bank's disposal. So-called *conventional measures* (used in times without stress) are for example targeting the short-term risk-free interest rate and impact the front-end of the yield curve. *Unconventional* measures are additional operations in the open market, typically through limited-time repo transactions or outright security purchases, called *Quantitative easing* (QE).

Central banks' discount windows (or standing facilities) are used to keep the interest rate at which depository institutions lend reserve balances to other depository institutions overnight close to the target established by the central bank. For example, the Federal funds (or Fed funds, for short) effective rate is the interest rate at which US depository institutions lend reserve balances on an uncollateralized basis to each other on an overnight basis. The Fed is steering this rate by "targeting" a *desired* rate level, called the Federal funds target rate. It is set by a meeting of the members of the Federal Open Market Committee (FOMC) which normally occurs eight times a year about seven weeks apart. Figure 3.3 shows how the US Fed has adjusted the target rate according to the economic environment: In 2001 and 2008, the target rate was reduced to stimulate the economy during recessions;

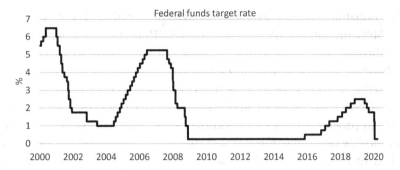

Fig. 3.3 Federal funds target rate, 2000–2020 (Graphic shows the federal funds target rate previous to the December 2008 rate change and the upper limit of the Federal funds target range since then. *Source* Federal Reserve Bank of St. Louis [2020])

mid-2004 to mid-2006, the rate was pushed higher to fight inflation. The reduction in the first quarter of 2020 is to fight the adverse effects of the COVID-19 pandemic.

Some economic textbooks make it appear that a change in the central bank target rate has an impact on the market. This is wrong. What actually causes a market reaction is a deviation from market *expectations*. If the market already expects a 25 bp increase in the target rate and the central bank delivers precisely such a 25 bp increase, there will be likely hardly any change to (short-dated) interest rates in the minutes following the announcement. However, if the market widely expects a 25 bp increase and the target rate is kept unchanged, this would possibly create a market reaction akin to an unexpected decline of the target rate.[27] For a proper analysis of the anticipated market reaction function to central bank activity one needs as a starting point a good estimate of what is already *priced in* by the market. Sometimes, there are liquid traded instruments that can be used to extract the implied market expectation. For example, for the future Fed funds target rate, one could look at the Fed funds futures market.[28] However, by simply comparing the Fed funds futures-implied interest rate to the current target rate, one cannot gauge the *precise* market expectation. This should be illustrated by the following example.

Let's assume it is one day prior to an FOMC meeting in May with the current Fed funds target rate being 1%. The June Fed funds futures trades at a price of 99, implying an average daily Fed funds effective rate in the month of June of 1%.[29] With this information alone, it is not possible to say whether market participants expect an unchanged target rate with a

100% probability or, for example, a 50% probability of a 25 bp increase and a 50% probability of a 25 bp decline. Thus, futures prices only offer probability-weighted expectations and are not very useful to gauge information about the *dispersion* of believes.[30]

Extracting market expectations from surveys of economists can be tricky as well. Chief economists of major broker-dealer firms are regularly polled and ask to provide a forecast for various economic releases. Each economist has to provide one single forecast and then the various forecasts are provided as a list, often together with some statistical analysis. Table 3.4 illustrates how a typical format of such a consensus forecast table looks like. If all economists were to see a high probability of an unchanged target rate and a low probability of, say, a Fed hike, they would all report an unchanged rate as their forecast. This would then look like there is no expected probability of a Fed hike, because nobody is projecting this scenario.

Besides the *conventional* central bank policy measures aimed at changing the short-term interest rate, central banks engage in *open market operations*. Those include limited-time transactions in the repo market as well as outright security purchases, so-called *quantitative easing* (QE). Quantitative easing inflates a central bank's balance sheet as more and more assets get absorbed (see Fig. 3.4 for the US Federal Reserve). The spike in the first half of 2020 is due to central bank action on the back of the COVID-19 pandemic. The reduced float of remaining assets in the market can create scarcity problems, as the cap for central bank holdings of individual securities is set quite high (70% for the Fed). Table 3.5 shows the Fed's holding for selected Treasury securities as of May 2020. Although central banks try to mitigate undesired impacts on market functioning,[31] temporary market

Table 3.4 Illustrative table of economists' forecasts of the Fed funds target rate

Fed target upper bound	Q3 2020	Q4 2020	Q1 2021	Q2 2021	Q3 2021	Q4 2021	Q1 2022
Median	0.25	0.25	0.25	0.25	0.25	0.25	0.50
High forecast	0.50	0.50	1.25	1.50	1.75	2.00	2.50
Low forecast	0.25	0.25	0.25	0.25	0.25	0.25	0.25
% of forecast at median	96	93	90	88	85	85	50
No. of forecasts at median	67	65	61	60	51	51	18
No. of forecasts	70	70	68	68	60	60	36

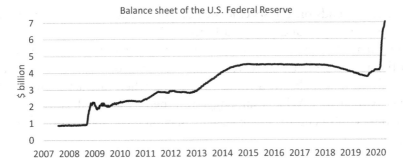

Fig. 3.4 Federal Reserve's balance sheet, 2007–2020 (Graphic shows the total assets of the Federal Reserve. *Source* Board of Governors of the Federal Reserve [2020])

Table 3.5 Federal Reserve's security holdings for selected securities

Instrument (CUSIP)	Maturity date	Coupon (%)	Par value (billion)	Total out-standing (%)
912828SF8	15 February 2022	2	$45.1	60.8
912828SV3	15 May 2022	1¾	$44.2	64.1
912828TJ9	15 August 2022	1.625	$44.1	66.8
912828QN3	15 May 2021	3.125	$40.0	60.6
912810QU5	15 February 2042	3.125	$31.5	66.7
912810QE1	15 February 2040	4.625	$	70

Table shows the domestic security holdings for selected Treasury Notes as of May 17, 2020
Source Federal Reserve Bank of New York (2020)

dislocations and dysfunction may arise. Therefore, it is important to closely monitor how much of a particular security a central bank buys and whether this had caused any price dislocation.

3.2 Key Concepts of Financial Theory

Financial theory is a very wide field stretching from simple concepts of *financial mathematics*, such as net present value (NPV) calculations, over complex theories of *financial economics*, such as the capital asset pricing model (CAPM) to psychological aspects of human behavior in *behavioral finance*. It is impossible to cover *all* of them in one section. It is also not possible to objectively select the most important ones, as their applicability and usefulness depends on the specific area of use. What follows here is a selection of concepts I found particularly useful in a sales, trading and research environment. The choice is subjective. Ultimately you need to compile your own theoretical toolkit that serves you best, that allows you to differentiate yourself and that makes you more convincing when interacting with other market participants. What I am suggesting here is what I believe to be the theoretical equivalent to a screwdriver, hammer and pliers in a beginner toolbox.

3.2.1 Choice Under Uncertainty and Risk

Financial markets are all about information. Is there some information not yet reflected in the market price? Can we extract information from the observed market dynamics? Do we have information about what could happen next? Typically, one of the first questions before even starting the most basic financial analysis is: *What do we know?* This seems obvious, but this is an area where often wrong assumptions are made already. At the early morning of Tuesday, September 11, 2001, everyone believed to *know* that trading on the following day, a non-holiday Wednesday, would be possible on the New York Mercantile Exchange. And yet, after the attack on the World Trade Center, the exchange was closed for a week.

Donald Rumsfeld, in a speech given on February 12, 2002, popularized the distinction between different levels of knowledge:

> *"[T]here are known knowns; there are things we know we know.*
> *We also know there are known unknowns; that is to say we know*
> *there are some things we do not know.*
> *But there are also unknown unknowns – there are things*
> *we do not know we don't know."*[32]

Unknown unknowns are rare, but problematic events, because market participants have not considered their impact at all. Risk management, pricing, hedging and many other techniques are doomed to fail. Going forward, terrorist attacks on critical financial market infrastructure are no longer unknown unknowns, as we are now aware of the possibility of this to happen again. For example, infrastructure safeguards have been put in place (backup server locations, etc.). But eventually, there will be something happening again, that no one has considered to be realistically feasible.[33]

More common than unknown unknowns are *known unknowns*. Here, we know that something is unknown. For example, we know that we don't know a central bank's target interest rate two years from now. Still, we have to make choices such as whether or not to protect a floating-rate liability against increasing interest rates on the back of monetary tightening. What is the rational choice to make? Going back to a distinction made first by Frank Knight in 1921,[34] there are known unknowns for which the probabilities of the relevant outcomes are both meaningful and known, and there are known unknowns where the probabilities of the relevant outcomes are completely unknown or not even meaningful. In the former case, one is facing *choice under risk*, in the latter *choice under uncertainty*.[35] See Table 3.6.

Table 3.6 Taxonomy of randomness

	Known Knowns	Known Unknowns		Unknown Unknowns
		Risk	Uncertainty	
Examples	• Risk-free rate • Risk-free cash flows • Maturity of (non-callable) bond • Calendar	• Probability of a traded option to be in-the-money at expiry • Change of interest rates	• Default of a customer loan • Greece leaving EU • Terrorist attack	• Unexpected wars • Environmental disaster • Regime changes • Aliens coming from outer space
Assessment	Unproblematic	Risk Management & Hedging	Probabilities must be assumed	Problematic

When facing a choice under uncertainty, the probability of an event must be assumed (i.e., guessed or estimated) to make a rational decision. For example, if a bank extends a loan to a customer,[36] the amount of reserves established depend on the assumed probability of the loan taker defaulting. When facing a choice under uncertainty, probabilities are known, which allows for some degree of risk management or even hedging. If a market hedge exists for a known unknown, the *implied* probability of the hedge instrument is often used as a proxy of the "real" probability and the choice is considered to be one under risk.

The taxonomy of randomness can be a useful tool for anyone holding a sales, trading or research position. Two examples may illustrate this.

You are a risk manager. To hedge a position against interest rate risk, you did establish a long position in a bond future contract. The cheapest-to-deliver (CTD) of a futures contract is the security one assumes the short position in the futures contract will deliver, because delivering any other security that is part of the deliverable basket would be more expensive. Also, one assumes that delivery takes places at the day during the delivery month that is most advantageous to the short position. Let's assume that widely available futures research suggests that long positions in a particular futures contract should expect to get the CTD security delivered on the last date of the delivery month. Let's also assume that you have no interest (or even worse: not the technical ability) to take delivery of the CTD; in fact, you plan on closing out the futures position prior to delivery. Taking the futures research analysis as a known known, you hold on to the futures position during the delivery month, "knowing" that delivery will not happen until the very last day of the delivery month. This is an example of how dangerous it can be to blindly trust known knows. While it may be true that a *rational* actor would not deliver prior to the last delivery day if that is not the most profitable course of action, there is no guarantee that the long position in the futures contract could in fact deliver the CTD, or any other deliverable security, prior to the last delivery day. This could put you in a very uncomfortable position of having to take physical delivery of the underlying.

Another example relates to implied probabilities. Let's assume you are a salesperson covering a corporate customer who fears that interest rates could increase. This would drive up financing costs, as the corporate customer issues 10-year corporate bonds as the main debt financing instruments. Your customer asks you what the probability of an increase in 10-year corporate bond rates of 100 bp over one year is. He needs this information within 5 minutes, because he wants to use it in an internal meeting that is about to start. In a situation like this, it is more important to provide the customer with an approximative answer in time, rather than taking too long for a precise solution. There is no time to make assumptions about the expected change in the corporate bond spread, so you assume for simplicity that the probability of a 100 bp increase in the corporate financing rate is approximately the same as the probability of a 100 bp increase in the 10-year swap rate. You then ask the swap desk to indicate to you what the delta of a one-year-into-10-year receiver swaption struck 100 bp above the current spot rate is. The delta of an option is not the same as the probability of execution,[37] but as a very rough approximation this will need to do. If the delta of the swaption is, say, 0.25, you could indicate to your client that the probability of a 100 bp rate increase over a 1-year period is somewhere around 20–30%.

3.2.2 The Efficient-Market Hypothesis

The efficient-market hypothesis (EMH) was developed by Eugene Fama in 1970.[38] EMH is a theory in financial economics that states that an asset's prices fully reflect all available information. It comes in three versions:

- *Weak-form EMH*—Future prices cannot be predicted by analyzing prices from the past. Excess returns cannot be earned in the long run by using investment strategies based on historical data;
- *Semi-strong-form EMH*—Prices adjust to publicly available new information very rapidly and in an unbiased fashion, such that no excess returns can be earned by trading on that information;
- *Strong-form EMH*—Prices reflect all information, public and private, and no one can earn excess returns.

What makes the EMH such a valuable contribution to financial theory is that it made people *think* about market efficiency. Whether or not a market is efficient is often a question of perspective. To a market participant executing trades via voice channels, a market in which prices adjust in the blink of an eye is totally efficient. To a hedge fund that has a 3 milliseconds advantage in transmitting orders between New York and Chicago through a dedicated microwave network, the same market may look inefficient, allowing for latency arbitrage opportunities.

It is dangerous to leap to a conclusion about a market's efficiency. If the assumption is that a market is *strong-form efficient*, it would be impossible to systematically outperform (or, "beat") the market on a risk-adjusted basis by analyzing information. This notion was probably first formulated in 1973 quite eloquently in the Malkiel (2014) book *A Random Walk Down Wall Street*: "A blindfolded monkey throwing darts at a newspaper's financial pages could select a portfolio that would do just as well as one carefully selected by experts."[39] On the other hand, the notion of a market being informationally *inefficient* appears suspicious, also. How come other market participants are not taking advantage of this by trading on information not yet reflected in the price, generating a profit for themselves and driving the market price toward informational efficiency by doing so? If you claim having found an inefficiency (mispricing, arbitrage opportunity, etc.), you must be prepared to answer some tough questions. Are you faster than everyone else in transmitting information (e.g., latency arbitrage)? Are you more efficient in analyzing information (e.g., utilizing AI and machine learning)? Do you have access to privileged information (e.g., insider trading)? Are you able or willing to act other market participants are prevented from doing (e.g., being unaffected by regulatory restrictions or willingness to break the law)?

How can a market be efficient and, at the same time, incentify market participants to process information (conduct financial market research, etc.) that drives the market toward efficiency? Grossman/Stiglitz raised this question in 1980 and proposed that markets cannot be completely efficient.[40] There appears to be an *efficient degree of inefficiency* that creates an *equilibrium* between market participants searching for, and profiting from, market inefficiencies and participants relying on market prices: "Prices are pushed away from their fundamental values because of a variety of demand pressures and institutional frictions, and, although prices are kept in check by intense competition among money managers, this process leads the market to become *inefficient* to an *efficient* extent: just *inefficient* enough that money managers can be compensated for their costs and risks through superior performance and just *efficient* enough that the rewards to money management after all cost do not encourage entry of new managers or additional capital."[41]

As a sales, trading and research market professional, you will perform two different roles in *efficiently inefficient* markets. At times, you will need to rely on market prices to extract implied information. Here, you assume the market to be (sufficiently) efficient and benefit from the informational value of market prices. For example, you observe Eurodollar futures prices and calculate the implied Eurodollar rate (100 minus the futures price) without questioning whether the market is efficient enough to have properly converted yields into prices in the first place. At other times, you will find yourself in the position to hold information that are not yet fully reflected in the market price yet (or so you think), in which case you will assume the market to be temporarily inefficient. You will probably consider this to be a market dislocation and may want to take advantage of it (e.g., by trading or communicating your observation to other market participants that will compensate you for it one way or another).

At times, you will face contradictions regarding market efficiency. Take this example: You believe to have found a mispricing in a traded option. In order to benefit from the market inefficiency, you plan to trade the option and hedge it with a delta-equivalent position in the underlying. But what is the delta of the option? If you don't trust the market to calculate the correct option price, you surely can't assume the market to provide you with the proper delta (sensitivity) either. Should you, therefore, hedge according to hedge ratios generated by your own model? Or does your internal risk management group force you to use risk parameters from the market? There is no easy answer to this question.

3.2.3 Arbitrage

Arbitrage is another important concept in financial theory. In this section, we will be covering three nuances of the concept of arbitrage: *pure arbitrage*, *market micro-arbitrage* and *relative value*. Then we look at one specific example of arbitrage, *institutional arbitrage*.

3.2.3.1 Pure Arbitrage

The theoretical definition of arbitrage, often referred to as *pure arbitrage* or *riskless arbitrage*, is *simultaneous buying and selling* of identical securities that requires *no capital* (i.e., "self-financing" trades), locks in an instant *profit* or *profit opportunity* and creates *no risks* of any kind. Theory does not define arbitrage in a constructive way to help market practitioners make money. For that, the definition is way too restrictive.[42] How many trade opportunities are there that create absolutely no risk (not even reputational or regulatory risk)? Is there any way to trade with absolutely no capital (given that some regulatory requirements demand a minimum capital adequacy from many institutional investors)? Scholars came up with the definition of arbitrage primarily to test whether a theory is *arbitrage-free*. Because a theory or a model that allows for arbitrage opportunities would violate a number of assumptions financial theory is based on. For example, neoclassical models tend to assume all actors to be *rational* (e.g., maximizing profit or maximizing utility). It would be a contradiction to assume rationality and at the same time to assume that subjects are not increasing profits and utility by exploring existing arbitrage opportunities. It would also violate the assumption that prices *react* to changes in supply and demand (taught in microeconomics 1.0.1 courses) when we allow for arbitrage trading to persist without prices to move toward an arbitrage-free equilibrium.

3.2.3.2 Market Micro-Arbitrage

It is fair to say that for the majority of market participants it would be a total waste of time to be looking for arbitrage opportunities in liquid, developed financial markets. Also, traders considering themselves "arbitrageurs" typically do not look for *pure* arbitrage but for *good bets*. Those bets are still risky. The kind of arbitrage opportunity that present itself every now and then in the real markets is so-called *market micro-arbitrage*. This type of arbitrage is less restrictive than then pure arbitrage found discussed in textbooks and can be characterized as follows:

- Simultaneous buying and selling of different, but *highly related* securities;
- Usually of *short-term* nature;
- No, or little, market directionality;
- Exploiting *temporary market imbalances* due to lagging price adjustments in different markets and sudden, large order flows.

Almost always when proposing a potential market micro-arbitrage opportunity, the question comes up what had *caused* the dislocation in the first place. If you cannot explain the driver of the dislocation, you cannot assess how likely it is that the dislocation will disappear again. A good micro-arbitrage trade takes advantage of a dislocation created by some events in the market that are known to be *transitory* in nature. Those trades are sometimes pitched as *mean reversion trades*. However, markets can stay "dislocated" for a long time, so timing is critical. For example, if you have identified buying of US Treasury securities by the Chinese central bank as a cause for US Treasury bonds trading expensive, it would not be a good market micro-arbitrage trade idea to propose selling US Treasury bonds vs. buying some other highly correlated assets unless you also believe that buying by the Chinese central bank is about to stop. If, on the other hand, your analysis suggests that there is a lot of US Treasury bond buying during the last weeks of a year due to major market participants' window dressing in the balance sheet, then selling Treasury bonds in December and buying them back in January may be a reasonable market micro-arbitrage trade idea.

3.2.3.3 Relative Value

Market micro-arbitrage opportunities are actually hard to find. Very often, what is labeled as "arbitrage" is upon closer inspection nothing more than a trade someone considers attractive. A better name for this would be is *relative value* and can be described as follows:

- A general term that includes arbitrage but also refers to positions with *residual risks;*
- Potential gains seem to *outweigh* potential losses (*attractive risk/return profile*);

- Historically *unusual* price constellations which are expected to *revert back* to mean.

Relative value analysis is a process of gaining insight into the relationship between different instruments and the forces driving the process. The concept of relative value bases on two economic principles:

- If two securities have identical payoffs in every future state of the world, then they should have identical prices today ("law of one price");
- If two securities present investors with identical risks, they should offer identical returns.

3.2.3.4 Institutional Arbitrage

Internal policies and self-imposed restrictions of many institutional investors (pension funds, money market funds, insurance companies, etc.) restrict their investment behavior. When it comes to bonds, they often use credit ratings as a basis for their investment decision. For example, it is common practice to invest only into *investment grade* bonds (rated "BBB" or better by the major rating agencies) and not into *sub-investment grade* (also called *high yield*, or *junk*) bonds. This institutional limitation creates excess demand for investment grade instruments, which drives down their yield. Through slicing a sub-investment grade pool into tranches which are partly investment grade, one creates more demand from institutional investors, resulting in an overall lower yield (higher price) of the structured product (see Fig. 3.5).

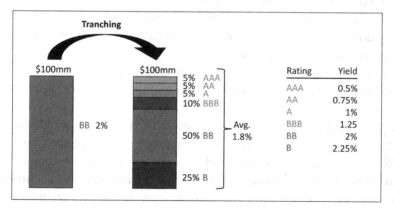

Fig. 3.5 Institutional arbitrage through tranching

Another way to look at this is to observe that rating agencies fail to assign ratings to individual tranches that would *prevent* institutional arbitrage. Therefore, one could also view this as *credit ratings arbitrage*.

3.2.4 Agency Theory

Agency theory is a very powerful concept that helps explain a lot of behavior in the financial markets. Formalized first in Jensen and Meckling (1976), it concerns itself with the problems arising when one person, the *agent*, makes decisions on behalf of another person, the *principal*. The theory acknowledges that the principal and the agent both act in their *own* interest, which may *diverge*, creating conflicting interests.

Additionally, the agent has information unknown to the principal, referred to as *asymmetric information*, which makes it difficult for the principal to ensure that the agent acts properly. Asymmetric information can lead to adverse selection, a situation in which the principal can no longer trust the agent and has to assume the worst. Adverse selection can cause market participants to withdraw from the market, with the potential for a market collapse.[43]

Without agency theory, it is virtually impossible to address questions like those in a meaningful way:

- Why does bank management pay itself huge boni (even in years when the bank is losing money)?
- Why do traders often take more risk than what is beneficial for their employer?
- Why do financial market participants with an explicit or implicit government guarantee engage in overly risky business practices?
- Why do portfolio managers sometimes make asset allocations that are not in the best interest of the end-investor?
- Why did rating agencies systematically underestimate the risk of structured mortgage securities prior to the financial crisis of 2007–2008?

Agency theory formally challenges the notion that agents should always be assumed to act in the best interest of the people they represent. In fact, it would be quite naïve to think so. Hypothetically, if medical doctors' compensation would only depend on the price of the medication they prescribe, would you be surprised to learn that patients are prescribed more drugs than is good for them? Because if not, you shouldn't be surprised about many observations in the financial markets either, such as that mergers and acquisitions (M&A) departments (that receive the majority of their compensation only if an M&A transaction takes place) are promoting more M&A transactions than necessary and that a large number of M&A transactions turn out to be a disaster for the buyer as a consequence.

Often, there is a *chain* of principal-agent problems in the financial markets. For example, end-investors appoint mutual funds to manage their money; mutual funds hire portfolio managers to make financial decisions within the mutual funds' investment policy; portfolio managers appoint broker-dealers to assist in the execution of trades; broker-dealers hire registered representatives (salespeople) to cover portfolio managers. Salespeople executing trades and end-investors impacted by the performance of those trades will likely never meet face-to-face.

There are several *interests* and *information asymmetries* along the chain connecting the ultimate principal (the end-investor) and the ultimate agent (sales agent). The sales agent may receive a bonus partially based on the amount of transactions he/she conducts, creating an incentive to trade more than necessary. The portfolio manager may receive a compensation based on the annual outperformance vis-a-vis a given benchmark with no participation in case of a loss, creating an incentive to invest in assets that are expected to outperform the benchmark most of the time, but occasionally lead to significant losses.

The *longer* the chain connecting the ultimate principal to the ultimate agent, the more severe the quality of decision making is impacted by diverging interests. It appears that over time the chains have become longer and longer in the financial markets. For example, the predominant investment banks used to be partnerships. The head of bond trading, being one of the partners, would have *skin in the game* and would personally make sure that only an appropriate level of risk is been assumed by the bond trading desk. Nowadays, the same head of bond trading reports to the head of interest rate trading, who reports to the head of FICC trading, who reports to the regional chief executive officer (CEO) of a country, who reports to the global CEO, who is appointed by the board of directors, who represent the shareholders. Is it still reasonable to assume that the head of bond trading will always act in the best interest of the shareholders?

Because of diverging self-interest and information asymmetries, both the principal and the agent occur cost, called *agency cost*. According to the Jensen/Meckling framework, this includes:

- *Monitoring expenditures* by the principal. For a buy-side client mandating a sell-side broker firm with trade execution this could mean: Annual review of broker execution quality; putting trades in competition; investing in own pricing models/systems.
- *Bonding expenditures* by the agent: For a sell-side broker firm this could include client entertainment expenditures to strengthen the relationship.

There is a third cost element, described by Jensen/Meckling as *residual loss*. It results from inefficient behavior due to conflicting interests. For a buy-side client mandating a sell-side broker firm with trade execution this could mean: Excess transaction cost due to overtrading and sub-optimal risk allocations.

Notes

1. A broker-dealer is a sell-side financial market participant that trades securities with customers. When trades are executed on behalf of the customer at a third-party trading venue (e.g., a stock exchange), the broker-dealer acts as a broker; if the broker-dealer assumes the other side of the trade (e.g., in an over the counter swap transaction), it is acting in the capacity of a dealer.
2. Sometimes, the differentiation between buy-side and sell-side gets complicated. For example, the asset management group of a sell-side firm would be considered to be the buy-side from another sell-side firm's point of view.
3. We are going to discuss the general concept of principal-agent problems causing conflicts of interest from a theoretical point of view in Sect. 3.2.4.
4. Lautenschläger (2017).
5. For example, there are very few issuers of AAA-rated instruments, while demand from institutional investors is quite high.
6. Shadow banking is sometimes also referred to as "non-bank financial intermediation."
7. A repo, short for repurchase agreement, is a collateralized, short-term financing transaction between institutional investors. Details of repo transactions will be discussed in Sect. 5.9.1.
8. Financial Stability Board (2019, 4).
9. Source: OECD (2020).
10. USA, UK, Australia, Netherlands, Canada, Japan and Switzerland.
11. Rudden (2019).
12. BlackRock (2019, 15).
13. E.g.: Newlands and Marriage (2016).
14. Source: Schramm (2019).

15. In a cut-throat price war among low-cost index funds, other asset managers have lowered their fees to similar levels, e.g., BlackRock, Lyxor and State Street.
16. Vanguard (2020).
17. They also include private equity funds, infrastructure funds, commodity funds, real estate funds or other special funds.
18. Russell (1989).
19. Zuckerman (2019, 333).
20. Taub (2019b).
21. Hope (2015) and Two Sigma (2020).
22. Taub (2019a).
23. A complex transaction that involves the execution of more than one instrument is said to have several "legs," with each *leg* referring to a specific part of the multi-asset trade. For example, a bond-switch (buying one and simultaneously selling another bond) has two legs. Also, in derivatives, a leg refers to an isolated cash flow. For example, a generic fixed-to-floating interest rate swap has two legs, the *floating leg* that specifies the cash flows based on a floating rate and the *fixed leg* that defines the reoccurring, fixed payments based on a fixed interest rate.
24. It should be inserted here parenthetically that not *all* hedge funds are as smart and sophisticated as the well-known leaders in the hedge fund industry. Because of the high fees, many former salespeople and traders are inclined to try their luck in establishing a hedge fund, only to find out that they lack the skills to generate excess returns. Some hedge funds have little information advantage and all they do is providing leveraged exposure to a particular asset class. If that asset class turns out to perform well, they look good and succeed in raising more money. Eventually, the asset class underperforms, causing the hedge fund to go out of business. However, up to that point the hedge fund collects significant fees (typically 2% of AUM annually).
25. Alarm bells would go off with the trader if, immediately after a sizable transaction with a hedge fund had been confirmed, the hedge fund would ask whether another transaction of the same, or even larger size, could be done at the same price level.
26. Reserve management can also have a market-moving impact at times. Central banks primarily hold reserves to defend the exchange rate against destabilizing outflows and to be able to provide foreign currency liquidity support to domestic banks.
27. This is a simplification because in reality the accompanying announcement of the central bank also needs to be taken into consideration. For example, if the market had expected a 25 bp increase, the central bank then kept the rate unchanged but also announced strong indications that a 25 bp

rate hike, and possibly more, is to come soon, the market may not react as strongly at all.

28. Fed funds futures contracts are based on the simple average of the daily Federal funds effective rate for the delivery month. For non-business days, the Fed funds effective rate of the previous business day is used. Fed funds futures offer only an *approximation* of the expected Fed funds target rate for a number of reasons. First, the Fed funds futures contract is based on the average daily Fed funds *effective* rate, not the *target* rate. While those two rates are typically very close to each other (as the Fed actively trying to achieve this), there can be a systematic difference between them. Also, while forward rates are the best unbiased predictors for future yields, future-implied rates are not due to the bias created by margining requirement (technically, a convexity adjustment would be necessary to eliminate this bias).

29. Fed funds futures are quoted as a price that is calculated as 100 minus the implied interest rate expressed as a percentage number. We make the following simplifying assumptions: There is no chance that the Fed has an unscheduled meeting (i.e., between formerly announced FOMC dates) in June; the spread between the effective and the target rate is zero; the convexity adjustment between futures and forwards is neglectable; the FOMC will always move rates in 25 bp increments.

30. To estimate the dispersion of believes, one could try to extract conditional probabilities from the option market.

31. For example, by lending out securities in the repo market and by excluding securities in high demand (on-the-run Treasuries, cheapest-to-deliver securities into a futures contract, securities trading special in repo) from the purchase program.

32. Donald Rumsfeld, Defense Department Briefing, February 12, 2002, accessed at https://www.c-span.org/video/?168646-1/defense-department-briefing.

33. Some investors prefer to be long convexity (long optionality) for this reason alone. Something unexpected may happen at any point in time, and it is better to own securities that benefit from unexpected events than those that lose value.

34. Knight (1921).

35. Angner (2016).

36. Assuming that there is no market for credit protection for this particular customer (e.g., credit default swaps) that would allow to extract the implied default probability, or any credible credit assessment (such as a rating by a rating agency) available.

37. This is the case for a number of reasons. First, the delta of an option, using a Black Scholes option pricing formula, is $N(d1)$, while the probability of the option to be struck in the risk-neutral world in $N(d2)$. Second, even when using $N(d2)$, this is a risk-neutral probability (or, technically speaking, an

object of the $\mathbb{Q}$ measure) as opposed to a real probability (i.e., a $\mathbb{P}$ measure). To convert from the $\mathbb{Q}$ to the $\mathbb{P}$ measure, one would have to have independent knowledge of the market's utility function or the market price of risk.

38. Fama (1970).

39. Ever since, a number of experiments have been conducted with monkeys and with people simulating monkeys. In 2016, the Financial Times evaluated the performance of portfolio managers, not vis-a-vis monkeys, but compared to the average market performance, and found that "(…) 99 per cent of actively managed US equity funds sold in Europe have failed to beat the S&P 500 over the past 10 years, while only two in every 100 global equity funds have outperformed (…)"; see Newlands and Marriage (2016).

40. Grossman and Stiglitz (1980).

41. Pedersen (2015, 4).

42. There are two examples of mispricing that come very close to pure arbitrage, although they are both from the 1980s and disappeared (i.e., got "arb'ed out") over time. The first relates to trading long dated FX forwards vs. currency swaps. For a few years, FX forwards traded as a separate market where prices were quoted by brokers based on supply and demand. At the inception of the currency swap market, one was able to trade currency swaps against FX forwards and arbitrage the two markets under a single ISDA agreement. The second example bases on the convexity of Eurodollar futures. In the early days of the interest rate swap market, the longer dated Eurodollar futures traded at comparable yields to interest rate swaps, although, unlike swaps, futures have zero convexity. As a result, one was able to set up risk-free positions with positive convexity. Thanks to Richard Leibovitch for pointing those examples out to me.

43. See Akerlof (1970).

References

Akerlof, George A. 1970. The Market for 'Lemons': Quality Uncertainty and the Market Mechanism. *Quarterly Journal of Economics* 84 (3): 488–500.

Angner, Erik. 2016. *A Course in Behavioral Economics.* Basingstoke: Palgrave Macmillan.

BlackRock. 2019. Re-engineering for Resilience: Global Insurance Report 2019. https://www.blackrock.com/institutions/en-us/literature/whitepaper/global-insurance-report-2019.pdf. Accessed on January 20, 2020.

Board of Governors of the Federal Reserve System. 2020. Balance Sheet Trends— Accessible: Total Assets of the Federal Reserve. https://www.federalreserve.gov/monetarypolicy/bst_recenttrends_accessible.htm. Accessed on May 23, 2020.

Deutscher Derivate Verband. 2018. Inforum, February. https://www.derivateverband.de/DE/MediaLibrary/Document/DDV-Informationsdienst%20INFORUM,%20Februar%202018.pdf. Accessed on January 20, 2020.

Fama, Eugene F. 1970. Efficient Capital Markets: A Review of Theory and Empirical Work. *Journal of Finance* 25 (2). Papers and Proceedings of the Twenty-Eighth Annual Meeting of the American Finance Association New York, N.Y. December, 28–30, 1969 (May), 383–417.

Federal Reserve Bank of New York. 2020. System Open Market Account Holdings of Domestic Securities. https://www.newyorkfed.org/markets/soma/sysopen_accholdings. Accessed on May 17, 2020.

Federal Reserve Bank of St. Louis. 2020. Federal Funds Target Range. https://fred.stlouisfed.org/series/DFEDTARU. Accessed on May 18, 2020.

Financial Stability Board. 2019. Global Monitoring Report on Non-Bank Financial Intermediation 2018. https://www.fsb.org/wp-content/uploads/P040219.pdf. Accessed on January 20, 2020.

Grossman, Sanford J., and Joseph E. Stiglitz. 1980. On the Impossibility of Informationally Efficient Markets. *American Economic Review* 70 (3): 393–408.

Hope, Bradley. 2015. How Computers Trawl a Sea of Data for Stock Picks. *The Wall Street Journal*, April 1. https://www.wsj.com/articles/how-computers-trawl-a-sea-of-data-for-stock-picks-1427941801. Accessed on January 20, 2020.

Jensen, Michael C., and William H. Meckling. 1976. Theory of the Firm: Managerial Behavior, Agency Costs and Ownership Structure. *Journal of Financial Economics* 3 (4): 305–360.

Knight, Frank H. 1921. *Risk, Uncertainty and Profit*. Boston, MA: Houghton Mifflin Company.

Lautenschläger, Sabine. 2017. 3-6-3: Banks and Change. Speech by Sabine Lautenschläger, Member of the Executive Board of the ECB and Vice-Chair of the Supervisory Board of the ECB, at the Bankwirtschaftliche Tagung of the BVR, Berlin, May 31. https://www.bankingsupervision.europa.eu/press/speeches/date/2017/html/ssm.sp170531.en.html. Accessed on January 20, 2020.

Malkiel, Burton G. 2014. *A Random Walk Down Wall Street: The Time-Tested Strategy for Successful Investing*. New York, NY: W. W. Norton.

Mutual Fund Directory. 2020. Mutual Fund Companies Ranked by Assets Under Management (AUM). https://mutualfunddirectory.org/latest-directory-ranking-here. Accessed on January 20, 2020.

Newlands, Chris, and Madison Marriage. 2016. 99% of Actively Managed US Equity Funds Underperform: Almost all US, Global and EM Funds Have Failed to Beat Their Benchmark Since 2006. *Financial Times*, October 24.

OECD. 2020. Pension Funds' Assets (Indicator). https://data.oecd.org/pension/pension-funds-assets.htm. Accessed on January 20, 2020.

Pedersen, Lasse H. 2015. *Efficiently Inefficient: How Smart Money Invests and Market Prices Are Determined*. Princeton, NJ: Princeton University Press.

Rudden, Jennifer. 2019. Total Assets of Insurance Companies Worldwide from 2002 to 2017. Statista, March 14. https://www.statista.com/statistics/421217/assets-of-global-insurance-companies. Accessed on January 20, 2020.

Russel, John. 1989. Alfred W. Jones, 88, Sociologist and Investment Fund Innovator. *New York Times*, June 3, Section 1, p. 11. https://www.nytimes.com/1989/06/03/obituaries/alfred-w-jones-88-sociologist-and-investment-fund-innovator.html. Accessed on January 20, 2020.

Schramm, Michael. 2019. What Is Passive Investing? We Break Down What It Is and How It Works. Morningstar, September 27. https://www.morningstar.com/articles/946546/what-is-passive-investing. Accessed on January 20, 2020.

Sovereign Wealth Fund Institute. 2020. Top 88 Largest Sovereign Wealth Fund Rankings by Total Assets. https://www.swfinstitute.org/fund-rankings/sovereign-wealth-fund. Accessed on January 20, 2020.

Taub, Stephen. 2019a. The Rich List. Institutional Investor, April 30. https://www.institutionalinvestor.com/article/b1f61584d2sl0q/The-Rich-List. Accessed on January 20, 2020.

Taub, Stephen. 2019b. Inside the Geeky, Quirky, and Wildly Successful World of Quant Shop Two Sigma. Institutional Investor, June 28. https://www.institutionalinvestor.com/article/b1g1fp7k736xlv/Inside-the-Geeky-Quirky-and-Wildly-Successful-World-of-Quant-Shop-Two-Sigma. Accessed on January 20, 2020.

Two Sigma. 2020. About Two Sigma. https://www.twosigma.com/about. Accessed on January 20, 2020.

Vanguard. 2020. Vanguard 500 Index Fund Admiral Shares (VFIAX). https://investor.vanguard.com/mutual-funds/profile/VFIAX. Accessed on January 20, 2020.

Zuckerman, Gregory. 2019. *The Man Who Solved the Market: How Jim Simons Launched the Quant Revolution*. New York, NY: Penguin.

4

Sales

4.1 Anatomy of the Trading Floor

While the work environment of Sales has changed over the last decades, the archetypical setup is that Sales is typically co-located with trading on the trading floor. The close proximity allows sales staff to interact with traders in a fast and efficient manner. This was particularly important during times in which electronic communication was not as developed as it is nowadays. Still, even now it is not uncommon for universal banks to ensure physical proximity of sales and trading on one trading floor (see Fig. 4.1).

Sales is clustered in groups covering particular client groups, e.g., central bank sales, hedge fund sales, real money sales. Those units are then positioned close to the trading groups that are most relevant to them. For example, hedge fund sales is positioned closely to the swap (trading) desk and real money sales close to the Treasury (trading) desk. Mid- and back-office functions are situated on the sides, or on different floors.

An illustrative trading floor schematic is provided in Fig. 4.2. Hedge fund sales is close to the repo desk (because hedge funds need leverage), the derivative desk (swaps, volatility) and the Treasury desk. Central bank sales is close to the Treasury desk (central banks mostly just buy government bonds). Real money sales is close to the Treasury and Repo desks (e.g., money market funds buy Treasuries and post money in the repo market). Proprietary (Prop) trading and research are usually located on the side. There is a large conference room, in which the daily morning meeting is conducted.

© The Author(s) 2020
F. Tata, *Corporate and Investment Banking*,
https://doi.org/10.1007/978-3-030-44341-2_4

Fig. 4.1 Former UBS trading floor in Stamford, Connecticut (2005) (Credit: Douglas Healey/Polaris)

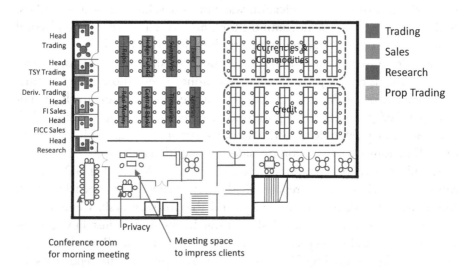

Fig. 4.2 Illustrative FICC trading floor setup

All Sales desks look quite similar. They mostly consist of multiple monitors and a trading floor phone. Their workspace setup is almost identical. There is a reason for this: If a client calls and the responsible salesperson is on the other side of the trading floor, he/she could pick up the phone from someone else's desk, feels familiar with the computer setup and can conduct the transaction. Also, when someone is not present (on vacation, on a client visit, etc.), someone else will typically take the place (trading floor space is in high demand).

The majority of banks have a "clean desk" policy, meaning that everyone is expected to maintain a tidy workspace with no client- or trade-related information laying around. This is important so that nobody unauthorized (visitors, employees from different departments) can gather privileged client information when walking by. It also ensures that important information (trade details, client data, etc.) are entered into the appropriate electronic systems right away and not kept on paper or locked away in drawers.

Bloomberg is one of the most important tools for sales; it used to be operated as a stand-alone Bloomberg terminal. Nowadays, Bloomberg is an integrated desktop application. Bloomberg serves many functions, including

- Email (many clients prefer to communicate via Bloomberg email);
- News (helps to discuss current market events with clients);
- Pricing tools (e.g., to convert a bond price into a yield);
- Market prices (to know approximate prices before asking trader).

A Bloomberg terminal costs roughly $20,000 a year per user; to be considered a serious market participant (especially in FICC), it helps to have a Bloomberg email address.

A trading floor phone turret is a comprehensive system that handles all audio communication requirements; some of the settings are standardized, so that an employee can use any phone within the sales and trading unit; other settings are configurable (such as direct lines to key clients). Phones are also used to directly address any person on the trading floor without dialing (called *squawk box* or *hoot-n-holler*), e.g., to ask for a price quote. Some lines are permanently open for announcements and commentary.

Although Sales does not establish a firm price that gets quoted to the client (only a trader is supposed to do that), a good salesperson knows the price level at which a financial instrument is trading at. Often, traders will only quote the last part of the price, assuming the salesperson knows the general price level. For example, instead of quoting "offered at 102-16+," the trader may just say "offered at a plus." If trades have multiple legs or if the trader only quotes hedge points of a trade, the salesperson needs to combine the information from the trading desk within a pricing model.

Salespeople often have multiple pricing tools in front of them, including:

- Bloomberg (usually good enough for bond pricing);
- Swap and swaption pricing tools (usually black-box models);
- Exotic derivative pricing tools (often spreadsheet-based);
- Additional pricing and trade-booking tools.

4.2   Role of Sales

This term "Sales" is a bit of a simplification of what encompasses the role. There is quite a difference between, say, the (fictional) shoe salesman Al Bundy and a salesperson covering institutional investors. First and foremost, the goal is to develop a lasting (sometimes called "strategic") relationship with the client, allowing the trading areas of the bank to capture an appropriate portion of the client's order flow. Maybe terms like client advisory, solutions marketing, relationship management or account management would better describe the role of a Global Markets sales, but for simplicity it is just called Sales.

A rather insulting reduction of a Global Markets salesperson's quality is to merely "smile and dial," implying that it suffices for a career in sales to be nice to clients and to know how to work the phone. Nothing could be further from the truth. In fact, what makes it particularly hard to be a salesperson is the large number of functions and often conflicting expectations associated with a sales role. Also, to be a successful salesperson you likely need a very broad skill set. People skills are equally important as technical abilities (pricing trades, etc.). A healthy self-confidence is required, as well as the ability to be modest and to de-escalate potential conflicts and friction inherent in the trade execution process. Product knowledge is required not only in one single product class, but often across various financial market instruments, across geographical regions, in various currencies. Basic knowledge about legal, regulatory, tax-related and self-imposed restrictions of clients is desirable. Foreign language skills are sometimes necessary as well.

There is, to my knowledge, no comprehensive list of what is expected from a Global Markets' salesperson, and even if that list existed, it would not guarantee a successful career in Sales. Each seasoned salesperson has, over time, developed his or her own *style* that works best. I have seen salespeople who arrived late, skipped the morning meeting, didn't seem to have superior product or market knowledge, lacked technical skills and did not appear to make much of an effort to serve their clients' needs. And yet, they would execute big-size trades for important clients of the bank. Later, I found out that they were close friends with their clients, often regularly playing golf with them on the weekends or engaging in other recreational activities together. If you have that kind of close relationship with key clients, you may put down this book. However, it is highly unlikely that you will *start* your career in Sales being in such a comfortable position. More likely, you will have to earn yourself the trust of a set of clients by diligently serving their needs over many years. Also, you will not know a priori what is needed to set you apart from other salespeople covering your clients, so you may have to pretty much try everything you see other sales professionals do, and only later skip some activities you find unnecessary in the context of your specific client relationship. For example, you will be told on your first day to always show up for the daily morning meeting and to take notes, so that you are prepared for your client calls. You will likely do this for a very long time, before you are in a position to skip this meeting.

What follows is a list of roles expected from an archetypal employee in Global Markets sales. It is subjective and far from complete. Yet, it provided an insight about the activities of a typical work day in sales.

4.2.1 Prospecting for New Clients vs. Managing Existing Relationships

The sales department is entrusted with the development and maintenance of client relationships necessary for other units of the bank to conduct client business. The first step is to locate new clients and to bring them on. After contacts at new clients have been established, the *onboarding* process starts with convincing the client that additional *coverage* makes sense on top of what is provided by other broker-dealers it already has business relationships with. Then, various agreements need to be negotiated and signed with the client, such as the ISDA Master Agreements governing over the counter (OTC) derivative transactions. The whole process can take a year or more to complete and requires a fair amount of persistence. From a mid-career hire into Sales it is almost always expected to help onboard clients covered in previous sales positions. New hires are expected to gradually develop relationships with smaller clients and to help onboard them once they have grown and start trading in reasonable size.

Newly established client relationships then need to be *managed*, often (but not always) by the same salesperson that has opened up the account. Managing existing client relationships requires a skill set that is different from the one needed for onboarding, and while some salespeople are better in prospecting for new clients, others are better in managing existing client relationships. That's why clients are sometimes passed from the onboarding salesperson to another (seasoned) salesperson. Given the turnover on the buy-side, it is important for a sales department to have a good mix of sales-people with respect to their skills in onboarding and managing relationships, and to maintain a pipeline of prospect clients for future onboarding.

4.2.2 Trade Execution

One of the most obvious roles of Sales is to facilitate *flow*. *Flow busi-ness* describes clients' trading activity, mostly triggered by client-specific needs (need to invest money, need to hedge, etc.). Sales aims to capture an as-large-as-possible share of each client's flow business, therefore maximizing the trading flow for their own *flow traders*. Flow traders *monetize* the client relationship by charging a fee (often in the form of a bid-ask-spread) and also gain valuable insight into general market flows. Therefore, a salesper-son is entrusted with ensuring a smooth trade execution. While the salesper-son aims at pleasing the client (to maintain a lasting client relationship), the primary goal is actually to *protect the trader*. "Protecting the trader" means making sure that the trader does not inadvertently loses money (e.g., by not knowing the client's trading strategy). Losses in the trading book are *real*, while future benefits from making a client happy are only *potential*, so a salesperson is well advised to always look out for the trading desk's interests.

Executing trades is not limited to picking up the phone and revealing a trader's price to the client. There are many additional elements to a smooth trade execution, including:

- Confirming that legal entity of client is authorized to trade (Know Your Customer, KYC) and that size of trade is within client's line (of credit);
- Gathering information about flow (total size, how many other parties involved, reasons for trade, etc.) and relaying this to traders;
- Lining up different legs of a trade (e.g., making respective traders aware of upcoming execution) and agreeing on quoting convention;
- Providing quote to client;

- Relaying to trader when client wants to execute and communicating to client when trade is done;
- Providing post-trade follow-up (fill on legs, "cover," etc.).

Sales also helps *streamlining* the communication, often "translating" a client's order into trading terms. Traders prefer to be asked for quotes in standardized, unambiguous and short language. Instead of "my client wants to buy 200 million worth of the current 10-year on-the-run Treasury security," they prefer "tens: offer 200." This becomes second nature to a salesperson after a while, but during the learning phase it can be quite stressful because one of the worst things that can happen to a salesperson is that a buy order is accidentally communicated to the trader as a sell order, or vice versa. Figure 4.3 shows a stylized example of the communication flow between a client (Fidelity investments, often referred to on the trading floor as "Fido" for short), a salesperson and the trading desk in a Treasury bond transaction.

Apart from the trade execution, a salesperson is expected to gather *intelligence* from the client, as far as trade motives, remaining flow, involved other counterparties or competitiveness of own quote is concerned. Markets have become so competitive that often enough the trading desk does not make any money in terms of bid-ask spread in a trade and the sole benefit from client interaction and transaction is the *informational value* of the client flow. If, for example, one large mortgage market participant starts executing hedging programs, there is some probability that other similar market participants will likely do so as well, which would create some flow imbalances

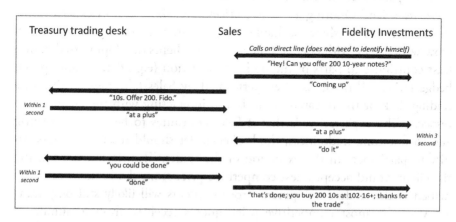

Fig. 4.3 Stylized example of trade execution

in the market and trigger price changes. Being able to *anticipate* this is extremely valuable for a trading desk because it allows them to adjust positions, recalibrate pricing or to fine-tune risk management.

As long as a trade gets executed smoothly, everything seems easy; the moment something is off, it is important for the salesperson to keep cool and to limit potential losses. There are many things that can go wrong during trade execution. Potential complications include:

- It takes the client longer than 3–5 seconds to react to a price quote and to protect the trader, client needs to be informed that prices are subject to change;
- Trader's quote seems wrong (compared to what is quoted on broker screens);
- Price moves after quoting to client;
- Client asks to adjust notional to odd-lot size (e.g., trades 50 million, then wants it changed to 50.1 million);
- When confirming the *handle*,[1] prices don't tie out (you probably quoted the wrong instrument);
- When calling back to confirm trade, you don't find the right contact person on the client side.

4.2.3 Iterative Trade Development

If a trade is developed solely on the client side, the sales side has little leverage to participate in the resulting trading flow other than by quoting an *aggressive* price.[2] Quoting aggressive prices is maybe the most expensive way to increase market share, so banks are interested in finding other ways to grow wallet share with clients. One is helping clients developing trades, or at least contribute to parts of the trade construction (e.g., determining proper hedge ratios). This role is often performed by Sales (although at times the trading desk or the research group is also interacting with the client in this respect). The expectation is that if Sales continues to help clients identify and to fine-tune trade ideas, the broker-dealer should receive the opportunity to participate in the execution of the trades. This does not mean that the client would accept a less competitive price from the broker-dealer that helped in the trade development process; clients will likely still only transact with the most competitive price quotes received from a number of competing broker-dealers. But it could mean that a helping broker-dealer at least gets *included* in a group of broker-dealers from which price quotes are requested from. Also, if the price quote is the most competitive price together with another broker-dealer that quoted the same price, the client would most likely award the trade to the broker-dealer that contributed most.

Even when Research has published a specific trade idea, there is a role to play for Sales. Sales, typically in close cooperation with Research, often turns a *generic* trade idea (e.g., one published as a PDF document and distributed to the entire client base) into a *client-specific* trade fitting the needs and execution abilities of a specific client. Clients often request from the salesperson to provide additional information, adjust the length of the time series, apply different hedge ratios, modify the instruments used, incorporate additional transaction cost, etc.

This iterative process of working with clients on trades is extremely valuable for Sales for a number of reasons:

- It gives insights into the clients "thinking process" (which is particularly helpful when it comes to clients that are notoriously secretive about what they do, like hedge funds);
- It increases the probability of being included in the trade execution;
- It helps finding conceptual flaws in own trade suggestion;
- It helps find new/better trades.

The process of iterative trade development is very well illustrated by Doug Huggins, co-founder and CEO at Markov, a financial services provider: "Under the traditional business model (...), we might perform a principal components analysis of the USD swap curve, regress a PCA-weighted butterfly spread against the price of front-month Brent futures, and then use Monte Carlo simulation to formulate a strategy for extracting value from the trade. (...) If our client likes the idea, he might send us an email asking us to repeat the principal components analysis using five years of data rather than three. Then we'd reply via email with the results. He might then ask us to regress the PCA-weighted spread against the price of WTI futures rather than Brent futures. Again, we'd update the analysis and send the results via another email. Finally, he might ask us to reassess the ex-ante Sharpe ratio of the trade over a horizon of two months rather than three, and with a stop-loss level 10 basis points away from the proposed entry level for the trade. Again, we'd update the analysis and reply with the updated results via email. All these iterations may take hours"[3]

4.2.4 Providing Market Color

Market color refers to the general market sentiment in the markets and anonymized flow information. Some clients tend to call various brokers to collect such market color, hoping to detect market trends and institutional behavior patterns before they become public information.

Often, there is a *Quid pro Quo*: Salespeople ask their clients whether they intend to transact shortly ("Anything I can help you with today?"), while clients ask for market color ("Do you see anything?"). Even when there is no trading of securities, there is a constant trading of information. But as a salesperson you only get told worthwhile information from your clients if you are able to feed them with something that is valuable to them. Since you are competing against many other salespeople from competing broker-dealers, you need ferret out information that sets you apart when you call your client. Maybe what you heard in the morning meeting will provide you with some valuable market color, but probably not. In order to assess the market sentiment and to anticipate flows, you probably need to talk to a number of clients first and get their reaction to what you know. There are some economies of scale in Sales when it comes to the ability to generate good market color: The more significant clients you cover, the better the feedback you receive when communicating the market color, which makes your market color better and more sought-after by other clients. Seasoned salespeople, after communicating market color and collecting the reaction of their clients, are often in the position to help other salespeople, and even trading desks and research groups, which improves their popularity. The flipside of this is that when you start in Sales and only have very few clients, many of which don't have much knowledge about the current market dynamics either, you have less information to offer during your client calls. Here, it helps if you allowed to sit next to a seasoned sales professional and are able to overhear his/her market observations.

Another source of market color (apart from what is shared internally and what you receive from your clients) is the trading flow you observe while sitting on the trading flow. The bigger the trading operation of the broker-dealer you work for and the more diverse the trading flow, the better the information you can extract from observed execution flows. Naturally, you are not allowed to share client-specific information with other clients. Examples of market color shared by email/Bloomberg or on the phone would be:

- "We are seeing good interest in the 10-year part of the curve";
- "There has been better buying in 10s";
- "Mortgage hedging has picked up";
- "Some real money accounts have been active in the front end today";
- "This trade idea had sparked some interest already; our own desk put some of it on already";
- "It has been a very quiet day so far."

There is the temptation for some salespeople lacking good market color (maybe working for a very small broker-dealer that has little flow business) to exaggerate or even to make up market color in order to appear more relevant to their clients. This is a dangerous and shortsighted strategy, however, because most clients receive market color from various broker-dealers and quickly detect this kind of behavior.

4.2.5 Sharing Traders' Axes

An axe in the financial market context is the inclination a trader shows in transacting; if a trader is not indifferent toward the direction of future order flows and would rather prefer to either buy or sell, he is said to be "axed." Those references toward the direction of transactions are typically based on the positions in the trading book or desired hedging flows. The term axe also represents a trader's sentiment about a given security.

The sales force is expected to help the trading desk to "fill" their axes. Often double or triple the regular sales credit[4] is given for filling axes. Trader axes are often communicated in the morning meeting, or else throughout the day. The purpose for Sales sharing the trading desk's axes with clients includes reasons like:

- It allows clients to focus on broker-dealers that are axed to do a trade, come trade execution (i.e., in a bidding process, not accidentally inviting traders that can't provide a competitive quote);
- It helps clients to gather a sense about liquidity in the market: If the majority of traders are axed to buy (sell), the price is likely to go up (down);
- It facilitates spotting arbitrage opportunities (i.e., finding opportunities to "cross" two traders);
- It helps matching and aligning traders' axes with clients' own execution needs.

Sometimes, the axe is used as an excuse for price quotes to the client that turn out to be not competitive:

Client: "Your quote was totally off the market!"
Sales: "Sorry, but our desk is not axed to do this trade."
Client: "You should have told me beforehand."

4.2.6 Sharing Desk Research and Strategy Publications

Clients are virtually bombarded with research publications, but often lack the time and inclination to read everything they receive (a problem that will be further discussed in Chapter 6). The job of Sales includes *alerting* clients about relevant publications, or to *highlight* the part of a broad publication that could be of interest to a particular client. Because different clients have different mandates, trading restrictions and views, a salesperson needs to read almost everything its own research department puts out (in the relevant product class and/or geographical region) to be able to judge, which bits and pieces would be worth to recommend to various clients during client calls or in individual emails/Bloomberg messages. Often, Sales acts as a "quality filter," ignoring the parts of the research publication that is of little value-adding.[5] Sales also offers to put a research analyst on the phone to have the research analyst talk the client through the relevant sections of the publication.

One example of analysis shared by Sales is research related to upcoming bond auctions. Many large institutional investors (especially "real money" investors) are active market participants in auctions because it allows them to buy security in large size (with less of a price impact and potentially lower transaction cost). Some other investors, such as foreign central banks and sovereign wealth funds, need to buy at bond auctions to replace maturing bonds and/or to peg their currency against the dollar.[6] Sales provides clients with a schedule of upcoming auctions, called auction pipeline. This includes information how previous auctions went, who were believed to be the main buyers, at which spread to the current benchmark security the newly auctioned instruments are expected to trade and how the new supply from the auction is believed to change the yield curve and/or create relative value opportunities.

Besides auction-related publications, Sales provides clients with various outlooks, commentaries, alerts, trade ideas, thematic research publications and other publications. The market outlook is particularly useful to engage the client because it covers a variety of markets and products; a salesperson can use an outlook to test a client's interest in an area where currently no customer business is conducted ("Our outlook has an interesting section about volatility; are you involved in volatility product at all?").

Some outlooks and other flagship publications are used as a reason for client visits, research roadshows or research conferences.

4.2.7 Client Entertainment

One main purpose of Sales is to develop a deep personal relationship with the client base that goes beyond the pure business relationship; it is not unusual for a salesperson to develop a friendship with key clients, often also involving spouses. There are examples of salespeople being invited to clients' weddings, or vice versa.

At the minimum, a salesperson will invite clients to business lunches and business dinners, a form of entertainment referred to as "wine and dine." In the 1980s and 1990s, strip-club visits were not uncommon; in the 2000s, the focus shifted to sport events; since the financial crisis of 2007–2008, the relationship between sales and clients has become significantly more professional. In fact, most institutional investors are no longer allowed to accept inducements (partly because of regulatory restrictions, partly because of self-imposed limitations to prevent manipulation).

Client entertainment used to be an easy way to steer up business with clients. To give a historical perspective, those would be typical steps:

- Annual or semi-annual client visit scheduled by salesperson.
- Salesperson, often accompanied by research analyst, trader and/or relationship manager, visits client at client location; short presentation of research analyst given.
- Going to restaurant picked by client (often a steak house); 3–5 clients attending; "wine & dine"; potentially additional client entertainment.
- Next day: client calls to thank for visit; "coincidentally" also doing one big-ticket transaction that essentially "pays" for the whole trip.

Client entertainment can be viewed as a form of agency cost in the context of agency theory (discussed in Sect. 3.2.4).

While the relationship between Sales and clients no longer includes the unprofessional behavior practiced in the past, it remains an integral part of any salesperson to organize client meetings and to engage in as much interaction with the client as possible.

4.2.8 Client Education

Sales also offers clients education in financial products, markets, pricing and hedging techniques and other areas as an inducement to increase execution flows and to foster a tighter relationship.

Some buy-side clients don't have a formal training program for their front, mid- and back-office employees and are rely on the sell-side to offer training. Usually, it is considered an honor to be asked by a client to perform an in-house training seminar.

Client education can also have the purpose of increases the breadth of a client relationship by getting the client to trade in a new product class.

Client education can finally be viewed as a form of marketing in which the broker-dealer showcases its sophistication and market/product knowledge. Some of the educational material (research primers) rivals academic and practitioner literature or what is presented at industry conferences.[7]

4.2.9 Seminars and Research Conferences

The last task of a salesperson to be discussed here is to accompany clients to seminars and research conferences organized by the bank. Most large broker-dealers run annual conferences for key client groups. For example, there may be an annual Central Banks Conference, organized by your employer. If you cover central banks and some of your clients accept the invitation, you may be required to attend the conference as well. What sounds like a lot of fun can actually turn into a lot of work. You will likely not only join your clients to all presentations they chose to attend, but also accompany them on sightseeing activities, dinners and potentially even barhopping and clubbing. For some clients, the conferences are one of the few occasions in the year to get away from their family and they want to make the best out of it. Don't expect to get a whole lot of sleep when taking your clients to Paris, Las Vegas or London.

Still, seminars and conferences can be excellent opportunities to deepen a client relationship. If done right, your clients will have the opportunity to personally meet with some conference speakers, and as a salesperson you may learn about your clients' academic and theoretical interests, which product classes and markets they are planning to venture into going forward, what their macroeconomic concerns are, which theoretical frameworks and pricing models they use internally and other aspects that may not often come up during a regular client-sales relationship.

4.3 Agency Problems in Sales

As discussed in Sect. 3.2.4, the concepts developed in agency theory can be used to describe problems arising when one person, the *agent*, makes decisions on behalf of another person, the *principal*. In the context of a client-sales relationship, the salesperson is the agent, while the client is the principal. However, the salesperson is employed and paid by the broker-dealer. This means that a salesperson's *own* interest (maximizing compensation) may *diverge* from the client's interest (low transaction cost, risk reduction, etc.). This creates conflicting interests for salespeople, some of which have become quite obvious in the wake of the US subprime mortgage crisis that triggered the financial crisis of 2007–2008. Investors, many of them outside of the USA and with little knowledge about the subprime mortgage market, felt that banks used their sales force to purposely mislead them when selling mortgage-related structured products under false promises to unload risk from their own balance sheet.

A salesperson has to develop some sense of balance and fairness in the client relationship. While the salesperson gets paid by the bank that he/she works for, it is the client who conducts business and ultimately determines the salesperson's success. If a salesperson merely serves the trading desk (maximizing revenues, filling axes, enabling large commissions, etc.), clients will eventually take notice and start steering business toward competing banks. On the other hand, if a salesperson pushes traders all the time to improve their prices to the benefit of the clients, he/she risks developing the perception to work for the client, not the bank, and that the client business does not actually contribute much to the bottom line of the bank.

Also, the salesperson (agent) has information unknown to the client (principal), described as *asymmetric information* in agency theory. An example for such an information asymmetry would be a salesperson knowing that other clients are executing similar trades, but in an opposite direction. From a trading desk's perspective, it is beneficial to face offsetting flow from different clients; clients, however, may be more reluctant to enter into a transaction, knowing that their own competitors are doing exactly the opposite. Thus, a salesperson may choose not to tell a client that other market participants are currently establishing the opposite economic exposure. We have seen that asymmetric information can lead to adverse selection, where the client (principal) can no longer trust the salesperson (agent) and simply assumes the worst. From an information point of view, a good salesperson has to have a sense of balance. In the long run, clients will reward salespeople that help prevent bad decision making by providing sufficient information. The reward comes in form of a larger share of their wallet spend with the respective broker-dealer.

In some areas, price indications coming from Sales are not trusted anymore because of dodgy practices by some market participants in the past. For example, bid prices indicated by Sales were often set artificially high to create the illusion of a tight bid-ask spread during the process of selling a product; later, banks are no longer keen to bid back the product, leaving the buyer with an illiquid product that has a wide bid-ask spread.

4.4   Cognitive Biases

Being an institutional investor does not necessarily guarantee metacognitive competence. Especially if financial market professionals have been doing something in the same way for several years, have received social recognition for it (promotions, etc.), have been compensated well and been asked to act as a role model (trainer, etc.), they may develop an inflated view about their abilities and gradually lose their self-critical view about potential limitations.

In psychology, this cognitive bias is called the *Dunning-Kruger effect*, named after an article by Justin Kruger and David Dunning with the telling title "Unskilled and unaware of it: how difficulties in recognizing one's own incompetence lead to inflated self-assessments."[8] What the authors found is that unskilled people not only tend to make bad decisions, but their incompetence also robs them of the ability to realize this. In the context of a sales environment, salespeople benefit from clients exhibiting such a cognitive bias. Those are clients who don't know enough about a product, a market or a particular trade, and also don't know that they don't know enough. Maybe they know just a little bit from reading sell-side research material provided by the salesperson.[9] But those clients typically don't know enough to understand all risks and pitfalls of a proposed transaction. It is not an uncommon practice among salespeople to make clients feel good about their abilities by suggesting they are smarter than the average investor. "This is a trade idea we usually only show to hedge funds, but I think you should also take a look at it. It is similar to the kind of arbitrage trades you do." Many clients will feel flattered to hear something like that. Next thing you know is that German Landesbanks are investing in US subprime mortgage market products.

A naïve client is prone to suffer from cognitive biases because day in, day out he/she is told by multiple salespeople from different broker-dealers how smart his/her trading strategy is, even when salespeople suspect it is not. There is little reward for telling the truth. Thus, Sales is purposely cultivating what Satyajit Das calls "beautiful lies":

> 'Beautiful lies' are the lies that we like to believe; we know they are not true but everything makes us want to believe them – that is what makes them beautiful.[10]

Cognitive biases do not only affect clients. Salespeople can fall victim of them also. Salespeople often overvalue ideas they show out to clients, wanting to believe that they are low-risk/high-return trades. Their own boss and their own trading desk will likely reassure them in their view.[11]

4.5   Case Study: Fannie Mae Callable Debt

This is a case study about how Sales can help bring together two groups of market participants by constructing a trade such that they both benefit from it and, in addition, a profit can be made from the structuring. One group consists of highly rated bond issuers that aim to fund themselves as close to what the US Government is paying for its debt. We will use Fannie Mae as an example. The second group consists of investors looking for close to risk-free investments that offer a yield at a certain level above what the US Government pays. All interest rate levels used here are for illustrative purpose only.

4.5.1 Fannie Mae: Reducing Funding Cost

Fannie Mae is a government-sponsored enterprise (GSE) chartered by US Congress. It serves as a stable source of liquidity for purchases of homes and for refinancing existing mortgages. Fannie Mae operates in the secondary mortgage market. It supports the liquidity and stability of the US mortgage market by, among other things, purchasing mortgage loans and mortgage-related securities, primarily for securitization and sale at a later date. Fannie Mae obtains the funds to finance its mortgage purchases and other business activities by selling debt securities in the capital markets. Fannie Mae's goal is to obtain a funding level as close to that of US Government obligations as possible.

Fannie Mae's debt is very similar to that of US Government debt, except for a slight liquidity disadvantage. Fannie Mae is open to suggestions as to how reduce their funding level (without harming their reputation by issuing dicey instruments); Fannie Mae is only interested in plain-vanilla funding—any added complexity needs to be swapped out by the broker-dealer that creates the security.

4.5.2 Investors Looking for Yield

Buyers of Fannie Mae debt securities are among the most risk averse, conservative and restricted investors.[12] Many of them cannot buy corporate debt, take credit risk, enter into derivative transactions or buy non-dollar denominated debt. Buying callable debt is permissible, however. They are looking for securities comparable to US Government obligations, but with a higher yield.

From a credit risk rating perspective, Fannie Mae debt is comparable with US Government debt (see Table 4.1). Also, Fannie Mae debt obligations receive favorable regulatory treatment. They are deemed to be *exempt securities* within the meaning of the laws administered by the US Securities and Exchange Commission, to the same extent as US Government obligations; they fall in the class of "Agency Bonds." Agency bonds give investors the opportunity to gain a higher return than Treasury bonds, while sacrificing very little in terms of risk or liquidity.

Table 4.1 Long-term senior debt ratings of US Government and Fannie Mae

Rating agency	US Government[a]	Fannie Mae[b]
S&P	AA+	AA+
Moody's	Aaa	Aaa
Fitch	AAA	AAA

[a]As of February 3, 2018
[b]As of June 30, 2016

4.5.3 Problem Matching Market Participants' Interests

Assume the yield for 3-year Treasury non-callable, or bullet, notes to be 1.5%; investors are interested in buying Treasury-like 3-year notes at 2%. At the same time, Fannie Mae aims to fund itself at T+20 bp, i.e., 20 bp above Treasury yield. In case of a 3-year funding, T+20 bp would be 1.7%.

Fannie Mae's *funding target* and investors' *yield target* are not matching (see Fig. 4.4).

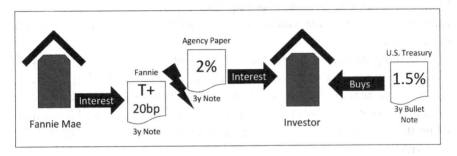

Fig. 4.4 No match between target funding level and target yield level

Buy-side investors now place a so-called *reverse inquiry* with Sales, indicating that they would be willing to buy 3-year Agency Paper at 2%. Sales is looking for a solution that allows Fannie Mae to issue debt for which there is demand from the buy-side.

4.5.4 Matching Target Funding Level and Target Yield Level

Fannie Mae can make its 3-year debt more attractive to investors by adding a call feature to it (see Fig. 4.5). The call feature can be a one-time European call, a Bermudian-style multiple call or an American-style continuous call.

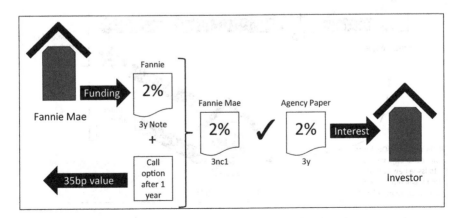

Fig. 4.5 Match between target funding level and target yield level

The lockout periodrefers to the amount of time for which a callable security cannot be called. For example, with a 3 non-call 1-year ("3nc1") debt security, the security cannot be called in the first year. The investor is compensated for being short the call option through a higher coupon payment. Many investors like the yield pickup they receive for essentially "selling" volatility, something they would not be allowed to do outright in the derivative markets.

By making its debt callable, Fannie Mae not only meets the target yield level of investors, it also diversifies its investor base by targeting a segment of borrowers that prefer investing in callable debt over non-callable debt. Fannie Mae is effectively buying a call option from investors and is compensating these investors with additional yield above comparable maturity bullet securities.

There is only one problem: Fannie Mae is actually not interested in purchasing call options, and rather have a broker-dealer swap them into a straight financing at their target financing level. In our example the broker-dealer pays 30 bp running for the option[13]; combined with the 1.7% from Fannie Mae (T+20), this gives the callable note a 2% coupon. As a result, Fannie Mae reaches its funding target, and investors receive their target coupon rate of 2%. The broker-dealer is paying 30 bp running for an option worth 35 bp running, thus pocketing 5 bp running (see Fig. 4.6).

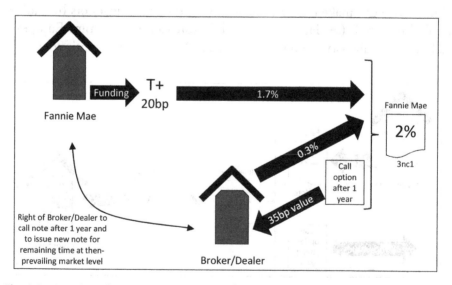

Fig. 4.6   Creation of Fannie Mae callable debt

4.5.5 Sales "Story"

Callable notes are often sold with a simple *story* illustrating the attractiveness of the coupon rate in comparison to non-callable, or *bullet* note yields. Assuming that current market levels of a 1-year bullet Fannie Mae bond is 1.5% and for a 3-year bullet is 1.9%, the story would go like this:

- "If you buy the 3nc1 instead of a 3y bullet and the callable does not get called, you earn 2% instead of 1.9%."
- "If the callable note gets called, you held a 1-year investment yielding 2% instead of 1.5%."
- "Thus, you win either way."

It seems the 2% yield of the 3nc1 "beats" both a 1- and a 3-year Agency note investment. But this is not true because the investor buying a callable bond has sold an option and is *short convexity*. Short convexity means that for large interest rate changes, the investment has inferior returns. If, for example Fannie Mae's 2-year funding level jumps to 5% a year from now, the callable bond will likely *not* be called and the investor is stuck with a 2% coupon payment in a 5% yield environment. If, on the other hand, Fannie Mae's 2-year funding level falls to 1% in a year's time, the callable bond gets called and the investor would have to *reinvest* the money at a lower yield level.

Investors aware of being short convexity may still like the callable note if they can be convinced that implied volatility is higher than historical or expected volatility. Implied volatility of an option is the volatility input entered into an option pricing model to calculate the theoretical value of optionality. Historical volatility is a backward-looking measure of the actual dispersion of returns of an underlying security over a given period of time.

4.5.6 Opportunities and Risks

Callable Agencies debt creates opportunities and risks for both, the issuer and the buyer. The role of Sales includes highlighting the advantages to the involved parties while qualifying the risks. Sales also needs to adjust the trade mechanics (maturity, call dates, lockout period, call feature, etc.) to satisfy clients' reverse inquiries and issuers' funding targets at the same time. Because callable debt issuance requires derivative-savvy salespeople, it is often conducted out of specialized sales units (Derivatives Sales, Investor Derivative Marketing, etc.). Table 4.2 summarizes opportunities and risks in callable debt to the issuer, the buyer and the broker-dealer.

Table 4.2 Opportunities and risks in callable debt

Market participant	Opportunities	Risks
Issuer (Agency)	Lower funding cost Tabbing into new markets	Lost opportunity to refund at lower yield (if call has been swapped out)
Investor	Higher return (if debt not called) Ability to sell volatility	Reinvestment risk (if debt gets called) Price risk if implied volatility increases
Broker-dealer	Fee income Cheap source of volatility	Hedging risk

4.6   Challenges Ahead

A publication covering Global Markets sales would not be complete without acknowledging a number of challenges ahead. Unfortunately, Sales does no longer have the high reputation among institutional investors it used to have. Partially responsible for this is that, over the course of the last 10 years or so, seasoned, experienced staff has been reduced by banks in an effort to save costs and been replaced by junior, inexperienced employees.

Sales has also lost some of its importance due to the fact that many of the fastest-growing areas in modern finance, such as high-frequency trading or passive portfolio management, require less sales support. Clients are increasingly more interested in connecting to the sell-side via APIs rather than through voice channel communication with salespeople.

The *reputation* of a sales unit can only be as good as the reputation of the broker-dealer it operates within. Since the financial crisis of 2007–2008, banks had to be disciplined by regulators with large fines for misconduct like toxic securities abuses, investor protection violation, interest rate benchmark manipulation, tax violations, securities issuance or trading violation, banking violation or anti-money-laundering deficiencies. It is hard for a salesperson to gain the trust of clients when there are widespread ethics concerns about banks in general.

Regulatory changes have made the sales environment more challenging. For example, a bonus cap that limits payouts to 100% of the base salary (i.e., the fixed component of the total remuneration) took effect in January 2014.[14] As a consequence, banks had to increase the fixed component of salespeoples' compensation (as qualified sales staff would otherwise leave for non-regulated entities), increasing the bank's fix cost (while revenues remained variable). This means that banks now need to aggressively reduce staff during low revenue periods, only to lack capacity once business picks up again. Exaggerated hire-and-fire policy is not only detrimental to sales staff, but also hurts clients who suffer from reduced sales support during busy periods. Some other regulation is prohibiting *inducements* (more on this in Sect. 6.8), ensuring that trade execution is based on price, and not on other "services" provided by Sales. In this market environment it becomes less clear how much value-adding is provided Sales and whether human salespeople could be replaced by some electronic execution platform used by clients. For example, a significant portion of the swap business is now mandated to be conducted on so-called swap execution facilities (SEFs). Those derivative trading platforms, operated by providers like Bloomberg and Tradeweb, are replacing some of the experienced salespeople.

While in the past, a client was sometimes covered by one single salesperson, Sales has turned into a *team* effort, where a group of 5–10 salespeople jointly serve a client on a wide product range. Each salesperson brings different product and market expertise and contributes as part of a diverse coverage team. The process of *institutionalizing* client relationships is often painful for some salespeople who feel that the "own" the client (and maybe even brought them on). However, clients tend to prefer the team coverage model, as it provides for the maximum product expertise and connectivity. Moving from a "buddy-to-buddy" to a team coverage model remains challenging for many banks, as they experience the exodus of frustrated seasoned salespeople.

Finally, Sales crucially depends on the *pricing ability* of the trading desk supporting it. When banks cut down their trading capacity, it impairs the sales forces' ability to offer liquid two-way prices. Banks also frequent shift their strategic focus (entering a new business, retrenching, merging, etc.), causing a great deal of management and staff turnover and increasing the volatility of a career in Sales.

4.7   A Career in Sales (by Peter Joel)

How Do You Measure a Salesperson's Success? Just like a trader, a sales-person is judged by performance. This performance can take many forms. First, there is *production* with clients ("How much did you add to the bank's bottom line with your accounts?"). Then, there is client *penetration* ("I need an intro to the Chief Investment Officer at that firm. Can you help?"). Also, there is *connectivity* between your firm and the clients ("We are the Prime Broker for XYZ Hedge Fund; would you be able to see if they have a need for interest rate coverage?"). I am working in Fixed Income that is predomi-nantly a principle-based market.[15] This means that most trades are such that clients are asking to assume and to warehouse the other side of their trade (which, given the sophistication of clients can be problematic). As a salesper-son, you are the linkage between your firm and the client, and you're often caught in between. I liken it to having two bosses. *Balancing interests* is art in itself.

How I Became a Fixed Income Salesperson Coming out of under-grad, I was looking for an engaging career that would help me utilize my economics degree. Growing up in a large family and always doing sports, the organized chaos of the trading floor appealed to me. A fam-ily friend recommended that I look into a career in markets.[16] This eventually led me to JPMorgan where I became an assistant trader on the Government Bond Desk. Back in the early 1990s, the evolution was that the floor assistants were apprenticing and eventually promoted to become a trader or salesperson. There were a few that got hand-selected for the training programs, but I was not one of the lucky ones. Thus, I started as a US Treasury assistant trader, then became head of assistants, and finally a trader and salesperson on the repo desk. My first few positions helped me understand risk, operations and market structure. But the repo desk was also eye-opening to me for it is the underpinning of the bond mar-kets. This stoked my market curiosity. From that point on, I made a con-scious effort to focus on *continuous learning*. This is a key element to a long and successful career. While the markets have dramatically changed over the years, my adaptation to them is fueled by learning.[17] Thus, if you ever feel you are in total control it is time to leave the comfort zone.

Variety Is the Spice of Life (in Sales) The wider the array of clients you cover and the more products you help selling, the more engaging your work will be. Markets are often a zero-sum game. There are winners and losers. Fortunately, clients have different investment mandates. For a Central Bank, it may be to invest currency proceeds. Index fund managers are intended to track an index. Hedge funds seek to exploit profit opportunities. Pension funds and insurance companies are concerned about long-term liabilities. Having a wide spectrum of clients leads to a broad spectrum of thinking and engaging. It gives you a diversified portfolio in case things stagnate or go sour with one set of clients. The same can be said about products: the more the better. But only to a point. If you become an expert in a selected number of products, people will seek you out. If you try to cover all products, you become a jack of all trades, but a master of none.

Notes

1. The "handle," or "big figure," is the part of a price that comes before the decimal point. In institutional trading, the handle is often omitted when quoting the price in order to speed up the trading process. However, quoting conventions are different for different product classes and a salesperson in supposed to know them. Some quotes are in price terms, others in terms of yield. In some markets, the decimal quotation system is used, while in others prices are quoted in 32nds and 64ths.
2. Aggressive pricing is meant to maximize the probability of execution. This includes quoting an offer price at (or sometimes below) the mid-market price, or to quote a bid at (or above) the mid-market price. It also includes offering to transact at a transaction size significantly below or above what is typically associated with a price quote in the particular market.
3. Huggins (2018).
4. Sales credit is an assumed contribution by a salesperson to a hypothetical profit in the trading book that is used to measure a salesperson's performance.
5. Research staff is often forced to produce periodic publications, such as a "Daily," a "Weekly," a "Monthly," a "Quarterly" or some sort of year-end publication. Not all of it is of a quality high enough to be promoted to clients. Some salespeople ignore the research of their own broker-dealer because they think, a competing broker-dealer produces better analysis. Some go as far as referring their clients to those publications; this behavior is frowned upon, however.
6. As of November 2019, China owns about $1.1 trillion and Japan some $1.2 trillion in US government debt. Source: Department of the Treasury (2020).
7. An example would be the 7-part series "Understanding the Yield Curve" by Salomon Brothers, published in 1995–1996.

8. Kruger and Dunning (1999).
9. Some of the most complicated derivative trades have been sold to clients that were "educated" by the same bank they afterwards traded with. The training sessions were mostly meant to create a false sense of knowledge for the client.
10. Das (2012, 62).
11. "Just remember: It's not a lie if you believe in it"—George Costanza, Seinfeld (TV Series), 1995.
12. They include commercial bank portfolios and trust departments, investment fund managers, insurance companies, pension funds, state and local governments, and central banks.
13. Contractually, the broker-dealer has the right to call the note (in Fannie Mae's name), issue a new note (a 2-year bullet note in one year's time) at then-prevailing yield levels, while continuing to receive 1.7% from Fannie Mae.
14. European Union (2013), Article 94(1)g(i).
15. As opposed to an exchange-based market.
16. Never underestimate contacts and conversations! As for me, I would rather die trying rather than just hope good fortune rolls my way. Talk to anyone that will talk to you! Good fortune will then find you.
17. In the mid-1990s, there were separate Treasury government bond, agency bond, derivative, option and futures salespeople. These silos started to give way to a sole "Rates" area in which traders and sales are able to interact in all products. If you didn't adapt, you didn't keep your seat.

References

Das, Satyajit. 2012. *Traders, Guns and Money: Knowns and Unknowns in the Dazzling World of Derivatives*. Harlow, UK: Pearson.

Department of the Treasury. 2020. Major Foreign Holders of Treasury Securities. https://ticdata.treasury.gov/Publish/mfh.txt. Accessed on January 20, 2020.

European Union. 2013. Directive 2013/36/EU of the European Parliament and of the Council of 26 June 2013 on Access to the Activity of Credit Institutions and the Prudential Supervision of Credit Institutions and Investment Firms, Amending Directive 2002/87/EC and repealing Directives 2006/48/EC and 2006/49/EC Text with EEA Relevance. *Official Journal of the European Union*, L 176/338, 27 June. https://eur-lex.europa.eu/legal-content/EN/TXT/?uri=celex%3A32013L0036. Accessed on January 20, 2020.

Huggins, Doug. 2018. What Is Research as a Service? LinkedIn Pulse, February 8. https://www.linkedin.com/pulse/what-research-service-doug-huggins/. Accessed on January 20, 2020.

Kruger, J., and David Dunning. 1999. Unskilled and Unaware of It: How Difficulties in Recognizing One's Own Incompetence Lead to Inflated Self-Assessments. *Journal of Personality and Social Psychology* 77 (6): 1121–1134.

5

Trading

5.1 Trading Basics

Trading is the maybe most unforgiving environment for making mistakes within corporate and investment banking. Trades with institutional investors are typically large and even small errors can have painful consequences for a trading desk, or even the bank as a whole. As a result, the career in trading is typically a gradual one, starting as a junior trader in a support function, before eventually receiving more responsibilities as a head trader.

5.1.1 Market Maker vs. Market Taker

Market makers stand ready to buy and sell securities in the marketplace. By their willingness to provide a two-way market, market makers serve as providers of liquidity. The difference between the price market makers are prepared to buy, called the *bid* price, and the price at which they stand ready to sell, called the *ask* or the *offer* price, is the *bid-ask spread*, or just "the spread." The spread serves as a compensation for providing liquidity.

Market takers are *consumers* of liquidity; they take up market makers commitment to buy (a process called "hitting the bid") or to sell (called "lifting the offer"), thereby eliminating those trading opportunities for others. Market takers pass their long/short positions with the risk associated with them on to the market makers who now have to manage that risk. In return for having the ability to *pass on* the risk to someone else, liquidity takers have to pay the (bid-ask) spread (see Fig. 5.1).

© The Author(s) 2020
F. Tata, *Corporate and Investment Banking*,
https://doi.org/10.1007/978-3-030-44341-2_5

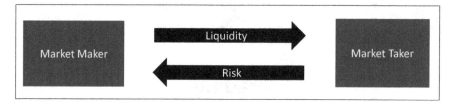

Fig. 5.1 Market maker vs. market taker

As long as the buy and sell orders from the market takers, called *order flow*, is *random*, they have no *systematic impact* on the price. In this case, market makers are able to *re-balance* their trading book at prices similar to the ones prevailing prior to the order arrival. The bid-ask spread, here, is merely a compensation for *transaction costs* (broker fees, trade booking, risk management costs, etc.). However, there is always the risk that some of the arriving orders are from *informed investors*, defined as investors who have nonpublic information about an expected price move. Because informed investors will buy from market makers if they expect the price to go up, and sell to market makers if they anticipate the price to fall, market makers are essentially *giving away options* to force them into a trading loss; this leads to a *widening* of the bid-ask spread (beyond what is charged to cover transaction cost) as a *protective measure*: Market makers need to generate a sufficient profit from uninformed order flow to offset the expected losses from informed order flow.

5.1.2 Stylized Example of Informed Order Flow

To illustrate the effects of informed order flow let's look at a situation in which market makers know that an informed market taker will transact with them shortly. Let's assume it is few seconds prior to an FOMC meeting announcement on which the Fed is expected to either keep interest rates unchanged or increase the target rate by 25 bp. Currently, the market assigns a 50% probability for both possible outcomes and bond prices reflect an implied rate increase of 12.5 bp. The price-yield relationship for a particular (roughly 10-year) bond may be assumed to be:

- Interest rates after FOMC equal those before FOMC: Bond price = $104
- Interest rates after FOMC 12.5 bp higher than before FOMC: Bond price = $103
- Interest rates after FOMC 25 bp higher than before FOMC: Bond price = $102

The market maker's current quote, assuming a fair value bond price of 103, shall be *$102.9 at $103.1* (meaning that the market maker is willing to buy the bond at $102.9 and to sell at $103.1).

Market makers, however, are aware that they may not have time to adjust price quotes between the FOMC announcement and the first order arriving from an informed market participant (e.g., due to the presence of low-latency high-frequency traders with superior data processing technology). Market makers know that the market price will jump either to $104 or to $102. At the same time, they are offering market takers an option to sell to them at $102.9 and to buy from them at $103.1. Either of the two options will be "in the money," resulting in a sure loss of $0.9 per bond to the market maker (see Fig. 5.2).

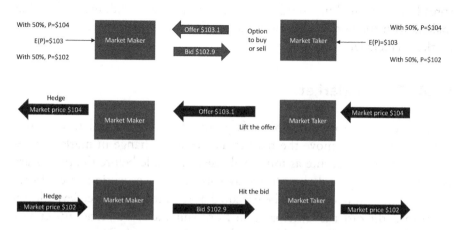

Fig. 5.2   Cash flows in stylized example of informed order flow

From this example it becomes obvious why traders are typically reluctant to make a market just moment prior to a market-moving event, such as the economic data releases or central bank announcements. Client inquiring about a price will be politely asked to wait until after the event and then to revert back.

5.1.3 Order Flow Toxicity

Order flow toxicity describes the problems arising from market makers not having direct control on the timing and direction of execution. Market makers are well aware that they are in competition with other market makers (it is not unusual for institutional investors to request price quotes from 3 to 5 traders). Order flow, in this context, is no longer *random*, as the probability of selling exceeds the probability of buying when a market maker inadvertently underestimates the value of a security, while the opposite is true when the value of the security is overestimated. Order flow, here, is *toxic* because it "adversely selects market makers, who may be unaware that they are providing liquidity at a loss."[1]

Order flow toxicity is an example of asymmetric information between market makers and market takers, leading to adverse selection. If the information asymmetry is such that market takers often have a better knowledge about the financial instrument's fair value (e.g., because they have more accurate pricing tools in case of derivatives) or imminent price changes (e.g. because of better information-processing capabilities), market makers will occur frequent losses. Those losses will first cause bid-ask spreads to widen, but could ultimately lead to a withdrawal of market makers with the potential for a market *collapse* (in which there are no more market makers left).

5.1.4 First to Market

Institutional investors often place large orders for execution; those orders are large enough to move the market, i.e., cause a change in market prices. Investors hope to execute as much volume as possible before the price starts changing adversely and to realize a favorable average execution price. In the best case, the entire order can be executed at the prevailing price level; in the worst case, the order is anticipated or front-run and has a price impact even before the first tranche of the investor's order is executed. Often, large orders are broken into smaller tranches that are executed simultaneously in different markets and/or sequentially over time (called "working an order").

First to market is an important principle of best execution, the legal responsibility of brokers to provide favorable execution of client orders. It ensures that a new order is arriving first for execution at the market (e.g., an exchange) before other orders based on the first order get executed. First to market prevents front running and minimizes the price impact of orders.

5.1.5 Backtesting

Backtesting is the process of applying a trading strategy or analytical method to historical data to see how accurately the strategy or method would have performed in the past. Basis for this is a good historical database. Importantly, the database has to be free from survivorship bias (i.e., it should include failed securities up to the point from which they no longer traded). Backtesting typically involves calculating the performance of trading strategies on a risk-adjusted return basis, e.g., expressed as a Sharpe ratio.

Common-sense rules for backtesting include[2]:

- Avoid look-ahead bias by using information that is not available in real time (e.g., day's high/low quotes prior to trading close);
- Avoid overfitting (overoptimizing parameters);
- Avoid training and testing model with same data set; instead, divide historical data into two parts and perform out-of-sample testing;
- Include transaction cost;
- Use historical data that span over (at least) one full business cycle;
- Make sure data series includes periods of stress (e.g., financial crisis of 2007–2008).

5.2 Pricing

5.2.1 Market Price

Traders in liquid financial products (for which market prices are observable and transactions at the prevailing market price are possible) will likely base their own pricing on market prices. Their own axe will determine whether there are better buyers or better sellers, causing (just small) deviations in their price quotes from market prices. A trader must, at any moment, know "where the market is"!

If there is a liquid market for a financial product, there are a number of reasons for using the market price as a basis for pricing:

- "The market is always right";
- Hedging is possible (only) at the market price;
- Mark-to-market of own positions will (likely) be vis-à-vis the market prices;
- Deviations from market price will potentially cause overwhelming client flow;
- Clients expect price quotes to reflect current market prices.

However, there are exceptions from merely relying on market prices, e.g.,

- The market price is "stale" (no recent trading);
- Size for requested quote is beyond average trading size in market;
- Odd-lot trading (quote not in typical increments of quantity);
- Non-standard terms in trading and/or execution;
- Counterparty risk.

5.2.2 Model Price

If there is no appropriate market price or the price is a function of related market prices, the trader needs to apply model-based pricing. To avoid being "arb'ed" by clients, the trader needs to know which pricing model and which calibration parameters are currently used by other market makers, even though the trader may use a different, proprietary pricing model.

If a model price needs to be established, the model needs to be *calibrated* to the market (transaction) prices of recent, liquid and relevant structures; for example: A swaption pricing tool utilized for pricing of 180 bp out-of-the-money receiver swaptions should be calibrated to a 200 bp OTM receiver swaptions, not to an at-the-money swaption.

When quoting a price established in a pricing model, model risk needs to be considered. Model risk is the risk associated with a mispricing or improper risk management due to the use of a model that does not reflect the reality. An example would be to use a lognormal model for interest rates that does assign a zero-probability for negative interest rates. Model risk also includes the risk of miscalibration.

5.2.3 Physics Envy

The intellectual milieu of economics established physics as the exemplar for economists, inevitably leading to the *mathematization* of economics and finance.[3] For example, the famous Black–Scholes option-pricing formula is also the solution to the so-called *heat equation* in Physics. More recently, fields like *financial engineering* and *algorithmic finance* are very closely linked to Physics and Computer Science. It appears that some finance professionals exhibit what Lo and Mueller (2010) call Physics envy.

However, human behavior is not nearly as stable and predictable as physical phenomena and quantitative aspirations of financial market participants may have created a false sense of mathematical precision in Finance. Simple, intuitive models at times serve as a better pricing and risk management tool than complex, non-intuitive mathematical calculations.

5.2.4 P&L Decomp

P&L decomp, short for profit and loss decomposition, is an exercise of splitting the total profit and loss to different root causes. It is also referred to by different names, including P&L explain or P&L attribution. The process starts with the mark-to-market (MTM) value of a position at the previous business day ("t-1," short for today-minus-one-business-day). Added to and subtracted from this value are all identifiable P&L components of the current trading day. For example, the position value may have changed due to a change in foreign exchange (FX) rates. More and more P&L drivers of the day are added. The MTM of t-1 plus the sum of all P&L drivers will (hopefully) approach the current day's MTM. There is likely a small *residual* that cannot be explained. See Fig. 5.3 as an illustration.

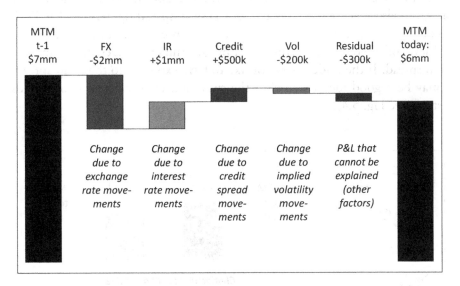

Fig. 5.3 Illustration of a P&L decomp for a UK callable bond

P&L decomp is very important to traders because traders need to know whether the trades are behaving the way they are supposed to work. A trader once told me that he prefers to lose money and to know why, rather than to make money for unknown reasons.

If a trade makes money for the wrong reasons, it will likely not perform as planned when the trader's views play out. In this case, it may be better to get out of the trade quickly and to find a better strategy to express a view in the market. The following example may illustrate this: Assume a trader expects 10-year interest rates to *decline*. The trader decides to receive fixed on a 10-year interest rate swap. The next day, the trader finds out that the interest rate swap position did not change in value although 10-year government bond interest rates *increased* on the day. It seems the trader was wrong and yet did not lose money. Is this a good thing? No, this worrying for two reasons. First, if the swap value does not change for an *increase* in government interest rates, then the swap cannot be expected to make money when government rates *decline*. Thus, the trade will likely not perform well when the trader's view materializes. Second, there are clearly some offsetting effects in the P&L that are not fully understood. This means that the trader is taking some risks he/she is unaware of. To understand what happened, a P&L decomp is performed. It turns out that while government interest rates increased, the swap spread declined by the same amount. The swap spread is the difference between the swap rate and the government (Treasury) rate.[4] Thus, the trade lost money because of the increase in government interest rates, but also made money because of the swap spread tightening. The P&L decomp shows that an interest rate swap creates exposure to both, the general level of interest rates (represented by government interest rates) and the swap spread. If the trader does not like to have exposure to the swap spread, it may be a good idea to unwind the swap and to buy government bonds instead (see Fig. 5.4).

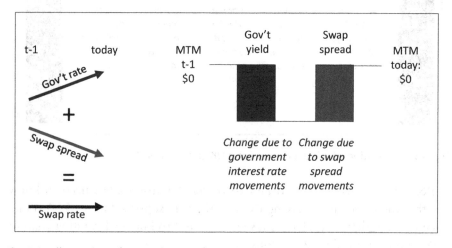

Fig. 5.4 Illustration of a P&L decomp for an interest rate swap

5.3 Flow Trading

Flow trading is the trading unit of a bank that serves clients. It is primarily conducting market making (i.e., providing liquidity) by standing ready to buy and sell at preannounced levels, as a service to clients.

Flow traders are also hoping that the arrival of buy and sell requests is such that they are mostly offsetting each other, meaning that the trader stays within the position limits; if order flow causes positions outside of the limits, there is the need to offset some of the trading book risk with other broker-dealers in the so-called *inter-dealer broker market* (in which case most/all of the bid-ask spread in the client trade is lost). To a flow trader, the biggest risk is to trade with informed clients buying (selling) just prior to a price increase (decline). The bid-ask spread needs to be set such that the trader covers transaction cost and recovers from occasional trading with informed clients (see Fig. 5.5).

For flow traders there is the inherent temptation to supplement income from charging bid-ask spreads with additional gains from front running client flow. *Front running* is the unethical practice of a flow trader to step in front of orders placed or about to be placed by clients to gain a

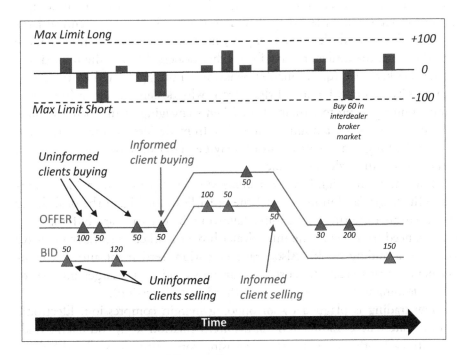

Fig. 5.5 Illustrative process of flow trading

price advantage. Flow traders asked for a quote could first execute a trade on their own behalf and quote a price to the client afterward; the client quote would reflect the prevailing market price after the trader's own execution and possibly (but not necessarily) be less attractive. Many institutional investors do closely monitor the market between asking for a quote and receiving a quote; if they see any sign of front running, they will stop trading with the particular dealer for a period of time (called "putting" the dealer "in the box").

A less severe misconduct of flow traders is what an anonymous market participant[5] calls *simul-running*, explaining it as follows: "some traders increase their lead-time by hitting bids [selling] or lifting offers [buying] in the brokers' screens as soon as a customer's direct wire flashes based on an educated guess—frequently obvious—as to which way he is going."

The dynamics between institutional buyers and sellers of Treasuries and broker-dealers providing liquidity is a complicated one. All involved market participants try to employ strategies that allow them to benefit from asymmetric information. It is not only flow traders trying to monetize flow information through *front running* and *simul-running*, but some institutional investors are also trying to benefit by *gaming* the bidding process. After contacting several dealers and making it look like they are put in competition for *one* single order, they then simultaneously execute identical large trades with *several* dealers. By doing so, institutional investors receive more liquidity than the dealers receive from other dealers through the inter-dealer broker market. This (questionable) behavior is not appreciated by the dealer community and may be one of the reasons why dealers engage in front- and simul-running to protect themselves. Clients engaging in this behavior may not receive the same amount of liquidity from dealers, so the tactic backfires in the long run; clients, instead, may be better of letting one dedicated dealer "work" the order over time.

Flow trading has significant *economies of scale*; it pays to be a "flow monster." The larger (and more diverse) the order flow, the higher the probability that there are offsetting transactions (allowing the bank to earn bid-ask without the need to hedge in the inter-dealer broker market or to carry excessive risk in the trading book). Also, trade execution, settlement and risk management systems create fix cost that can be spread over a larger number of trades, leading to lower cost per trade (fixed cost degression).

Flow trading is plagued by an ongoing margin compression. Electronic trading, alternative trading venues, disintermediation (e.g., end-clients trading with each other directly) and increasing competition has caused bid-ask spreads to decline.

Lower margins force dealers to either withdraw from market making in areas they don't have a competitive advantage in, or to monetize the client relationship in more creative ways, including cross-selling, benefiting from flow information or using client as liquidity providers. In some areas, flow traders hardly make any money off the bid-ask spread and are expected to generate profits from flow-related prop trading.

5.4 Proprietary Trading

Proprietary trading, prop trading for short, is using the bank's resources (capital, trading systems, risk management tools, access to information, human capital, etc.) to earn a sufficient risk-adjusted return on capital. Prop trading does not have clients of its own—prop trading *is* the client of other broker-dealers. Prop trading can involve providing liquidity as market makers, but there is no requirement to do so and typically the prop desk is a market taker (i.e., hitting bids and lifting offers).

The borders between flow and proprietary trading are often not crystal clear, as flow traders sometimes also place (hopefully small) directional bets or enter into relative value trades if they feel that they had extracted some insight from the client flow that gives them an informational advantage.

An entity that engages mostly in proprietary trading is also referred to as proprietary trading firm (PTF). Some PTFs are organizational structures with capital that allow prop traders to join on a contractor-basis, getting paid a part of the profit they generate.

Prop trading is a client to the "Street," i.e., gets covered by other dealers, receives research from other banks and does not need to execute through the sales trading desk. Often, there is room for tension between a bank's prop desk and the flow trading desk due to the risk of prop traders front running client flows.

Prop traders are not totally free to trade as they wish. They have to obey institutional rules, limitations and expectations, such as:

- Stay within risk limits and stick with authorized products (no rogue trading);
- Obey legal rules and regulations;
- Earn a sufficient return on capital;
- Don't jeopardize client relationships of the flow business or harm own flow traders;
- Aim to diversify bank's risk;
- Support flow trading in modeling and pass on market color.

5.5   Hedge Fund Trading

Traders at hedge funds have much more latitude than their colleagues at banks' trading desks because hedge funds are not depository institutions and therefore are not regulated as banks. Hedge funds, however, limit themselves to certain asset classes or to self-described investment styles and strategies. Common hedge fund categories include *Long-Short* (taking long and short positions in stocks to limit their exposures to the stock market), *Event-Driven* (taking positions on corporate events such as corporate bankruptcies and reorganizations), *Fixed Income Arbitrage*, *Global Macro* or what is vaguely described a *Multi-Strategy*.

Hedge funds employ a wide range of trading strategies, including trading on fundamentals, utilizing pattern recognition, using quantitative/statistical methods, technical analysis or trend-following strategies. Those trading techniques are not unique to hedge funds. Many of them are used by university endowments, pension funds, wealthy family portfolios and proprietary trading desks of commercial and investment banks.

Many successful hedge funds employ quantitative trading strategies to engage in *statistical arbitrage* and employ traders with a computer science, mathematics and engineering background. An increasing number of hedge funds also explore *latency arbitrage*[6] opportunities. Latency arbitrage takes advantage of an arbitrageur's ability to quickly observe order flow on one exchange and to transmit algorithm-based orders to other exchanges at low latency. The ability to quickly observe and analyze order flow on a given exchange place is typically facilitated through collocated blade computers with advanced low-latency customizable logic chips running fast/efficient algorithms. The ability to transmit orders to other exchanges is sometimes created through dedicated microwave networks (gaining a 3 milliseconds [ms] advantage on a distance New York-Chicago).

A stylized example of latency arbitrage is given in Fig. 5.6. An institutional investor, say a pension fund, wants to purchase 20,000 shares trading on both exchange A and on exchange B. On each exchange, there is an offer for 10,000 shares at a price of $100. The institutional investor sends two buy orders for 10,000 shares, one to each exchange. The expectation is to buy a total of 20,000 shares at a price of $100. When the first order arrives at exchange A and the institutional investor lifts the offer for 10,000 shares at $100, the computer algorithm of a hedge funds running on a blade computer collocated to exchange A's server picks up the trade and sends a buy order for the same share to exchange B. Because the hedge fund uses a

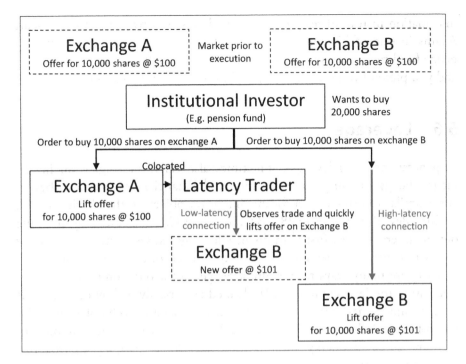

Fig. 5.6 Stylized example of latency arbitrage

low-latency connection to exchange B (say, a microwave network) while the order of the institutional investor travels via standard telephone lines, the hedge fund's buy order arrives at exchange B prior to the buy order of the institutional investor. By the time, the institutional investor's order arrives at exchange B, the offer for 10,000 shares at $100 is gone and there is a follow-on offer at a higher price, say $101. This means that the hedge fund was able to buy a security prior to the price impact caused by the institutional investor's second order, i.e., before the price went up.

Hedge funds are supposed to take all reasonable measures necessary to prevent *insider trading*.[7] Nonetheless, there are multiple instances of insider trading. For example, in 2013 the hedge fund *SAC Capital* agreed to pay a $1.8 billion settlement to resolve a criminal indictment for inside trading.[8] Three years later, the Securities and Exchange Commission (SEC) charged a research analyst working for the hedge fund *Artis Capital*[9] with insider trading in advance of a merger of two technology companies based on non-public information he received from his friend who was an executive at one of the companies.[10] The temptation for hedge fund traders to use insider information instead of research is captured very well by the cartoonist Scott Adams in one of his comic strips, in which one character, representing a hedge fund manager, says to a prospect employee "I'll do the insider trading and you pretend you created an algorithm that makes winning trades."[11]

5.6   Leverage

In general, financial leverage, sometimes also called gearing, is an investment strategy of using borrowed money.[12] Financial leverage describes an effect similar to using a lever for moving heavy objects in the physical world. Archimedes of Syracuse (c.287 B.C.–c.212 B.C.) is credited by pointing out the leverage effect first.[13] In finance, leverage causes a smaller amount of equity to control a larger amount of balance sheet (or of a transaction).

There are many ways to measure leverage, but a very common one is by calculating the leverage ratio (LR), defined as debt divided by equity. A LR of zero implies that there is no debt financing at all and each dollar in equity controls one dollar of total assets. A LR of 1 implies an equal amount of debt and equity financing, meaning that each dollar in equity controls two dollars of total assets.

If the returns on assets (r_{assets}) are larger than returns on debt (r_{debt}), leverage will increase the return on equity (r_{equity}). That's because in this case the assets generate a higher return than is passed on to the debt holders, thus creating an additional yield for the equity holders. This is illustrated in Fig. 5.7 for two balance sheets, each consisting of $100 in assets that generate a return (r_{assets}) of 10%, or $10. In the first balance sheet, assets are completely financed by equity, i.e., with a LR of zero, resulting in a return on equity (r_{equity}) of 10%; in the second balance sheet, the same assets are financed with an equal amount of equity and debt, i.e., with a LR of 1, whereas debt holders receive 5%(r_{debt}).

Leverage played an important role in the downfall of the infamous hedge fund *Long-Term Capital Management* (LTCM). Long-Term Capital Management L.P. was founded in 1994 by John W. Meriwether, the former vice-chairman and head of bond trading at Salomon Brothers. Members of LTCM's board of directors included Myron S. Scholes and Robert C. Merton, who shared the 1997 Nobel Memorial Prize in Economic Sciences. Initially successful with annualized return of over 40%, in 1998 it lost $4.6

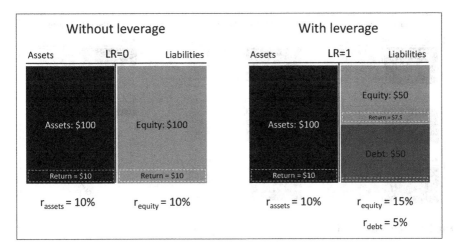

Fig. 5.7 Illustration of the leverage effect

billion in less than four months following the 1998 Russian financial crisis. LTCM was liquidated in early 2000. The impact of leverage before and after Russia defaulting on its debt, as well as the resulting change on the leverage ratio, is illustrated in Table 5.1.

Table 5.1 Long-Term Capital Management's leverage

	Equity	Debt	LR	r_{assets}	r_{debt}	r_{equity}
Before Russia default (August 1998)	$5 bn	$125 bn	25	7.31% ($9.5 bn)	6% ($7.5 bn)	40% ($2 bn)
Russia default	$5 bn	$125 bn		2.23% ($2.9 bn)	6% ($7.5 bn)	−92% (−$4.6 bn)
After Russia default	$0.4 bn	$125 bn	>300			

Leveraged investors often have a target leverage ratio. Thus, if losses cause a reduction to equity and lead to increasing leverage ratios, traders are forced to bring the leverage ratio down again by liquidating assets. This process is called *deleveraging* and is illustrated in Fig. 5.8. Deleveraging of many market participants at the same time can have a destabilizing effect on the market because the hastily liquidation of assets (sometimes similar to a fire sale) can amplify the decline in asset prices.

There are often several layers of leverage, causing the effective leverage ratio to increase even further. For example, hedge funds may invest with a modest LR of 5 into subordinated tranches of credit structures, that then get topped off by senior tranches; the resulting LR may be close to 30 (see Fig. 5.9).

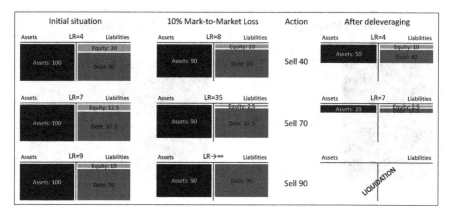

Fig. 5.8 Illustration of the effects of deleveraging

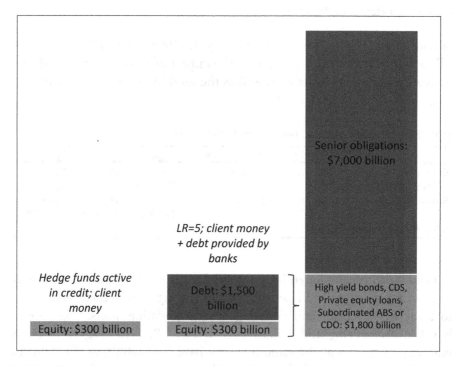

Fig. 5.9 Multi-stage leverage in the credit market (Adapted from Merritt and Fahey [(2007, 4])

5.7 Electronic Trading

Historically, trading took place bilaterally via the telephone. Some asset classes are still predominately traded in a voice-quoted fashion, e.g., single-name CDS, high-yield bonds and repo. In the 1990s, the inter-dealer broker market started to shift to electronic trading, followed by the dealer-to-client market.

Electronification takes several forms: Electronic trading, according to a definition by the BIS, "refers to the transfer of ownership of a financial instrument whereby the matching of the two counterparties in the negotiation or execution phase of the trade occurs through an electronic system"[14]; if this system is powerful enough to autonomously make trade decisions, it is considered automated trading; high-frequency trading is a subset of automated trading in which orders are submitted and trades executed at high speed, usually measured in microseconds (see Fig. 5.10).

Electronic trading is the result of advances in technology (i.e., lower costs of creating and maintaining electronic trading infrastructure). For most asset classes, electronic trading results in significantly lower transactions costs, increased competition and faster price discovery. In certain situations, electronic trading can also have disadvantages, such an information leakage or disruptive activity (such as the spoofing algorithms causing the Flash Crash of 2010).

Automated trading refers to a subset of electronic trading that relies on computer algorithms for decision-making and execution of order submissions. Automated trading requires special risk management as the increased speed of execution creates operational risks (e.g., malfunctioning algorithms). Also, automated trading has the potential to increase volatility in

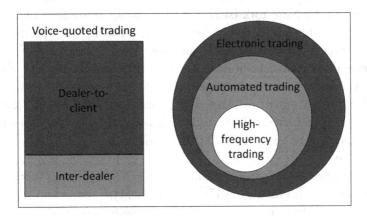

Fig. 5.10 Taxonomy of trading styles

financial markets by transmitting and amplifying idiosyncratic shocks from one market to other markets.

Automated trading can be used particularly in three areas of trading:

- Trade execution (e.g., trying to minimize the price impact of a transaction by splitting one large order into several smaller orders, executed sequentially and/or across different trading venues);
- Market making (e.g., algorisms generating price quotes, so-called auto-quoting);
- Execution of algorithmic strategies (e.g., algorisms identifying price discrepancies across different trading venues and executing pair trades that take advantage of that).

High-frequency trading was developed in the 1990s on the back of advances in computer technology and the digitalization of trading venues. It evolved from classical technical analysis, extending it to using high-frequency (i.e., intra-day, tick-by-tick) data and using significant computational power and ultra-low latency direct market access.[15] There is a debate on whether high-frequency trading may disadvantage a large part of the trading community. According to the BIS, market participants seeking to realize performance improvements of only a few milliseconds (dubbed "latency arms race") causes them to overinvestment in technology. "They overinvest because the race to trade on new information often has a 'winner take all' payoff. The race can impose externalities. As other participants invest in speed trading, less sophisticated traders may experience deteriorating market liquidity."[16]

The evolution of the inter-market latency is discussed by Laughlin et al. (2014), using the data connection between the Chicago Mercantile Exchange and the New York-based exchanges as an example of the development of ever-faster infrastructure for securities trading. The speed of information transport between Chicago and New York has increased due to the emergence of line-of-sight microwave networks connecting the financial centers, causing latency to improve by about 3 ms (0.003 seconds). The physical limit is a signal traveling at the speed of light (300,000 km/s) on the geodesic path between New York-Chicago, which results in a one-way transmission time of about 4 ms (0.004 seconds).

According to some estimates, roughly 85% of all trading is now computerized, controlled by "machines, models, or passive investment formulas that move in unison and blazingly fast"[17] (see Fig. 5.11).

Trading algorithms are an example of an application of electronic trading. They are predefined sets of rules for execution. Johnson (2010)

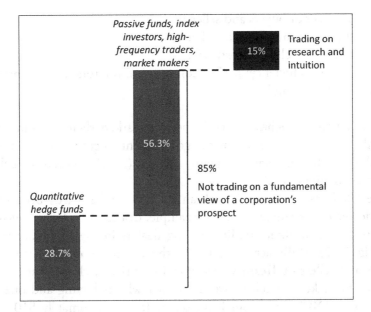

Fig. 5.11 Computerized trading accounting for around 85% of trading volume (Adapted from data quoted in Zuckerman et al. [2018])

differentiates between *impact-driven, cost-driven* and *opportunistic* algorithms. *Impact-driven algorithms* are splitting larger orders into smaller child orders, trying to minimize market impact costs and to reduce signaling risk.[18] *Cost-driven algorithms* try to reduce the overall transaction costs. *Opportunistic algorithms* seek taking advantage of favorable market conditions, e.g., based on price or liquidity.

Trading desks saved significant cost from replacing traders with trading algorithms. As a result, the number of traders required for a broker-dealer to provide liquidity in a particular market has declined. For example, Goldman Sachs is reported to have reduced its number of equity traders from 500 to three between the late 1990s and 2018.[19]

5.8 Case Study: Trading in the US Treasury Market

Along with the FX (foreign exchange) market, the US government bond (Treasury) market is considered to be one of the most efficient financial markets, exhibiting all signs and requirements economists attribute to perfect competition in perfect markets:

- Large number of buyers and sellers;
- Market participants are price-takers;
- Transactions are close to costless[20];
- Informational efficiency; perfect communication; total price transparency;
- Instantaneous equilibria.

Economic theory teaches us that in perfect markets there is no market failure. Also, there is no reason for the government to get involved, other than to make sure that the market remains efficient (e.g., by preventing collusions and price manipulation).

The US Treasury market is such an efficient market partly because of the high degree of intermediation. For example, dealer-to-dealer, or *inter-dealer*, brokers (IDBs) facilitate trading among dealers in the secondary market[21] (see Fig. 5.12). IDBs act as agents in the dealer community; they match buyers and sellers of Treasury securities in a private, closed market. If they are able to make a match between a dealer who is buying and one who is selling, the IDB is paid a small brokerage fee (approximately $10 per million of US Treasury notes transacted). The inter-dealer broker market gives dealers anonymity, so that no information about their own hedging needs is conveyed to other dealer (which may otherwise take advantage of this information and could try to front-run the flow.

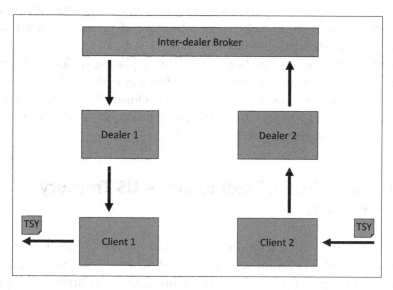

Fig. 5.12 Inter-dealer brokers connecting brokers

Traders have IDB broadcasts that display live trading prices directly from inter-dealer brokers; they are commonly referred to as "screens." Traders can execute either by calling direct phone lines ("voice broking") or online through IDM software ("electronic broking").

Prices in the US Treasury market are quoted as clean prices (without accrued interest) in the fractional, or tick, format: 102-086 means:

102 "Handle" or "Big figure" giving the percentage price
- Dash
08 32nds of a percentage
6 8ths of a 32nd of a percentage (a "+"-sign stands for 4 8th, or a half, of a 32nd)
⇒ 102.2734375%

A stylized IDB screen is shown in Table 5.2, displaying the (at the time) most recently auctioned Treasury securities. They are called the "on-the-run," "current" or "benchmark" issues. Securities up to one year are money-market instruments and quoted on a yield-basis. The screen prominently shows when an aggressor (market taker) sells into a bid ("hit a bid") or buys at an offer ("lift an offer") by flashing "HIT" and "TAK" in bold emphasis, along with the trade size. Not for all securities are two-way market available. For example, a size of "1x" means "$1 mm bid /no offer."

Besides from buying or selling Treasuries *outright*, they can also *exchange* Treasuries on inter-dealer broker platforms in the so-called Treasury *swap box*. The name "swap box" can be misleading, as it has nothing to do with swaps (derivatives). A swap box functions as follows: The on-the-run (OTR) TSY is "locked" and off-the-run (OFR) TSY prices quoted against it. Off-the-run issues are all securities that no longer hold the on-the-run status. All trades are executed as a "swap" (exchanging one Treasury for another), weighted to be DV01 (duration)-neutral; this means that there is no directional risk in trading the swap box.

Table 5.2 Stylized IDB screen for US Treasury bonds

	Coupon	Maturity	Price	Size	Yield
3M		10/27/2011	0.08+/0.08	1x1	0.082/0.081
6M		01/26/2012	/0.14	x5	/0.141
12M		07/26/2012	0.20+/0.20	10x1	0.205/0.202
2Y	0.375	07/31/2013	100-02 /022	5x10	0.343/0.342
3Y	0.625	07/15/2014	/	x	/
5Y	1.500	07/31/2016	**HIT** 101-01+/02	**10**x2	1.280/1.276
7Y	2.250	07/31/2018	101-15 /	1x	2.025/
10Y	3.125	05/15/2021	103-14 /14+ **TAK**	5x5	2.724/2.721
30Y	4.375	05/15/2041	105-07 /08	1x1	4.078/4.077

Prices at which OTR are locked are adjusted throughout the day and are close, but not necessarily identical, to current market prices.

Table 5.3 shows an illustrative inter-dealer swap box for US Treasuries. If someone wants to buy $10 mm (million) of the TSY 1 3/4% of 6/23, there would be *two separate* transactions:

- *Immediately* buy $10 mm 5Y OTR (to eliminate directionality) in the outright market;
- then, exchange the OTR for the TSY 1 3/4% of 6/23 in the swap box.

Table 5.3   US Treasury swap box[a]

Security	Bid Y	Bid	Offer	Offer Y	BSize	x	OSize	LSize
2 D/21	-4.88	97.122	97.12+	5.13	10	x	18	32
2 1/8 D/21	-5.20	97.25+	97.26	5.69	10	x	19	24
1 1/2 1/22	-4.77	95.212	95.216	5.25	15	x	20	10
1 7/8 1/22	-4.57	96.286	96.292	5.05	20	x	10	
1 3/4 2/22	-4.89	96.132	96.13+	5.12	20	x	10	26
1 7/8 2/22	-4.38	96.262	96.26+	6.62	10	x	10	135
1 3/4 3/22	-4.22	96.10	96.10+	4.68	10	x	10	
1 7/8 3/22	-3.91	96.23+	96.236	4.14	20	x	10	10
1 7/8 4/22	-3.47	96.206	96.21	3.70	10	x	20	10
1 3/4 5/31/22	-3.18	96.036	96.04	3.40	10	x	10	10
1 3/4 6/22	-2.76	96.006	96.012	3.19	20	x	20	
1 7/8 7/22	-2.58	96.13	96.13+	3.01	10	x	12	31
5YR	28.58	99.16	99.16	28.58	10	x	10	

[a]Stylized reproduction of a typical display of the inter-dealer broker ICAP

5.9   Case Study: Impact of Regulatory Changes to the Repo Market

Since the financial crisis of 2007–2008, global regulators created new constrains to regulated banking entities. One of the main drivers of change was the Basel III capital regulation, and specifically the limitation of leverage through the *supplementary leverage ratio*, or SLR. SLR regulation has tilted the playing field between (regulated) banks (Sect. 3.1.2) and (non-regulated) shadow banks (Sect. 3.1.3). This has an impact on the liquidity and the functioning of the repo market.

5.9.1 The Repo Market

Repo stands for "repurchase agreement," which is a contract to sell a financial market instrument at a specified price to a counterparty with the commitment to repurchase the instrument at a future date for a pre-agreed price. The annualized interest rate implied by the price at which the security is sold and bought back represents the repo rate. A transaction in which a market participant sells a security and implicitly borrows money is referred to as repo, while the opposite transaction (buying a security and implicitly lending out money) is called *reverse* repo. While most repo transactions are overnight (so-called overnight, or O/N, repo), they can span over several days, weeks or months (called term repo).

Different market participants are involved in the repo market for various reasons. Trading desks of broker-dealers use the repo market to finance the inventory of securities resulting from their market making activity (by lending out securities to receive cash); derivative trading desks use combinations of cash and repo transactions to create self-financing positions to hedge their derivative exposure or to obtain high-quality collateral used for margining; some investors (pension funds, insurance companies, etc.) invest cash on a short-term basis in return for receiving collateral; central banks also engage in the repo market for the purpose of injecting or withdrawing liquidity on a temporary basis (see Fig. 5.13).

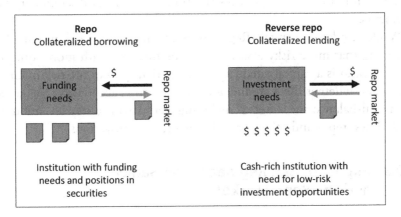

Fig. 5.13 Repo and reverse repo transactions

Repo trades can be settled as *bilateral* repo, *triparty* repo or through a *CCP*. Bilateral repo is a transaction between just two counterparties. Triparty repo involves a third party that intermediates between the two repo counterparties and facilitates clearing and administration. Both, bilateral repo and triparty repo create credit risk between the buyer and seller. If that risk is assumed by a central counterparty (CCP) clearing house, we have the case of a CCP-cleared repo transaction. Large broker-dealers are members of CCP clearing organizations, allowing them to apply a fair amount of exposure netting to inter-dealer repo business, but smaller broker-dealers are often not CCP members, and neither are non-broker-dealers.

5.9.2 Supplementary Leverage Ratio Regulation

An internationally agreed framework for banking regulation referred to as *Basel III*[22] was introduced by the Basel Committee of Banking Supervision (BCBS) as a response to the financial crisis of 2007–2008. Basel III consists of several features, including requirements to increase the level and quality of capital, enhancing risk capture and improving liquidity. Another very important element is the constrain with respect to leverage of banks. In order to reduce the risk of a deleverage spiral in a crisis, a supplementary leverage ratio limits the amount of debt to fund investments and activities. Banks must meet a 3% leverage ratio minimum requirement at all time. Global systematically important banks (G-SIBs) must maintain an even higher enhanced supplementary leverage ratio (eSLR) requirement of 5–6% (depending on whether at the bank holding level or the bank level) to avoid limitations on capital distributions and certain discretionary bonus payments.

While regulatory capital (Reg Cap) is calculated on a risk-weighted basis (meaning that more risky assets need to be financed with more equity), the leverage ratio is a capital adequacy measure that ignores the risk intensity of assets, and whether these are included in the bank's accounting balance sheet or are off-balance sheet items, including derivatives, undrawn amounts on credit lines, repos and other securities financing transactions.

5.9.3 Impact of SLR Regulation on Banks and the Repo Market

Because the SLR is not a risk-based measure, it requires banks to hold substantial capital against very low risk and even riskless assets. Capital, however, is very expensive. Banks are faced with the following choice: either to move into riskier or into less liquid assets that carry a higher risk- and illiquidity-premium, or to pass on the addition capital costs to customers even for low-risk transactions.

The impact of SLR regulation can be illustrated by a simple example. Let's assume a broker-dealer subsidiary of a bank holding company lends a client money in a reverse repo, receiving high-quality government (Treasury) securities as a collateral. The assets created on the broker-dealer's balance sheet are close to risk-free, yet SLR or eSLR rules require the broker-dealer to hold 3–6% capital against them. Assuming a cost of capital of somewhere between 8 and 10%, the broker-dealer needs to charge the client some 25–60 bp running.

Empirical research has shown already that banks falling under the SLR regulation have reduced their repo activity, reducing the liquidity in the repo market, and that non-regulated entities, such as shadow banks, are in a good position to capture an increasing share of the repo business.[23] The consequences for the functioning of the repo market could be significant, as shadow banks tend to be more opportunistic in their behavior and may not provide the same degree of liquidity as banks during periods of stress.

5.10 Useful Skills for a Career in Trading

Prospect employers of candidates applying for an entry-level trading job will expect certain skills that can be demonstrated for example by having selected appropriate courses at the university. Seasoned trading professionals tend to point out four skills particularly useful for aspiring traders[24]:

- *Quantitative ("Quant") Skills*
  Ability to use complex mathematical procedures and analytics, as well as doing basic mental math;
- *Statistics*
  Standard deviation, probability calculations, etc. with the goal to find meaning in data that is not apparent to the naked eye;
- *Computer programming*
  Basic knowledge in programming beyond Excel, preferably in statistical tools (such as R or Python) and MATLAB;
- *Economics*
  Possession of macroeconomic appreciation of how changes in interest rates, monetary policy, etc. have an impact on prices.

Because trading is a craft learned on-the-job, there is no guarantee that the command of a specific set of skills will make somebody a good trader; however, acquiring those skills before applying for a job in trading demonstrates devotion and sets one apart from other candidates during the hiring process.

5.11 A Career in Trading (by Fabrice Pilato)

I feel very fortunate to have been working as a derivatives trader & trading desk manager for over 25 years. I have worked my entire career for only two firms, both located in New York City, but for a one year on a temporary assignment in London. In my current role, over the last five years, I have had to bring together my various trading and risk management experiences in macro, credit and exotics of the previous 20 years. In keeping with the adage that we are never too old to learn, I have also had to build fluency in markets like commodities, secured & unsecured funding that were not as familiar to me.

As I was graduating from university, I originally considered a very unoriginal career in either consulting, investment banking or in sales and trading. With such narrow "interest," a minimal amount of homework and outreach to a couple helpful Alumni led me to realize I was (best) suited for *Sales and Trading*. Like many of my friends, I submitted my resume and got selected for interviews on campus by some major Wall Street firms. Having fallen victim to a particularly inclement Ithaca winter when both planes and buses got repeatedly canceled, I was unable to make it to New York for my 2nd rounds with the now defunct Salomon Brothers and Bankers Trust. A finance professor whose Ph.D. seminar I was attending connected me with one of his former students. I was able to visit him at his Wall Street office and I was back on track. *Never ignore lady luck!*

I started my Wall Street career (at that time, my first employer did have one of the rare Wall Street addresses) as an interest rate derivatives trader and, in succession, made markets in US interest rate swaps, US vanilla and exotic options and, eventually, became part of a relative value trading desk within the options desk. These first five years were formative. I got my first exposure to markets as a trading professional with its imperative of rationality and coolness, to brutal "Darwinism" in an exciting and apparently limitless industry, and to being a full-time employee in a large, complex institution. Most importantly, I made a couple of lifelong friends (like the one who asked me to write this section for the book!). I still vividly remember the excitement when I first successfully took large market risks (as well as getting stopped out on a couple of spectacularly unsuccessful trades), staying in the office for over 24 h and catching a couple hours of sleep at my desk as we were bidding on the Orange County structured note portfolio and, more prosaically, the infamous O.J. car chase and verdict. Looking back, it was an "age of innocence," we all felt invincible and "up" was the only way forward for us.

Eventually, I moved from Downtown to Midtown and there, I started what turned out to be an interesting 20 years and counting. I was back on a US interest rate trading desk doing the same thing I had been doing before, but with more opportunities. I eventually got to move around, started a new business for the firm and learned about new markets: the humbling Canadian bond and fixed-income derivatives market where I felt like an outsider for the first and last time in my career, the large and always interesting US municipal market and eventually the technically captivating US corporate structured credit market. Those early years were scarred by the 9/11 terrorist attacks on the World Trade Center on September 11, 2001. My earliest memory of this tragedy was the Telerate 500 (Cantor Fitzgerald's omnipresent US Treasury) inter-dealer broker screen going blank and an announcement on the trading floor that a plane had hit the twin towers where Cantor had their office. We all lost family, friends and colleagues that day and it was never the same afterward. Eventually, the financial crisis of 2007–2008 hit. For our industry in particular, it was a watershed. A few firms went under or were bought out, many jobs were lost and regulation was justifiably back in force. I remember my boss coming back Sunday afternoon after meeting with the NY Fed for a second day and letting us know that Lehman Brothers would file for bankruptcy either later that day or the next morning, Lehman personnel going in the office that evening to pick their belongings not knowing whether they would be allowed in the building on Monday morning and, eventually, the TV trucks moving from the Lehman building to our building like sharks circling a prey.

I am occasionally asked to talk about my experience with the new analyst class. Since no one has antiquarian interest in my career, I usually stick to offering a number of *career tips* to those starting their careers in our industry. Those are:

- Most importantly, post the financial crisis of 2007–2008, this industry has changed a lot and may not have the unchallenged prestige it once had, but it still offers an extremely stimulating work environment, a relatively flat hierarchical structure where initiative and entrepreneurship are valued and unmatched opportunities for ambitious young men and women including geographic mobility given its global footprint.
- The challenge to be met during the first rotations is to figure out your interests and skill set. Management will assist as it is in its interest to properly place young graduates, but this is the ultimate "self-honesty" test.

- In my opinion, it is not a good idea to try and get placed in a function or department you think is attractive at the expense of a good fit. Since it will take years to fully enjoy financial rewards, it is practically too hard to call years ahead what market or function will be "hot" then and, as importantly, our industry is way too competitive for "competitors" not be at their best. For the sport-inclined reader, there are very few Bo Jackson around!
- Whatever first job you are initially given as an analyst, do your absolute best. This first impression will "follow" you for a long time. It will get you promoted or, if it is not the right fit, it will be much easier to get management's ear with your wish for internal mobility if you've doing a good job.
- Paradoxically, at least for the first few years, while working for a large firm, you are actually self-employed. You have to develop your own skill set and your own network. These are yours not your employer's. They will help move up or move out. In addition, senior salespeople and traders will really only spend time and invest in hardworking young employees showing signs of promise. In other words, the optimal strategy is always to do your best.

Notes

1. Easley et al. (2012, 1).
2. See Chan (2009, 31–67) and Chan (2013, 1–38).
3. Mathematization can be traced back to Louis Bachelier's dissertation thesis, completed at the Sorbonne in 1900. See Davis and Etheridge (2011).
4. Swap spreads are impacted by a number of factors, one of them being the general level of credit risk. Thus, if there is an increase in perceived credit risk, causing corporate spreads (the difference between interest rates paid by corporate bond issuers and government bond yields) to widen, swap spreads typically widen as well.
5. Anonymous (2000).
6. Latency arbitrage is strictly speaking not a pure form of arbitrage because it involves some risk.
7. Insider trading is an activity in which securities are traded based on material confidential (nonpublic) information. It is illegal in most countries.
8. Source: Kolhatkar (2013).
9. The analyst was ultimately charged by criminal authorities and has since received a prison sentence. Artis Capital agreed to settle the SEC's charges by disgorging the illicit trading profits that its trader generated for the firm totaling $5,165,862, plus interest of $1,129,222 and a penalty of $2,582,931.

10. U.S. Securities and Exchange Commission (2013).
11. Adams (2011).
12. de Haan et al. (2015, 290–291).
13. "Give me a lever and a place to stand and I will move the earth" (Δῶς μοι πᾶ στῶ καὶ τὰν γᾶν κινάσω).
14. Bank of International Settlement (2016, 4).
15. For more detail on high-frequency trading see Aldridge (2010).
16. Bank of International Settlement (2016, 22).
17. Zuckerman et al. (2018). An even lower estimate for fundamental single stock pickers making up for less than 10% of total equity trading is presented in Fletcher and Aliaj (2019).
18. A very simple impact-driven algorithm could time-slice the execution of a large 10,000 unit-order into a series of 10 1000 unit-orders.
19. Basak and Palmeri (2018).
20. Bid-ask spreads are often only a fraction of one-quarter of a basis point, customers pay no commissions when they trade OTC with dealers, dealers pay less than $10 per million to trade with inter-dealer brokers.
21. IDMs include Tullett Prebon, Broker-Tec, ICAP (formerly Garban), BGC Partners (formerly Cantor Fitzgerald), Liberty, TradeWeb and Tradition.
22. Basel Committee on Banking Supervision (2017).
23. See, for example, Kotidis and van Horen (2018).
24. See, for example, Friesen (2017, 64–67).

References

Adams, Scott. 2011. Dilbert Cartoon Posted on 12 August. https://dilbert.com/strip/2011-08-12. Accessed on January 20, 2020.

Aldridge, Irene. 2010. *High-Frequency Trading: A Practical Guide to Algorithmic Strategies and Trading Systems*. Hoboken, NJ: Wiley.

Anonymous. 2000. Letter by an Anonymous Market Participant Describing Imperfections in the United States Treasury Bond Market Sent to a Former Commissioner of the Securities and Exchange Commission on July 14. http://ustreasurymarket.com. Accessed on January 20, 2020.

Bank of International Settlement. 2016. Electronic Trading in Fixed Income Markets. Report submitted by a Study Group established by the Markets Committee, January 2016. https://www.bis.org/publ/mktc07.pdf. Accessed on January 20, 2020.

Basak, Sonali, and Christopher Palmeri. 2018. A Goldman Trading Desk That Once Had 500 People Is Down to Three. Bloomberg, April 30. https://www.bloomberg.com/news/articles/2018-04-30/goldman-trading-desk-that-once-had-500-people-is-down-to-three. Accessed on January 20, 2020.

Basel Committee on Banking Supervision. 2017. Basel III: Finalising Post-crisis Reforms, December. https://www.bis.org/bcbs/publ/d424.htm. Accessed on January 20, 2020.

Chan, Ernest P. 2009. *Quantitative Trading: How to Build Your Own Algorithmic Trading Business*. Hoboken, NJ: Wiley.

Chan, Ernest P. 2013. *Algorithmic Trading: Winning Strategies and Their Rationale*. Hoboken, NJ: Wiley.

Davis, Mark, and Alison Etheridge. 2011. *Louis Bachelier's Theory of Speculation: The Origins of Modern Finance*. Oxford, UK: Princeton University Press.

de Haan, Jakob, Dirk Schoenmaker, and Sander Oosterloo. 2015. *Financial Markets and Institutions: A European Perspective*. Cambridge, UK: Cambridge University Press.

Easley, David, Marcos M. López de Prado, and Maureen O'Hara. 2012. Flow Toxicity and Liquidity in a High-Frequency World. *Review of Financial Studies* 25 (5): 1457–1493.

Fletcher, Laurence, and Ortenca Aliaj. 2019. How Quants and QE Shook the Cult of the Stockpicker. *Financial Times*, 22 November. https://www.ft.com/content/489345c6-0c6b-11ea-bb52-34c8d9dc6d84. Accessed on January 20, 2020.

Friesen, Garth. 2017. *Bite the Ass off a Bear: Getting in and Standing out on a Hedge Fund Trading Floor*. Austin, TX: Lioncrest Publishing.

Johnson, Barry. 2010. *Algorithmic Trading & DMA: An Introduction to Direct Access Trading Strategies*. London, UK: 4Myeloma Press.

Kolhatkar, Sheelah. 2013. SAC Capital to Pay $1.8 Billion, the Largest Insider Trading Fine Ever. Bloomberg, 4 November. https://www.bloomberg.com/news/articles/2013-11-04/sac-capital-to-pay-1-dot-8-billion-the-largest-insider-trading-fine-ever. Accessed on January 20, 2020.

Kotidis, Antonis, and Neeltje van Horen. 2018. Repo Market Functioning: The Role of Capital Regulation. Bank of England Staff Working Paper No. 746, August. https://www.bankofengland.co.uk/-/media/boe/files/working-paper/2018/repo-market-functioning-the-role-of-capital-regulation.pdf. Accessed on January 20, 2020.

Laughlin, Gregory, Anthony Aguirre, and Joseph Grundfest. 2014. Information Transmission Between Financial Markets in Chicago and New York. *Financial Review* 49 (2): 283–312.

Lo, Andrew W., and Mark T. Mueller. 2010. Warning: Physics Envy May Be Hazardous to Your Wealth! *Journal of Investment Management* 8 (2): 13–63.

Merritt, Roger, and Eileen Fahey. 2007. Hedge Funds: The Credit Market's New Paradigm. Fitch Ratings Special Report from June 5.

U.S. Securities and Exchange Commission. 2013. SEC Charges California-Based Hedge Fund Analyst and Two Others with Insider Trading. Press Release, 26 March. https://www.sec.gov/news/press-release/2013-2013-47htm. Accessed on January 20, 2020.

Zuckerman, Gregory, Rachael Levy, Nick Timiraos, and Gunjan Banerji. 2018. Behind the Market Swoon: The Herdlike Behavior of Computerized Trading: The Majority of Trades Comes from Machines, Models, or Passive Investment Formulas That Move in Unison and Blazingly Fast. *Wall Street Journal*, December 25. https://www.wsj.com/articles/behind-the-market-swoon-the-herd-like-behavior-of-computerized-trading-11545785641. Accessed on January 20, 2020.

6

Research

6.1   The Market for Investment Research

Investment research, sometimes also labeled *Strategy*, has come under tremendous pressure during the past two decades. Demand from institutional investors has declined, regulatory requirements have limited the role research plays in the sales and trading environment and technology has made some of the legacy research products obsolete. Still, from a professional development perspective, research departments can be attractive steppingstones in a Global Markets career as they help acquiring broad product and market knowledge, make it possible to accompany salespeople on client trips and to learn about a wide range of trade ideas, hedging and speculative strategies.

Research consumes a lot of resources of an investment bank and is paid from various sources, asset management firms being the largest one. With roughly $105 trillion of assets under management (AUM) and an estimated average operating profit margin of 10 bp, global asset managers have the ability to pay for research out of an annual revenue pool of roughly $100 billion. But research is also paid out of banks' internal budget since banks hold large portfolios of securities themselves, conduct proprietary trading, need to support their Treasury department or use research as a marketing tool.

Based on commissions, the global research market is estimated by some to be anywhere between $12 billion and $15 billion.[1] Roughly half of this amount goes to research providers in the Americas (primarily USA and Canada), and the rest is split between Europe and Asia/emerging markets. The majority of this goes to sell-side research.

© The Author(s) 2020
F. Tata, *Corporate and Investment Banking*,
https://doi.org/10.1007/978-3-030-44341-2_6

Following the financial crisis of 2007–2008, investment banks have been allocating significantly less capital to research as part of widespread cuts to restore profitability. According to some estimates, the number of analysts at the 12 biggest banks fell from more than 6600 in 2012 to fewer than 6000 in 2016.[2] Banks have also been cutting the cost per head by replacing experienced analysts with younger, cheaper staff, a trend labeled "juniorisation."

Research analysts are under pressure to publish a large amount of research publications.[3]

Most research is still distributed by email; email distribution groups are generously extended and often include recipients that have little interest in reading specific research publications.

According to some estimates, more than 2 million different research publications are distributed every year, but only 2–5% of those are actually read on average.[4]

Modern tracking methods allow research providers to monitor which research publications have been accessed by the clients, but banks are reluctant to disclose the precise percentage (most likely out of embarrassment).

6.2   Providers of Research

Investment research analysts can be categorized according to whom they work for. If they work for intermediaries that offer financial services to other institutional investors (brokers, dealers, investment banks, advisors, etc.), they are referred to as *sell-side* analysts; if they are employed by financial institutions that bear the economic exposure of the trades suggested by the research services, they are characterized as *buy-side* analysts; if they are offering research services independently and are neither part of the buy-side nor the sell-side, they are called independent research providers (IRPs).

The tools used to conduct research are often similar, or even the same, for the three types of research analysts, yet the motivation differs. *Sell-side analysts* provide the buy-side with a wide range of research products, including thematic publications, trade ideas, market commentary, product and market research and technical analysis, hoping to *increase deal flow* with or gain advisory mandates from the client. *Buy-side analysts* conduct research to help the buy-side institution *outperform* the market and to create a distinguished investment proposition for the institutional investor's own clients. *IRPs* sell their research product to the buy-side for a *fee*.

6.2.1 Sell-Side Analysts

Sell-side research mainly serves one goal: *increasing sales*. Each business area within a sell-side firm instrumentalizes (monetizes) research for its own purpose. For example, a low interest rate view developed by research analysts in the Rates Strategy group will serve as a basis to suggest *buying bonds* in the bonds unit, *receiving fixed* on a swap in the derivative unit or *buying stocks* in the equity group. The performance of sell-side analysts is measured to a large degree against how it helps the sell-side firm to increase trade execution flow with clients. For example, if a sell-side strategist publishes a trade idea and a salesperson can confirm that this trade was executed with a client afterward, the analyst wins recognition. Also considered a positive contribution by Research is which a proposed trade idea does not get executed precisely in the terms laid out but can be used by Sales to initiate a client conversation that leads to *other*, related trades. This is harder to measure, but salespeople have a good sense about whether the day-by-day work of a particular research strategist helps them strengthening their client relationship and to increase business. As part of the annual performance measure process, research analysts are often asked to have a few salespeople provide feedback about the use of their research work.

Sell-side research serves additional purposes, apart from increasing sales activity. The output of research units also has *internal* consumers, such as risk management groups, the Treasury department, accounting, proprietary trading desks, senior management and units responsible for regulatory reporting. For example, if the bank needs interest rate forecasts for their business planning process, Research is typically asked to provide the information. Sell-side research is also used by banks to *showcase* their expertise in products and markets. Research is posted (for free) on the bank's website, presented on conferences and client events, etc. Research then becomes a *marketing* tool.

As a sell-side analyst, you may be assigned to different research areas depending on the bank's needs and your interests and abilities. To some degree, it is a process of trial-and-error. For example, at some point you will likely ask to accompany a salesperson on a client visit. Depending on how that goes you would be allowed to see more clients (salespeople share among each other experiences they had with research analysts). If you have good people skills and your presentations are appreciated by clients, you will gradually transition into a mostly *client-facing* position; otherwise, you will more likely be utilized in a more analytical capacity within the research production process. What is nice about the research environment is that it offers a home for people with almost any skill set. If you are very eloquent, big-picture (thematic) research could be your thing; if you a very technical, market micro-arbitrage trade generation would potentially be suitable. If you are a skillful writer, written publications could become your focus; if you more of a verbal person, presenting at morning meetings, during client calls or on conferences could be your strength. Sell-side areas can be differentiated according to various research disciplines. To just name a few dimensions:

- Global markets vs. investment banking/advisory;
- Fixed income vs. equities vs. commodities vs. derivatives vs. global asset allocation;
- Big-picture thematic research vs. quantitative modeling;
- Pure strategy vs. desk-research (transactional analysis conducted on the trading desk);
- International market vs. local market research;
- Product-specific vs. cross-product analysis;
- Fundamental vs. technical analysis;
- Micro-arbitrage vs. macroeconomics;
- Institutional vs. retail research.

Nearly all areas within capital markets and investment banking have their own "embedded" research unit, creating the risk of duplication, overlap, competition and inconsistency in research. A great deal of energy is spent within the sell-side institution on who "owns" the right to set the official prediction (house view, or "call") on a product, asset class, rate or price. Even when this was decided, some analysis may promote their own opinion as "risk scenarios" or "alternative views."

6.2.2 Buy-Side Analysts

A buy-side analyst is an analyst who supports the fund managers at mutual funds, pension funds, hedge funds, trusts and other buy-side institutions in the investment making process. The results of buy-side analysts are for the better part confidential and not for public consumption.

The research conducted by buy-side analysts helps the buy-side firm increase the risk-adjusted return on their capital. Analysts are usually engaged in monitoring current news and trends, tracking down valuable information, compiling and evaluating research received from the sell-side, building proprietary financial models and conducting ad hoc requests by the buy-side traders.

Because buy-side research typically does not get distributed outside the firm sponsoring it, buy-side analysts don't have to worry much about appearance, language and regulatory requirements (disclaimers, etc.) of what they produce; however, more rigor is applied to backtesting and risk analysis because buy-side research is often the basis for actual market transactions with an immediate P&L impact (while sell-side research is more often than not merely an invitation to consider a proposed idea).

Because buy-side firms often hire seasoned sell-side analysts, starting your career as a sell-side analyst at a reputable sell-side firm may be advisable even if your goal is to ultimately become a buy-side analyst. Also, while working as a sell-side analyst you have the opportunity to network with a wide range of buy-side firms, allowing you to identify the best fit for you.

6.2.3 Independent Research Providers

The Centre for the Study of Financial Innovation (CSFI) defines IRPs as "standalone research firms, owned by neither buy- nor sell-side. Their clients are mainly asset managers and their USP is their independence, which avoids the conflict of interests that come with serving corporate clients. They receive most of their payments directly, in the form of subscriptions, payments for be-spoke research and consultancy, although some receive a sizeable amount via dealing commissions. The sector is fragmented – the research ranges from macro to micro and includes technology-driven modeling and analytics. Most are niche operators. The advantage is their focus and depth of knowledge; the disadvantage is the lack of diversified revenues and of a big balance sheet to tide them over in tough periods."[5]

There are a number of reasons to expect that IRPs will be playing a bigger role going forward. First, the reputation of sell-side research has been harmed as conflict of interests have become more obvious to the public (see Sect. 6.7), especially after a group of investment banks agreed to pay roughly $1.4 billion in a settlement with regulators related to their behavior in rating technology stocks in the dot-com bull market of the 1990s. Second, as an increasing number of sell-side firms keep reducing the number of seasoned research professionals for cost reasons, experienced research staff is offering their specific expertise on an independent basis. Third, regulation has made the business model of selling research more attractive due to limitations imposed on using research as an inducement (Sect. 6.8).

6.3   Value-Adding of Research

Whether or not investment research is providing much of a value is a hotly debated topic. On the one end of the spectrum are people suggesting that research (especially when coming from the sell-side) has only *entertainment value*[6] and does not help recipients to systematically outperform the market. The argument goes along the lines that markets are rather efficient to start with and even if there were temporary pockets of inefficiency, it would be highly unlikely that a research analyst identifies and publishes them before they have disappeared already. A somewhat cynical response of someone from this camp when receiving a research trade idea would be: "If you think this to be such a great trade, why don't you (or your trading desk) put it on yourself?". Of course, this point of view is rather extreme and ignores the fact that research is not just producing trade ideas but also helps compile and analyze data for decision makers on the sell-side, among other services. On the other end of the spectrum of opinions is the view that markets cannot become efficient without *some* market participants researching the market and taking advantage of dislocations, a notion related to *efficiently inefficient* markets discussed in Sect. 3.2.2. A balanced view between those opposing standpoints is maybe to assume that *some* research is useful, but not *all*. Like with other products and services, the principle of *caveat emptor* should be applied to investment research, meaning that because recipient of research assumes the economic risk it is imperative for them to always use their own judgment instead of blindly following research propositions.

In the following section, we will discuss a number of research service offerings (mostly from a sell-side perspective) with respect to their value-adding, perceived or actual, to clients.

6.3.1 Buy/Sell/Hold Recommendation

Similar to what credit rating agencies (e.g., Moody's, S&P and Fitch) do for debt instruments, research analysts evaluate and rank equity instruments (e.g., stocks and corporate bonds). The evaluation typically includes some form of buy, sell or hold recommendation. This rating helps portfolio managers in their decision process regarding which securities of an otherwise diversified portfolio to over- and to underweight in an attempt to generate alpha.

Research analysts' recommendations often carry weight with small investors as they tend to lack sophisticated financial data and seldom dig through corporate filings. Larger (institutional) investors have their own (buy-side) analysts performing ratings on existing and potential stocks in their portfolio; they often use sell-side ratings as a sanity-check for their own work.

Upgrades and *downgrades* by research analysts often move stock prices because they imply that something has changed. They are often used to initiate a discussion with clients, often involving the research analyst(s) who worked on the research piece. As with many other research publications, the goal is often to give salespeople a good reason to call their clients.

As will be discussed at greater lengths in Sect. 6.7, research analysts typically shy away from issuing *sell* recommendations because of conflict of interests. However, there is also a very practical reason why a buy recommendation can be monetized by Sales more efficiently than a sell recommendation: Sell recommendations can only be executed by clients that already own the security, while buy recommendation can be executed by anyone that is allowed and willing to trade in the security's asset class.[7]

6.3.2 Actionable Trading Opportunities

Often, salespeople call their clients on a daily basis (sometimes even multiple times a day); they need something to talk about! Being able to present an attractive trading opportunity is usually a good way to get a client's *attention* during which an experienced salesperson can extract some valuable information from the client (client's thinking process, type of trades conducted, existing positions, need for future transactions, etc.) that helps to strengthen the relationship and to generate some execution flow, even if completely unrelated to the trade idea used to initiate the conversation.

Trading opportunities have to meet a number of qualifications to be suited to be shown to a particular client. The most important are:

- Trade does not include instruments the client is not allowed to trade (e.g., long-dated bonds when talking to a money market fund manager);
- Trade fits client's risk appetite and market views;

- Trade idea is actionable (meaning that execution levels suggested in the research publication are in line with current market levels, even after bid-ask spreads and other transaction costs are taken into consideration, and that traders are willing to execute in the size suggested);
- Trade idea is not completely meritless.

Some investor types, like hedge funds and proprietary trading desks, are mandated with ferreting out attractive trade opportunities. Sell-side research analysts assist those investors by providing a constant flow of trade ideas. Some are merely observations of presumed *temporary dislocations* pointed out to suggest a possible convergence back to historical averages (so-called *convergence trades*), others involve a detailed, model-based analysis. There are some institutional clients that are reluctant to be called by salespeople unless a specific trade idea is presented.

Trade ideas will be discussed in more detail in Sects. 6.4–6.6.

6.3.3 Thought-Provoking Thematic Analysis

Research analysts have, or are supposed to have, enough time to think outside the box, presenting big-picture ideas that help clients to enrich their thought process. Those publications center around a *theme*, such as inflation, global trade, political events, environmental issues.

Often, institutional investors have to develop and present their own thematic analysis internally or to their own investors; thus, help from the sell-side to develop those ideas is almost always appreciated.

Thematic research is mostly a reaction to the buy-side ignoring highly *redundant* research reports generated by almost every broker-dealer in a similar fashion, put out on regular production cycles even if there is nothing new to be reported (so-called *maintenance research*), or publications replicating what other already put out before ("me-too" publications). Essentially, the buy-side's request is simple: "Don't call me unless you have something interesting to say!"

Thus, research groups now offer, or claim to offer, "new themes," "novel perspectives," "thought-provoking" arguments and "alternative views." If delivered as promised, it helps investment managers to position for shift in trends, structural changes in the economy, geopolitical events and other overriding topics, such as the impact of the COVID-19 pandemic (COVID-19).

6.3.4 Corporate Access

Some investors don't just want to read research about financial instruments, but also want to meet with the firms originating them. Specifically, institutional buyers of stocks and corporate bonds like to visit the corporation's headquarters or production facilities and speak to the corporation's management. Corporate customers of a bank, in turn, may have an interest to present themselves in a positive light to potential investors in their stocks and bonds. Research analysts are often entrusted with arranging this.

Research analysts are arranging access of investors to corporate executives, so-called *corporate access*, in multiple ways:

- Non-deal road shows: Analysts taking company executives to meet current and potential investors;
- Investment conferences: CEO, CFO or other senior managers give presentations, followed by one-on-one meetings with investors;
- Company visits: Analysts take investors to company's headquarters where they meet management;
- Group meals: Analysts invite investors to wine & dine with company executives.

Many investment banks track the number of times their research analysts take company executives on the road to meet clients and use the number to help decide analysts' annual compensation.

Analysts who want corporate top executives to attend private events with their investor clients have to show they are brand ambassadors. However, it is difficult for an analyst to be considered a *brand ambassador* if they have a *sell* rating on a stock. This creates some serious conflict of interests for the research analyst.

6.3.5 Analytical Research Platforms

Starting some 20 years ago, broker-dealers have been increasingly giving clients access to web-based analytical research tools and databases, so that they can do their own research and analysis. The purpose of those tools is mainly to make sure that clients come back next time they have transaction needs, i.e., to make them *sticky*.

Historically, access to those all-in-one platforms was limited to clients that reward the broker-dealer with a certain amount of deal flow. More recent regulation (see Sect. 6.8) limits most inducements of this kind.

Analytical web platforms typically consist of several elements. First, they give access to an extensive database, consisting of reliable historical securities data from a wide range of asset classes, currencies and indices. Often, economic data are included also. Real-time or close-to-real-time data are provided for some time series as well. Second, analytical functions are offered to the user, allowing the user to perform calculations on price histories of individual securities or entire portfolios of securities. This could be as simple as calculating the spread (difference) between two security prices, or to show a moving average. Third, the platform will likely also give access to in-house models for risk management and relative value analysis. Those include mortgage prepayment models, derivative pricing models or term-structure model. Fourth, analytical platforms give the user the ability to display data in multiple ways. Elaborate graphing tools help identify market dislocations, track price relationships on an ongoing basis, create a graphical representation of the performance of a specific trade or monitor entire portfolios. Finally, web platforms typically also provide links to the provider's research reports, market commentary and video/podcast content.

Because some clients prefer to use their own graphical user interface (GUI) many banks' analytical research tool provide direct access to the platform's analytical components through an application programming interface (API). Also, an increasing number of platforms also provide trading capabilities (access to liquidity and trade execution). Those platforms collect the client's trading activity in one place, provide transaction oversight along with individual pre-trade, trade and post-trade activities.

6.3.6 Machine Learning, Artificial Intelligence and Alternative Data

A transformative new trend impacting both, the buy-side and the sell-side, is the augmentation of investment decision processes by machine learning and artificial intelligence (AI) tools. Machine learning in the context of financial market analysis is a data-driven attempt to discover previously unknown relationships between prices and other market data with the goal of being able to forecast the market dynamics and to construct successful trading strategies. AI describes the ability of machines to exhibit human-like cognitive behavior.

Many significant market participants are already devoting significant resources to those developments in computer science. For example, on the buy-side the investment manager BlackRock has established a lab for AI in Palo Alto, California.[8] On the sell-side, JPMorgan Chase's technology budget in 2019 is some $11.4 billion[9] and about a quarter of Goldman Sachs' workforce is made up by computer engineers.[10]

Increasingly more important are data beyond what is typically used (corporate earnings, economic releases, etc.). Those data are referred to as *alternative* data and can be used for novel analysis such as:

- Analyzing traffic through corporate websites;
- Use of text analysis tools to analyze transcripts of earning calls;
- Use of geolocation data from smartphones;
- Analysis of credit card purchases and social media;
- Satellite imagery machine learning and computer vision algorithms.

Alternative data can be generated by individuals (e.g., billions of individuals constantly radiating data about what they are doing on social media), by business processes (e.g., credit card transactions) or by sensors (e.g., satellite data).[11] While alternative data may provide new insight, the length of alternative time series is often too short for identifying long-term trends that span over a whole business cycle.

The inroads advanced technologies have made on research can be illustrated in the field of satellite imagery machine learning. Space tech has become much cheaper and venture capital has fueled commercial satellite launches. Computer vision techniques applied to satellite imagery allows for the identification of cars, buildings or changes in landscape. Several hundred remote sensing satellites are already launched into orbit. Data from space is on such a massive scale[12] that only AI can process this. With this new technology, it has become possible to predict retailers' profits by counting cars on the parking lots (see Fig. 6.1) before the firm's annual/quarterly report is published, to forecast crops' yields, to estimate the world's oil inventory by detecting shadows on them,[13] to monitor activity and inventory of dry bulk cargo at ports or containers at ports, and to count ships to establish baseline activity and monitor for abnormalities.

Fig. 6.1 Car counting as satellite imagery machine learning example (Image source: Orbital Insight)

6.3.7 Other Contributions of Research

Research often plays an instrumental role in the *onboarding* process driven by Sales (see Sect. 4.2.1). Research capabilities are presented to prospect clients as a way to differentiate coverage from what the client already receives. Sometimes it is even a research analyst that initiates a client onboarding process. Clients tend to develop a strong relationship not only with their sales coverage, but also with some research analysts. If the research analyst moves to another broker-dealer, some of the clients covered by him/her may be willing to add the analyst's new employer to the list of broker-dealers execution is conducted with.

Research can increase the *market value* of a bank. Some broker-dealers describe themselves as a "research house" and use research rankings as a unique selling proposition (USP). Research publications can be prominently displayed on a bank's website and research findings are often quoted in the press, creating free publicity that is often more effective than paid-for advertisement.

Research can become an important part of the customer journey that typically begins with the *awareness* stage. As many broker-dealers compete for the attention of institutional customers, showcasing strong research capabilities can be a competitive advantage when trying to win execution business in an otherwise quite homogeneous service offering.

Research contributes to client *education* (see Sect. 4.2.8) and *seminars/ conferences* (see Sect. 4.2.9), organized by Sales. Research analysts tend to do most of the talking at those events (while Salespeople often focus on the social program following the formal presentations).

Last but not least, research also provides valuable services within the organization to "internal clients," such as the Treasury or risk management departments. For example, banks have to run so-called stress tests (complying with IFRS 9 regulation[14]) and may use different interest rate scenarios developed within the research group.

6.4 Trade Ideas

Trade ideas are recommendations to *consider* a potential *actionable* transaction. Calling them *ideas* highlights that there are merely opinions and observations that are to be used to inspire recipients and to be the basis for a further discussion. However, the idea is presented such that it includes a market transaction that can be executed in the market. An analysis predicting that Japan's unemployment is going to fall is *not* a trade idea because there is no actionable trade; a specific Dollar-Yen transaction based on Japan's unemployment projection is.

Trade ideas have various formats, are based on different type of information and serve different purposes. While it would be beyond the scope of this book to list them all, if that is even possible, a selection of most relevant types is discussed in this section. Most trade ideas come from the fixed income area.

6.4.1 Carry and Roll-Down Trades

Carry and roll-down represent the expected return to hold a fixed-rate instrument position assuming an unchanged yield curve over a defined period. *Carry* represents the cash return determined by the spread between fixed payments of an instrument (e.g., the coupon payments of a bond) and the short-term funding cost (e.g., the overnight repo rate). *Roll-down* measures the expected price change of a position, assuming the fixed income instrument matures (rolls down) on an unchanged yield curve over a defined period.[15]

Positive carry describes the situation in which a position gains in value if "*nothing happens*" (except the passage of time); negative carry indicates an expected loss in value in the absence of any changes.

The empirical failure of the pure expectation hypothesis (stating that the effects of higher carry will be perfectly offset by a price decrease due to higher expected yields in the future, et vice versa, and that all bond positions have the same near-term expected return) appears to provide some justification for carry- and roll-down-strategies.

Some investors have a strong preference for positions with positive carry. While they may have already established a number of trades that express a particular market view (requiring the market to move one way or another), they also want to hold trades that are expected to perform well if nothing happens. Those investors will then ask the research area for trade ideas that generate the maximum amount of (positive) carry and roll-down. Figure 6.2 shows an example of a three-month carry and roll-down calculation.

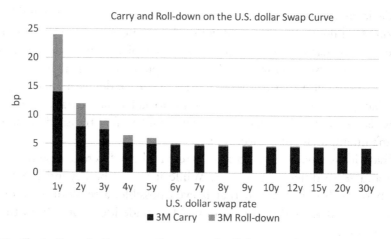

Fig. 6.2   Illustration of a three-month carry and roll-down analysis

Sometimes, carry and roll-down are risk-adjusted for comparison, due to the different volatility across the curve. Those trades are referred to as *carry-to-risk trades* and calculate carry-to-risk ratios to rank asset pairs across government bonds, swaps, credit, equities and currencies.

6.4.2 Curve Trades

Curve trades express a view about the *steepness*, or *slope*, of the yield curve. Since the steepness of a yield curve can be explained by many factors (expectations, risk premia, segregated markets, convexity, etc.), it is often not obvious whether a curve is too steep or too flat.

Typically, curve trades are based on historical observations. "*The curve has never inverted in this part of the curve*" or "*the last time the curve was this steep/flat was n years ago*" are typical statements found in curve trade publications. Curve trades often bet on a reversal (convergence toward what is believed to be a "normal" or average slope).

To avoid cash flows due to carry during the holding period of the trade, curve trades are often constructed in *forward space*.[16] If done, one needs to "beat" the forward slope (not the spot slope). The forward slope, however, is often less attractive (i.e., most of the expected convergence is consumed by negative carry). This means that there is actually no trade to be done, or the trade only works if one gets an almost immediate curve adjustment.

Figure 6.3 shows a comparison between a spot curve and a forward curve, representing market levels for US swaps observed in November 2006. Because the 1s10s[17] swap slope was much steeper in forward space, forward flattener trades appeared attractive. At the time, those trades were expected to perform well if the 1s10s slope would remain flatter than what forward slopes implied them to be in the future.

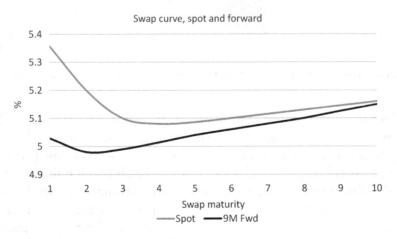

Fig. 6.3 Illustration of a curve slope analysis, levels as of 11/17/2006

6.4.3 Momentum Trades

The core principle of momentum trades is to identify, as early as possible, a pattern of market returns inconsistent with randomly moving prices.

There is some empirical evidence supporting the notion of *trending* behavior in financial markets. If the presence of market *momentum* can be found, a trend-following strategy would suggest a trade constructed to benefits from a continuation of this momentum. One of the most common explanations for trending behavior is that markets do not respond instantaneously to new information as it *takes time* for information to get incorporate in market prices, leading to only *gradual* price adjustments.

Momentum trades can be based on *absolute* or on *relative* momentum strategies. Absolute momentum strategies aim at identifying price trends of an individual asset, while relative momentum strategies rank assets on a relative basis (see Fig. 6.4).

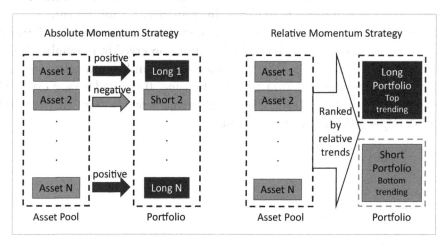

Fig. 6.4 Types of momentum strategies (Adapted from Kolanovic and Wei [2015, 19])

Similar to momentum trades are trades based on seasonality. While momentum trades are based on trends in *consecutive* time periods, seasonality trades are based on assumed trends in *non-consecutive* time periods. An example would be a year-end trade based on the observation that the market is exhibiting a reoccurring price pattern at or around year-end. For example, many market participants are adjusting their trading positions prior to the year-end to show a more favorable balance sheet, to be published in the annual report. Such behavior could lead to price effects for certain assets. Apart from year-end seasonality, there could be quarter-end-effects, month-end-effects and many other possible seasonal effects.

6.4.4 Fair Value Model Trades

Fair value models are empirical models that attempt to quantify the linkage between macroeconomic fundamentals and market prices as well as between market prices themselves. They are not pure forecasting models, but require projections for economic and financial fundamentals to translate a view on the business cycle into fair values for assets consistent with this view. *Fair value model trades* are trade ideas based on a perceived deviation of market prices from model prices.

6.4.5 Volatility Trades

Volatility trades are often based on a dislocation on the *volatility matrix*, which is a grid that summarizes implied volatility for various option maturities and tenures). Other factors being a basis for a volatility trade idea are changes in volatility skews (i.e., differences between at-the-money, in-the-money and out-of-the-money options) and dislocations between swaption volatility and cap/floor[18] volatility or between exchange-traded volatility and OTC volatility.

Various investor classes transact in different volatility products, which can lead to relative value opportunities due to supply-demand imbalances; on the other hand, volatility products are typically priced off a unified model, which is constructed to be arbitrage-free. Thus, true arbitrage opportunities in volatility space are nowadays very rare.

Some volatility products have a wide bid-ask spread (compared to, say, Treasury securities). Spotting volatility dislocations often help those investors required to buy volatility product (e.g., mortgage convexity hedgers) to identify cheap pockets of volatility.

6.4.6 Technical Analysis

Technical analysis (TA) is a collective term for a number of quantitative methods to extract information from historical price patterns to forecast market trends. It includes *chartism* (pattern recognition), *candlestick analysis*, *Elliott wave theory* (dividing price paths into impulsive and corrective phases) and *Dow theory* (identifying sector rotations).

The rationale of TA is hotly debated. Some people point out that it is a direct contraction to the efficient-market hypothesis, even in its weak-form version, because it assumes that there is information in historical data sets and graphical representations of them not fully reflected in the current market prices. Others point out that acknowledging some *behavioral* patterns in human investment decision making can help anticipate the future price evolution.

Some market participants claim not to believe in TA per se, but are observing it anyway because they know that *other* people are believing in it and, by doing so, are creating a *self-fulfilling prophesy*. From a practitioner's perspective, it does not really matter whether TA works because it correctly predicts the future, or TA works because many people act upon the TA's prediction.

For research, the discussion whether TA is a useful technique is a moot point. If clients want to receive it, it better be provided or else they will ask another broker-dealer for it. Not all clients want to receive TA, and some are even insulted by it, so it makes sense to produce it in stand-alone publications and to distribute it only to a selected group of investors.

Some clients do not use TA as the sole and exclusive source when making an investment decision, but rather as one of many signals along with fundamental analysis, relative value arguments, flow-driven information, supply/demand imbalances and other aspects.

Some of what technical analysts are producing, such as simple pattern recognition in chart analysis, can be automated with the help of machine learning. It is fair to assume that in the long run the market won't need any longer an army of chartists to analyze the same data sets.

6.4.7 Central Bank Trades

Research analysts dedicated to observing, interpreting and predicting the US central bank are sometimes called "Fed watchers."

Within the Federal Reserve (Fed), the Federal Open Market Committee (FOMC) is responsible for open market operations. It holds eight regularly scheduled meetings per year. At these meetings, the Committee reviews economic and financial conditions, determines the appropriate stance of monetary policy, and assesses the risks to its long-run goals of price stability and full employment. Changes to the Fed's target rate are most of the time announced on FOMC meetings (although they happen, on occasions, also between meetings).

Predicting the Fed's next policy move leads to trade ideas. The best trade ideas are those expected to be profitable for a wide range of FOMC outcomes.

There are central bank trades based on the expected behavior of other central banks as well, like trades based on the ECB or the Bank of England.

Expressing a view on the central bank's target rate policy typically involves money market instruments (Eurodollar and Fed funds futures and futures options), while trades based on changes to Quantitative Easing (QE) involve longer-dated bonds, bond futures, bond options and swaps.

6.4.8 Trades Related to Economic Releases

Economic releases, such as the *nonfarm payrolls* release in the USA, can give important impulses for trading. Prior to the economic release strategist put out trades that are supposed to perform well if the data release matches their own expectation (or the official forecast/call of the broker-dealer).

Often, investors have a view on data and request from research information about the following two questions:

- What is the "reaction function" of various financial instruments to a surprise in economic data?
- Which trades capture best any client-specific expected deviation from market consensus?

Investment banks often employ one analyst dedicated to the tracking, interpretation and prediction of economic data releases. This analyst is typically co-located with sales and trading to comment on a data release right away (by shouting out loud on the trading floor or on the so-called squawk box or *hoot-n-holler* ("hoot" for short).

In the minutes and hours following an economic release that significantly deviated from consensus, clients often experience adverse mark-to-market fluctuations on their trades and call the research strategist for an opinion about the further pricing dynamics.

6.4.9 Conditional Trades

Conditional trades are trades that create an economic exposure if, and only if, a specified scenario materializes; they are constructed through option products.

One class of conditional trades is *conditional curve trades*. They create a curve trade if interest rates move above or below a certain level. If, for example, a client faces curve risk, an offsetting curve position can be established conditionally; often, this is cheaper than an unconditional hedge.

Another type of a conditional trade is a *conditional swap spread trade*. Swap spreads, being the difference between the swap rate and the government (Treasury) rate, are market directional. Often, investors are hesitant to express an *outright* swap spread widening view because of the risk of tighter spreads in a rally or in a roughly unchanged market. A significant rally is often accompanied by mortgage convexity hedging which leads to tighter spreads. A significant sell-off, on the other hand, often leads to wider swap spreads due to hedging flows and leveraged accounts expressing bearish views on the swap curve. So-called *Put-Payers* are *conditional* asset swap-widening trades in a sell-off. They are a combination of a bond futures put option) and a payer swaption. Typically, an investor sells a bond futures put and buys a payer swaption that matches optionality, cash-flow and strike levels. If the market does not sell off beyond the strike level (i.e., in a rally or an unchanged market environment), both options are expected to expire worthless without creating an economic exposure. If interest rates push above the strike level, both options are expected to be exercised. The investor gets delivered the cheapest-to-deliver (CDT) from the bond futures option, while simultaneously entering into a pay-fixed interest rate swap. Thus, the investor gets long the asset swap spread of the CTD at the strike-spread.

6.5   General Rules About Trade Ideas

Unfortunately, a large percentage of research "ideas" are just recycled recommendations that experienced institutional investors have already seen multiple times throughout their career. Sophisticated investors are not interested in wasting their time going through extended research publications in search for actionable suggestions—they want to see them right away to make a quick assessment whether they are worth further consideration. *Trade ideas* can play an important role as the focal point of an effective sales-client communication that saves clients time and helps "cutting to the chase."

Vague recommendations are generally not helpful, as they *lack specifics* and often ignore negative aspects (negative carry, risks, illiquidity, etc.). Most investors expect *precise* details from a trade idea (and sometimes don't even want to hear any further explanation about the analyst's reasoning). While research recipients have different preferences with respect to the research format, there has been an *evolution* from essay-style toward trade idea-based publications (see Table 6.1).

Table 6.1   Evolution of investment research format

Publication style	Disadvantages
Essay-style text without recommendation	Text with specific trade idea upfront
Text with recommendation at the end	Takes too long to find the actionable recommendation
Text with recommendation upfront	Lacks specifics (instruments, hedge ratio, risks, etc.)
Text with specific trade idea upfront	Sophisticated investors often don't need reasoning for trade idea
Text with specific trade idea upfront	Less sophisticated investors may not understand motivation for trade idea

Most institutional investors (with the notable exception of some hedge funds) face institutional restrictions as to what kind of trades they are allowed to establish. There are limitations with respect to the *asset class* (e.g., no derivatives), the *maturity* (e.g., only money market instruments up to one-year remaining maturity), the type of *credit exposure* (e.g., only investment grade), the envisioned *holding period* or the *maximum risk* (e.g., DV01 of a trade not exceeding a certain amount). To allow investors to quickly check those restrictions, trade ideas need to highlight the relevant specifics prominently.[19] Table 6.2 lists the main elements that need to be part of a trade idea.

Table 6.2   Main elements of a trade idea and their purpose

Element	Purpose
Instrument selection	Confirming that investor is allowed to trade those products
Reason(s) for dislocation	Suggesting the driving forces that have caused a deviation from a general market balance
Reason(s) for reversal	Proposing reasons for why dislocation will reverse/normalize
Weighting	Proposing risk-weightings for different legs in trade construction
(Max.) notional	Telling investor up to which maximum amount trading desk is willing to provide liquidity
Execution levels	Realistic, actionable levels that include bid/offer and other transaction cost
Risk	Allowing investor to stay within own risk limits (DV01, Vega, Gamma, etc.)
Carry	Indicating whether trade has positive or negative carry
Holding period	Suggesting expected time for trade to perform
Expected profit	Price level at which profit-taking (i.e., unwinding the trade) is suggested
Stop-loss limit	Price level at which trade should be unwound to limit (cut) the loss

6.6   Trade Idea Generation

The ability to come up with good trade ideas, possibly even on a daily basis, is a great value to any research analyst. Some are actually keeping their cards close to their chest and are reluctant to share their knowledge, out of fear they could lose their distinctive features within the pool of research analysts.[20] Also, the market is quite efficient in the sense that any framework developed to spot profitable trade opportunities will only work for a limited period, as more and more market participants start replicating the process and price inefficiencies are "arbitraged out." Thus, as a research analyst you have to constantly look out for new ways to ferret out interesting trade ideas.

Conceptually, there are four generic methods to generate trade ideas. The *first* is a data-driven approach. Here, large sets of data (closing data pulled from the bank's databases or, even better, intra-day and tic-by-tic data) are analyses with respect to any possible *dislocation*. Dislocation may be defined as a, say, 2-standard deviation move from historical averages. The analytical framework is likely set up to create near-risk-free positions that tend to remain relatively stable and are widely independent on what the overall market is doing, something said to have little *market directionality*. An example for such a relative value position is a position on one part of the yield curve in comparison with positions in neighboring points on the yield curve. Depending on the resources available to the analyst, the analysis may be run on an Excel spread or as dedicated programs developed and maintained by IT departments. Once the analyst is alerted by the model that there is a potential dislocation (and after checking that is wasn't just due to data issues), the second step would then be to understand what has caused the dislocation, why it is assumed to be temporary and what will cause a convergence back to historical relationships.

The *second* strategy in finding trade ideas turns the above process upside down. Since dislocations are typically caused by an *imbalance* in flow, one would try to identify one-way trading flows initiated by significant market participants. Research analysts following this strategy would literally walk down the aisles of the trading floor and question salespeople whether they have noticed unusually large flows. Once those flows have been identified, one would then check whether they resulted in a price dislocation. The advantage of this approach is that one does not have to scan through the entire universe of possible relative value relationships and can focus on relevant areas. Also, knowing what has caused the dislocation, if there turns out to be one, makes it much easier to determine whether this is a short-dated effect or a long-term structural change.

The *third* way to generate trade ideas is to monitor what type of trade ideas other research analysts are publishing,[21] to check whether they are still attractive given current market levels and, if so, creating a variation of it that is then promoted under one's own name. The majority of trade ideas are created that way, which also explains why the buy-side is bombarded with similarly looking trade ideas from different sell-side firms every day.

The *fourth* strategy is to *reverse-engineer* the *thinking process* of market participants that do not advertise their strategies but are known for executing profitable trades. Those are mostly hedge funds, proprietary trading desks and other relative value traders. Salespeople are often too busy executing orders to extract the informational value of the flow from those clients, but a knowledgeable research analyst with enough time at hand can infer from the different legs of a structured trade the underlying trade idea. However, arbitrageurs are well aware of this and frequently make detection of their trading strategy more difficult by executing the different legs of the relative value trade with different broker-dealers.

Once a trade idea has been generated, it is necessary to prepare for questions from the investor side. Questions may include:

- "How come no one else thought of this idea before?"
- "Why aren't other people putting on this trade?"
- "What has caused the dislocation in the first place?"

One should also be able to explain what caused the dislocation and why this force is about to fade away. Reasons for a potential dislocation are:

- Market is wrong and you are the first one having found about it;
- Others know about the dislocation but cannot take advantage of it (e.g., for legal reasons);
- Other market participants are causing the dislocation by trading the other way (for a good reason);
- You are wrong (i.e., there is no dislocation).

It is typically very convincing if one can demonstrate that one's own prop desk/trading desk has put on the trade already:

"Our own desk has put on this trade in size already, but we maxed out on risk and want to give our favorite clients a chance to participate in the trade."

Investors are suspicious individuals (as they should be). Many have had their share of bad experiences and only trust research analysts (and salespeople & traders) they have a long-term relationship with. To the question *Why are you showing me this trade idea?* they don't want to hear any of the answers listed in Table 6.3.[22]

Table 6.3 Why are you showing me this trade idea?—answers nobody likes to hear

Answers to "Why are you showing me this trade idea?" nobody likes to hear:
"I am a junior analyst and nobody else is interested in listening to my recommendations yet. You are the beta-tester of my idea"
"Smart money is doing exactly the opposite, but we need some dumb investors providing liquidity for them to get into the trade"
"Smart money already put this trade on a while ago, made good money, and want to get out of the trade now. We are looking for some uninformed investors providing liquidity for them to get out"
"Our trading desk is axed to do this"

6.7   Conflict of Interests

We already discussed the general concept of principal-agent problems causing conflict of interests from a theoretical point of view in Sect. 3.2.4. More than just being an academic matter, conflict of interests in Sales have been very obvious to most market participant all along. As mentioned in Sect. 6.3.1, the observation that only so few sell recommendations are issued by research analysts is *casting suspicion*. Assuming that stock prices follow, at least approximately, a random process, buy- and sell-ratings should be issued in roughly equal frequency. Studies show, however, that merely 6% of research analysts' recommendations on stocks in the S&P 500 index are sell or equivalent ratings.[23]

The fact that research analysts only rarely issue sell recommendations and forecasts are often excessively optimistic has led to questions about the robustness and quality of investment research.[24] It also led to *regulatory enforcement* action. For example, in 2016 the Securities and Exchange Commission (SEC) charged a former Deutsche Bank research analyst[25] with certifying a rating on a stock that was inconsistent with his personal view.[26] The SEC investigation established that although the analyst recommended *selling* stocks of Big Lots in conversations with several hedge fund clients he didn't downgrade Big Lots from a *buy* recommendation in his report because he wanted to maintain his relationship with Big Lots management. During an internal conference call, the research analyst justified his behavior by saying "we just had them in town so it's not kosher to downgrade on the heels of something like that."

Most large sell-side firms, besides producing investment research, also feature an Investment Banking Division (IBD). This area performs primarily advisory functions and includes Mergers and Acquisitions (M&A), Equity Capital Markets (ECM) and Debt Capital Markets (DCM). In order to increase the chance of winning (profitable) investment banking mandates it is tempting for the bank to win the clients favor by portraying the client in a positive light in research publications. Even after a corporate finance mandate has been secured, there is a benefit from "talking up" the value of a mandate's business as it increases the chance of a positive outcome (merger, acquisition, Initial Public Offering [IPO], etc.), increases the business deal's fees by inflating its market value and generates buying interest in the secondary market, which facilitate the profitable unloading of the banks own positions in the security.

There are two ways a sell-side firm can address conflict of interests within Research. The first is to create a so-called *Chinese Wall* between Banking and Research. The term *Chinese Wall* (or just "*Wall*" for short) is inspired by the Great Wall of China and describes the (previously only) ethical (and now also) legal obligation to create a boundary between insider information gathered during an investment banking process and information used in investment research. There are strict regulatory rules governing the kind of information a research analyst is allowed to receive. The second way to mitigate conflict of interests is to isolate research strategists within a stand-alone research entity. An example for this is Kepler Cheuvreux, a leading independent European financial services company specialized in advisory services and intermediation to the investment management industry. Research analysts and research management are owning 31.9% of the equity. Among the minority shareholders are the sell-side firms Crédit Agricole CIB, UniCredit, Rabobank and Swedbank (see Fig. 6.5).

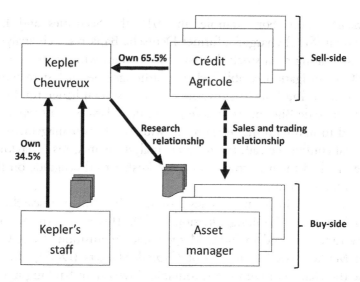

Fig. 6.5 Corporate governance at Kepler Cheuvreux

If you ever assume the role of a research analyst and keep defending your own integrity, along with the integrity of the institution you are working for, you will develop a reputation in the market that will benefit your career in the long run. It is primarily *your* responsibility to become aware of potential conflict of interests and to escalate them with management if they occur. Often, responsibilities can be realigned in quick and simple way that realigns your interest with that of the bank and its clients.

6.8 MiFID II

The *Markets in Financial Instruments Directive* of 2014,[27] commonly known as *MiFID II*, aims to ban any *inducement* for fund managers to act in a way that is not in clients' interests.[28] MiFID II for investment research states that brokerages providing both research and execution services will need to supply and price them *separately*. Any benefit received by the investment manager must enhance the quality of service to the client (asset owner) and does not distort or bias the provision of services. One aim is to combat the perception that research is provided by investment banks and brokers to asset managers as an inducement, or bribe, to trade with them.

Research in the context of MiFID II can be roughly defined as investment material or services concerning one or several financial instruments or other assets, the issuer or potential issuer of financial instruments, or something closely related to a specific industry or financial market. More specifically, those are explicit or implicit *recommendations* and investment *strategies*, providing substantiated *opinions* on financial instrument prices, or contain *analysis* and original value-adding *insights*.

Certain type of research provided to certain investor types needs to be priced to comply with MiFID II regulation. But what is the right price? The problem is that investment research had been given away for free in the past, so there is little knowledge of its price elasticity of demand.[29] Two possibilities are illustrated in Fig. 6.6. Increasing the price of research from zero could cause a gradual reduction in demand, or demand could collapse if even only a small price is charged.

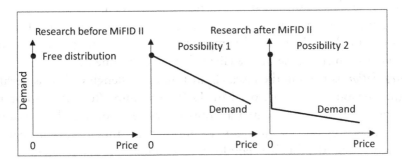

Fig. 6.6   Estimating the price elasticity of demand for investment research

Both academics and practitioners have been struggling, and still do, to establish a clear understanding of what the involuntary *unbundling* of research and execution services does to the research market dynamics. When looking for other markets where similar unbundling took place, some evidence can be drawn from the market of plastic bags (that used to be distributed freely by retailers as part of a service bundle). Aiming to reduce the waste of resources, laws in several countries forced retailers to stop offering plastic bags at a price of zero and to price them separately. Price elasticity of demand was found to be very high and demand dropped.[30] Is investment research the new plastic bag?

6.9   Challenges Ahead

Research used to be the first career stop for many new hires in Global Markets. Spending a year or two in research was considered to be a great way to acquire a broad knowledge about financial markets, products, clients and various coverage areas. Afterward, many research analysts would go on to work in sales, trading, risk management or other areas. It used to be quite easy to identify sympathetic employees from non-research areas and to have them help out in a research-related task. "I used to be in your shoes" was something along the lines they would say. Research no longer plays the same role of super-charging new hires due to shrinking research departments and for cost reasons. As a research analyst, it is now more difficult to find former research employees within the organization.

An increasing number of research publications (especially those considered to be maintenance research) are getting *outsourced* and/or *automated*. Fewer seasoned research staff is needed for this type of research and experienced research analysts are replaced by junior, unexperienced employees. Research analysts now must either have the necessary data science talent to facilitate automation (e.g., knowledge of the programming languages Python and R, skills in cloud computing[31]) or have strong people skills to deliver customized research in a client-facing environment.

Regulation is making the research area more challenging also, as discussed in the previous section. Before MiFID II came into effect, it was not atypical for many sell-side research analysts to spend a considerable amount of time and energy on *self-promotion*, trying to create the impression that their research is essential for their employer to maintain profitable client relationships. Since 2018, clients have started voting with their wallet about which research they actually like to receive. This is nothing short of a total game changer in the area of investment research. Although this is a long process to play out,[32] eventually the degree of value-adding of specific investment research services will be less of a matter of opinion and something that can be measured.

6.10 A Career in Research (by Vincent Chaigneau)

The quarter century that I have spent in investment research, on both the sell and the buy-side, has seen extraordinary changes in the way research operates, although the core objective of the job hasn't really: It is still about delivering good investment ideas.

Already at the time my own career started, Alan Greenspan, who served for nearly twenty years as the Chairman of the US Federal Reserve, was famous for his obsession with data: He was untiringly searching for on-the-ground evidence that would give him a faithful representation of the economic conditions. Since then data has exploded; so much that privacy has become a major challenge for business and society. Superior data provides an obvious edge to whomever has access to it and manages to use it effectively: that is true for policy makers as well as investment professionals. There is so much data now—free or not—that it is increasingly difficult for human beings to process it. That task is better left to the machine, hence the unstoppable rise of AI.

Hence, Research has evolved in a way that now gives a much bigger role to quantitative analysts, data scientists and programmers. One typical transformation in the making is the shift from VBA-based Excel-spreadsheets toward coding in the programming language Python. This evolution matches that of the industry, characterized by the rise of automated and algorithmic trading, fintech and passive asset management. The latter development is profoundly transforming the buy-side, and the self-sustained trend very much relates to the role of research. If active portfolio managers—often supported by the work of traditional analysts—consistently fail to outperform market indices, it is hard for them to justify being paid large fees. Both the regulators and market forces—clients looking for a better returns and lower fees—contribute to the move toward passive investment, which is much cheaper to run. The falling fees lead to cost cutting, and a broader move toward automation. Pursuing a career in Research opens many doors, as there is a direct links with other positions such as a developer, trader or portfolio manager.

The beauty of starting in Research, event for a quant, data scientist and programmer, is that you may be asked to collaborate with other analysts with a very diverse set of skills. From them you may learn about how capital markets actually work (the products and structures that are traded, the actors, the drivers, etc.). Eventually, a well-rounded research analyst with a decent understanding of capital markets and a strong expertise in quantitative analysis and/or technology has likely a bright future in the industry.

For all that is said about the rise of passive investments and the failure of active asset management, there is still very much a role for traditional (some will say old-fashioned) analysts. In fact, the diversity of Research positions is remarkable, as the author of this book has shown. One may categorize them in three buckets: quantitative, top-down and bottom-up analysts. I will not say more about the quantitative analysts, the rising stars of an industry, irremediably caught in a race to the bottom (falling margins and fees). Top-down research, or global macro, includes economics, strategy and asset allocation. Bottom-up refers to equity or credit analysis, that is focused primarily on the business strategy and balance sheet of corporations. This is still at the very heart of active portfolio management. My conviction is that asset management is being "barbellized." Passive portfolio management will be dominated by firms that manage a huge quantity of assets (the BlackRocks and Vanguards of this world) on which they charge very small fees. Active portfolio management will be dominated by much smaller but agile boutiques that are specialized in specific strategies; the much smaller size allows them to deploy trades that the giants are simply too big to execute in areas where market depth is insufficient. Those stuck in the middle of that barbell will be squeezed.

The traditional analysts of course are also challenged by technology. Credit and equity analysts for instance face the competition of AI—tech companies offering products that generate signals about business or rating trends are burgeoning. Those AI signals may emanate from social media feeds, data from financial reports, text analysis, etc. Those however are likely to complement rather than replace the role of analysts who talk with the management of those companies, understand the industry trends and interact with investors. Take an insurance company for instance: With regulation having forced a reduction of duration gap, the quality of the balance sheet to a large extent depends on the credit where it is invested; those that can rely on a solid credit research will tend to better absorb shocks in the cycle.

Another example of competing or complementary developments lies in equity strategy. Traditionally, the strategists were focused on geographical and sectorial relative value and allocations. Nowadays, the equity market is increasingly dominated by factor analysis (value, growth, momentum, quality, etc.), which essentially is a quantitative activity. Again, there is still a role to be played for the traditional top-down analyst, and even more so if he or she is able to complement the own work by that of quantitative strategists.

Finally, it is impossible to write about the exciting world of research without mentioning environmental, social and governance (ESG), criteria used by socially conscious investors when screening investment opportunities. The whole financial industry is adjusting to what has become both a purpose and a requirement (the ESG brand is attracting increasing inflows). This area is still developing, given the huge amount of data available and the flurry of providers, none of which has established itself as the new industry standard. ESG is also an area where fundamental analysis will assist the machine, or vice versa.

While large segments of finance are being commoditized, let me finish with two important trends. First, there is the rise of private capital markets. The decline in interest rates has led investors to look for new investment opportunities, such as private equity and private debt, where they can capture an additional illiquidity premium. Those markets, being far less transparent and liquid compared to public markets, require different skills. Second, while electronic trading is dominated by the machines, many long-term investors still very much rely on thematic research. Secular stagnation, the saving glut, globalization (and now reshoring?), inflation (or the lack thereof), unconventional monetary policy are all examples of themes that have truly shaped Global Markets for the past quarter century. Research remains an area of great diversity, where very different individuals can flourish, for as long as they have a passion for finance.

Notes

1. Fuller (2017, 17).
2. CRISIL Coalition, cited in Wigglesworth (2017).
3. This includes daily, weekly, monthly, quarterly and annual reports, stand-alone/thematic research, trade alerts and regional/sector compilations.
4. Wigglesworth (2017).
5. Fuller (2017, 3).
6. Financial market research can be quite repetitive, causing many research analysts, including myself, to seek out creative, funny or even poetical ways to transport otherwise uninspiring information. See, e.g., Phillips (2011).
7. Assuming clients are not engaged in so-called *short selling*, which is true for the majority of buy-side firms. Short selling is the process of borrowing a security from another market participant, selling the security in the market and then having to buy it back later to return the borrowed security to its lender.
8. Source: Wigglesworth (2018).
9. Source: Davis (2019).
10. Source: Franck (2018).
11. Kolanovic and Krishnamachari (2017, 12).
12. Even a relatively small $200,000-satellite is capable of sending several terabytes of data on a daily basis.
13. Most of the fuel tanks have floating top so it is possible to use trigonometry to calculate its volume and the amount of oil in it.
14. IFRS 9 refers to an International Financial Reporting Standard that replaces the previously used International Accounting Standard (IAS) 39. Since 2018, regulatory-mandated stress testing needs to be conducted following the IFRS 9 framework.
15. For example, the 1-year roll-down of a 5% 10-year bond currently trading at par would calculate how much above/below par a 5% 9-year bond would

be priced in the current yield environment. The expected roll-down is sometimes estimated by taking the difference between the current spot rate and a shortened rate on the same spot curve, and then multiplying this by the forward duration of the instrument.

16. "In forward space" means establishing a forward position. For example, instead of establishing a 2-year-vs.-10-year curve slope position using a 2-year and a 10-year spot-starting swap, it is constructed with a 3-month-into-2-year and a 3-month-into-10-year swap. This would then been called "putting on a 2s10s curve trade, 3 months forward."

17. 1s10s is short for 1-year-vs.-10-year, the yield difference between the 10-year rate and the 1-year rate.

18. An interest rate cap (floor) is a derivative instrument in which the holder receives periodic payments if interest rates exceed (fall below) an agreed-upon level.

19. Also, some investors expect the sale force to pre-scan research notes and to only forward those that do not violate restrictions or are inconsistent with their investment style.

20. There is even a story about a strategist who used to keep his relative value trade-detection spreadsheets on a USP stick that he would take home at the end of each workday, suspecting that if he were to save them on his work PC someone else would "steal" them from him.

21. This requires having access to competitors' research publications, which is getting increasingly more difficult. However, clients and prop desks are sometimes willing to forward research they receive from "the Street."

22. A research analyst with a strong relationship to a client may, however, playfully and jokingly suggest such an answer to tease the client, only to offer a convincing alternative explanation afterward.

23. Ng and Gryta (2017).

24. See, for example, Galanti and Vaubourg (2017).

25. The analyst agreed to settle the charges by paying a $100,000 penalty and was suspended from the securities industry for a year. Deutsche Bank agreed to pay a $9.5 million penalty to settle civil charges.

26. Source: U.S. Securities and Exchange Commission (2016).

27. European Union (2014).

28. MiFID II came into force in 2018.

29. Price elasticity of demand, or PED, is a microeconomic concept that measures the percentage change in the quantity demanded of a good resulting from a 1 percent increase in the price of that good.

30. E.g., in January 2010, Washington, DC, imposed a $0.05 tax on plastic bags at grocery stores and other retail establishments, causing a reduction of demand from an average 22.5 million per month in 2009 to 3 million bags in the first month of 2010. Similarly, Ireland introduced a €0.15 tax on plastic bags in 2002, causing a demand to fall by roughly 90%. See Yglesias (2010), Convery et al. (2007), and Tata (2019).

31. Parallel, distributed computing on shared, remote-access computing and storage resources.
32. Many sell-side firms are only offering research *bundles*, so it is currently not always possible to tell what the demand for specific publications or for publications of one specific research analyst is.

References

Convery, Frank, Simon McDonnell, and Susana Ferreira. 2007. The Most Popular Tax in Europe? Lessons from the Irish Plastic Bags Levy. *Environmental and Resource Economics* 38 (1): 1–11. https://www.researchgate.net/publication/5146973_The_Most_Popular_Tax_in_Europe_Lessons_from_the_Irish_Plastic_Bags_Levy. Accessed on January 20, 2020.

Davis, Michelle. 2019. Dimon Sounds a Cautious Note as JPMorgan Prepares for Recession. Bloomberg, 26 February. https://www.bloomberg.com/news/articles/2019-02-26/jpmorgan-to-spend-more-on-tech-as-rates-provide-revenue-boost. Accessed on January 20, 2020.

European Union. 2014. Directive 2014/65/EU of the European Parliament and of the Council of 15 May 2014 on Markets in Financial Instruments and Amending Directive 2002/92/EC and Directive 2011/61/EU Text with EEA Relevance. *Official Journal of the European Union*, L 173/349, 12 June. https://eur-lex.europa.eu/legal-content/en/TXT/?uri=CELEX:32014L0065. Accessed on January 20, 2020.

Franck, Thomas. 2018. Computer Engineers Now Make up a Quarter of Goldman Sachs' Workforce. CNBC, 30 April. https://www.cnbc.com/2018/04/30/computer-engineers-now-make-up-a-quarter-of-goldman-sachs-workforce.html. Accessed on January 20, 2020.

Fuller, Jane. 2017. A Level Playing Field for Investment Research? Challenges Facing the Buy-Side, Sell-Side and Independents. Centre for the Study of Financial Innovation publication, October. https://euroirp.com/wp-content/uploads/2017/10/CSFI-Full-Report-October-2017-A-Level-Playing-Field-for-Investment-Research.pdf. Accessed on January 20, 2020.

Galanti, Sébastien, and Anne-Gaël Vaubourg. 2017. Optimism Bias in Financial Analysts' Earnings Forecasts: Do Commissions Sharing Agreements Reduce Conflicts of Interest? Document de Recherche du Laboratoire d'Économie d'Orléans, 19 May. https://ideas.repec.org/p/hal/wpaper/hal-01724253.html. Accessed on January 20, 2020.

Kolanovic, Marko, and Rajesh T. Krishnamachari. 2017. Big Data and AI Strategies: Machine Learning and Alternative Data Approach to Investing. JPMorgan Global Quantitative & Derivatives Strategy, 18 May. https://www.cfasociety.org/cleveland/Lists/Events%20Calendar/Attachments/1045/BIG-Data_AI-JPMmay2017.pdf. Accessed on January 20, 2020.

Kolanovic, Marko, and Zhen Wei. 2015. Momentum Strategies Across Asset Classes: Risk Factor Approach to Trend Following. JPMorgan Global Quantitative & Derivatives Strategy, April. https://www.cmegroup.com/education/files/jpm-momentum-strategies-2015-04-15-1681565.pdf. Accessed on January 20, 2020.

Ng, Serena, and Thomas Gryta. 2017. New Wall Street Conflict: Analysts Say 'Buy' to Win Special Access for Their Clients. *Wall Street Journal*, 19 January. https://www.wsj.com/articles/new-wall-street-conflict-analysts-say-buy-to-win-special-access-for-their-clients-1484840659. Accessed on January 20, 2020.

Phillips, Matt. 2011. Some Poetical Thoughts on Bank Liquidity. *Wall Street Journal*, 19 August. https://blogs.wsj.com/marketbeat/2011/08/19/some-poetical-thoughts-on-bank-liquidity. Accessed on January 20, 2020.

Tata, Fidelio. 2019. Price Formation of FICC Research Following MiFID II Unbundling Rules. *Journal of Financial Regulation and Compliance* 28 (1): 97–113.

U.S. Securities and Exchange Commission. 2016. SEC: Deutsche Bank Analyst Issued Stock Rating Inconsistent with Personal View. Press Release, 17 February. https://www.sec.gov/news/pressrelease/2016-30.html. Accessed on January 20, 2020.

Wigglesworth, Robin. 2017. Final Call for the Research Analyst? *Financial Times*, 7 February. https://www.ft.com/content/85ee225a-ec4e-11e6-930f-061b01e23655. Accessed on January 20, 2020.

Wigglesworth, Robin. 2018. BlackRock Bets on Algorithms to Beat the Fund Managers. *Financial Times*, 20 March. https://www.ft.com/content/e689a67e-2911-11e8-b27e-cc62a39d57a0. Accessed on January 20, 2020.

Yglesias, Matthew. 2010. Bag Elasticity. ThinkProgress, 30 March. https://thinkprogress.org/bag-elasticity-eed0411b89d/. Accessed on January 20, 2020.

7

Derivatives

7.1 Why Derivatives?

Why derivatives? A bond salesperson, a stock trader or a macroeconomic research analyst does not need to know about them, right? Wrong! For anyone planning a career in Sales, Trading and Research, derivative knowledge is part of the required skill set. Here are two good arguments for knowing at least the basics about derivatives.

First, derivatives are truly transdisciplinary. Let's assume you had lost your job as a bond salesperson and were to transition into equity sales, you would probably have a hard time demonstrating that you have what it takes in the new position. If, on the other hand, your previous job included dealing with bond options, it would be very likely that you would be considered for a role in equity options. Derivative knowledge allows you to more easily move laterally across asset classes, bank businesses and functional roles. The debt capital markets (DCM) group uses interest rates caps, just like the investor derivatives group, advising corporate clients. The hedge fund sales group advises on swaptions, just like the corporate risk management (CRM) group uses them. Interest rate swaps are employed by institutional investors, just as they are part of asset and wealth management. Since the Global Markets environment is quite volatile, knowing about derivatives is a good career hedge.

Second, derivatives often allow for an unusual, surprising or creative analysis that helps set you apart from other market participants looking at the same market. This is particularly useful when you are in Sales or Research,

F. Tata, *Corporate and Investment Banking*,
https://doi.org/10.1007/978-3-030-44341-2_7

competing for the attention of your clients. In 2012, I detected a high correlation between inflation expectations extracted from inflation-linked bonds[1]
and the re-election odds of then-president Obama, as extracted from the
betting platform *Intrade*.[2] While not a typical derivative analysis, this unusual observation, illustrated in Fig. 7.1, helped me highlight how the US
presidential elections have, according to market expectations, an impact on
monetary policy and inflation (as the US president picks the chairman at the
Federal Reserve). Once I had the attention of my clients, it was much easier
to interest them in inflation and interest rate hedges.

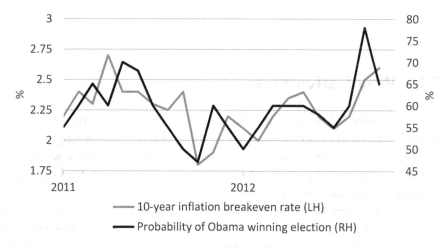

Fig. 7.1 Implied inflation expectations vs. expected election results (Author's own
calculation based on data by Bloomberg and Intrade)

7.2   Developing a Derivative Mindset

During my days working at financial institutions, I was regularly pulled into
meetings covering aspects of risk management, financial planning or project
evaluations. Usually, it took me less than half an hour to divide meeting participants into followers of what I would call linear thinking and those with a
derivative mindset.

Linear thinking, to me, is based on point-estimates of the future and of
some sort of discounted cash flow (DCF) analysis. Typically, a lot of energy
is spent among participants on agreeing on one specific scenario that appears
to be the plausible outcome in the future. Uncertainty, in terms of expected
deviations from this scenario, is then considered to be something negative.

The goal is often to fill an Excel spreadsheet with cash flow estimations and then to apply simple discounting rules to arrive at a single measure for decision making, such as the net present value (NPV)-rule.

People with a derivative mindset approach the decision-making process quite differently. First, there is the explicit understanding that the future cannot be represented by one single expected outcome. Instead, rather than spending time on compromising on one estimate, the range of possible outcomes is evaluated, and intellectual energy is spent in discussions about which theoretical framework or model would be best suited to represent such uncertainty. Second, uncertainty is never assumed to be negative per se. In fact, certain financial exposures (such as being long an option) benefit from uncertainty. Thus, a derivative mindset will always search for optionalities and aim to quantify their values to the involved parties. Third, a derivative mindset will never assume exposures to remain constant. While one IBM stock equals one IBM stock, option theory teaches us that one option on one IBM stock may have a certain IBM stock-equivalent exposure (called delta) now, but another tomorrow. This change of delta, called gamma, is nothing unusual to people even with only rudimentary derivative knowledge, but something outside of the comfort zone of linear thinkers. Fourth, a derivative mindset will thrive to define any exposure by its sensitivities to distinct factors, rather than by equating it to another observable financial market instrument. Those sensitivities, called Greeks in option pricing theory, are conceptually not very different from the beta utilized in the capital asset pricing model (CAPM) or the factor loadings of the arbitrage pricing model (APM), two frameworks linear thinkers often tend to struggle with as well. Having subscribed to thinking in terms of sensitivities, it comes naturally to people with a derivative mindset to focus on scenario analysis-type of "What-happens-if" questions and on the quantification of the impact of partial changes to the environment (e.g., interest rates going up, credit spread widening, volatility increasing).

It is almost bizarre to observe how each group, linear thinkers and derivative thinkers, tend to carry out their own discussions among themselves, without much interaction. Linear thinkers may, for example, have a heated discussion as to whether 2 or 3% would be the better forecast (or "baseline scenario") for a certain interest rate used in the planning process, based on what the economic research department has been predicting, what other market participants are thinking, how interest rates had been forecasted previously, etc. Meanwhile, derivative thinkers would discuss which statistical distribution (e.g., normal or log-normal) best captures the future interest rate environment and how those model assumptions create model risk in the risk management process. Every now and then, a member of the linear thinkers would address a derivative guy with a question like "are you o.k. with using 3% as our target rate?", to which the derivative guys would look baffled, and every now and then the derivative guys will ask the non-derivative guys something like "are you o.k. with applying a jump-diffusion process?", to which the non-derivative guys would look puzzled.

I don't want to create the impression that people with a derivative mind-set are smarter than those with a strictly linear understanding of the world. But I think it is safe to say that it is easier for someone with a derivative background to understand the thinking process of a linear thinker than the other way around. Thus, derivative knowledge is a useful skill set, similar to be able to speak in a foreign language or knowing legal and regulatory requirements.

A derivative mindset also often helps explaining seemingly improbable situations. Examples can be found in all areas of economic activity, but one of my favorites comes from the area of real estate development. There is a parking lot adjunct to the Holy Name Cathedral in Chicago that the Archdiocese in Chicago sold for some $110 million to a real estate developer in 2017.

One can only speculate about the Archdiocese's specific motives for having let the valuable parcel of land undeveloped for many years, before selling it only recently to a developer that now plans on building a $850 million 77-story apartment tower.[3] At least, option theory offers a convincing argument for such behavior. One could argue that the value of the property in front of the Cathedral is the sum of two value drivers: first, the value from the cash flow generated by the current use of the property and, second, the value from the option to decide later what to do with the property. A person merely applying linear thinking would aim at identifying the highest-NPV project for the use of the property. Running a parking lot is probably not generating much cash flows, and the NPV of future cash flows from collecting parking tickets (minus the cost of maintaining a parking lot) is almost certainly lower than the NPV generated by a high-rise apartment building. The second value driver concerns the option to delay development of the property. This option to wait has value, because in the future the specific type of building can be fine-tuned to the then-prevailing economic environment. If, for example, a 50-story building had been built 5 years ago, it would not be economical to tear down the building now and to replace it by a 77-story building, which is the most desirable structure from a current point of view.

In general, without the option of deciding when to invest, it is optimal to invest as long as NPV is positive. But when you have the option of deciding *when* to invest, it is usually optimal to invest only when the NPV is substantially greater than zero. Put differently, given the option to wait, an investment that currently has a negative NPV (such a parking lot) can have a positive value.

Assuming for a moment that the Archdiocese had applied a derivative mindset to the decision-making process, the incremental cash flow from turning the parking lot into a high rise would have to be compared to the option value of postponing the development by one additional unit of time. Calculating the value of the so-called *real option* is not trivial, but derivative theory helps us to better understand how some changes in the environment would impact the outcome. For example, we know that the option to wait is most valuable when there is a great deal of *uncertainty* regarding what the value of the investment will be in the future. The church, in derivative terms, was *long volatility*, benefiting from any increase in uncertainty.

Maybe somewhat surprisingly, a derivative mindset is not necessarily restricted to people working in a derivative environment. Many market participants that do not engage in derivative transaction, often because their institutional mandate prevents them from doing so, are just as derivative-savvy as derivative traders and salespeople. I once advised a portfolio manager at a central bank on picking the best government bond within a particular maturity bucket. Many central bank salespeople would simply point out an interest rates difference between neighboring securities on the yield curve to gain from what is called a yield pickup. The discussion I had with the central banker, however, centered on asset swap spread levels, differences in convexity and financing biases. Even though the central banker would, due to the central bank's mandate, never engage in interest rate swap transactions (as part of an asset swap), in convexity hedging, or repo financing, it was appreciated that I used relative value concepts employed by hedge funds and other sophisticated investors. This gave me an edge over other strategists and salespeople that treated the central banker as a less sophisticated investor and helped to win order flow. On another occasion, I was meeting with a portfolio manager of Fannie Mae, a US government-sponsored enterprise engaged in the mortgage market. The manager told me the following: "We are not a hedge fund, but treat us as if we were one." Many institutional investors may be prevented from trading derivatives at their current role, but they may have a strong derivative education nonetheless, are curious about derivative concepts or used to work in a derivative environment. They have a derivative mindset and expect anyone seeking to serve them to have one as well.

Finally, derivative knowledge can easily be used to shine. In fact, while working at the Derivative Marketing group of JPMorgan we used to joke that during pretty much any meeting one can torpedo a well-presented argument by raising the simple question "how about convexity?" Convexity is at the very heart of derivative theory, but unfortunately it comes in many different shapes and forms. A (de)convexity-adjustment is required to move from observable forward yields to implied market expectations, a convexity-adjustment is needed if payment dates differ from index dates (e.g., 10-year yields paid every 3 months), and pretty much every time the payout profile of a financial claim is nonlinear (which is even true for regular bonds, but even more so for mortgage products, bank's sight deposits, etc.) convexity matters. It is almost impossible to incorporate all facets of convexity. If you are not only alert to the possibility of convexity not addressed properly, but also manage to propose a theoretical concept or technique to improve the precision of calculation, you will be viewed as one of the smarter people in the room.

7.3   Fundamentals of Derivative Products

What is a derivative? A derivative is a contractual agreement whose value is derived from an underlying. In many cases, a derivative contract does not involve the exchange or transfer of principal or title. Rather the goal is to create an economic exposure to some underlying price change or event. Derivatives are zero-sum games between two contracting parties (see Fig. 7.2).

The term *derivative* refers to how the price of these contracts is *derived* from the price of some underlying security or commodity or from some index, interest rate or exchange rate.[4] Since derivatives are legal contracts between two consenting counterparties, pretty much anything could be used as the underlying; typically, the underlying should be easily observable and not subject to possible price manipulation by either side of the derivative contract.

Derivatives performed an uninterrupted, explosive growth up to the financial crisis of 2007–2008, as exemplified in Fig. 7.3 by looking at the outstanding notional of the over the counter (OTC) derivative market. Since then, it has been a mixed bag. Credit derivatives went on a decline, partially caused by the $30+ billion loss by American International Group

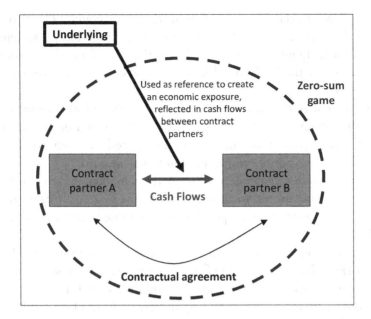

Fig. 7.2 Nature of a derivative contract

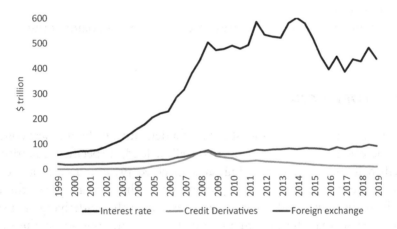

Fig. 7.3 Over the counter notional principal amount outstanding by risk category (*Source* BIS 2019)

(AIG) trading credit default swaps. Foreign exchange derivatives stabilized and even grew after the crisis, possibly because global world trade keeps increasing, making currency risk management more relevant than ever. Interest rate derivatives are impacted by a number of contrasting developments. Regulatory changes have moved an increasing part of derivatives from OTC onto exchanges. The zero-interest rate policy (ZIRP) of central banks and expectations for low rates for longer may have also dampened the need for hedging. On the other hand, the risk of an adverse increase in interest rates on the back of a less accommodative Fed creates some additional demand.

The notional principal amount or notional amount of a derivatives contract is the amount used to calculate the cash flows of a derivative contract. Typically, the notional amount is not exchanged between counterparties. Also, there is some double counting of notional amounts.

The gross market value shows the mark-to-market value of a derivative exposure. At trade inception, it is typically close to zero. Because of derivatives being zero-sum games, a positive market value to one counterparty is a negative to the other.

Central clearing has made very significant inroads into many OTC derivatives markets. More than 80% of outstanding OTC interest rate derivatives contracts are currently against central counterparties (CCPs). When a derivatives contract between two reporting dealers is cleared by a CCP, this contract is replaced, in an operation called novation, by two new contracts: one between counterparty A and the CCP, and a second between the CCP and counterparty B.

The four main types of derivatives contracts are forwards, futures, swaps and options.

7.4   Forwards

The simplest and perhaps oldest form of a derivative is the forward contract. It is the obligation to buy or borrow (sell or lend) a specified quantity of a specified item, called underlying, at a specified price or rate at a specified time in the future, called the expiration date. The forward price (the price at which the buyer and seller agree to exchange the underlying) is usually negotiated so that the present value of the forward contract at the time it is traded is zero. The contract partner committed to buy the underlying at expiration is said to hold a *long* position in the future, while the side committed to sell is *short* the future. There are no cash flows during the life of a forward contract; the only payout occurs at expiration.

The value of a forward contract at expiration can be displayed as payout profiles (see Fig. 7.4). Because forwards are zero-sum games, meaning that a profit to one contract partner must be a loss of equal amount to the other contract partner, the payout profile of a long position in a forward is a

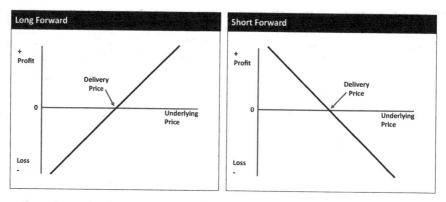

Fig. 7.4 Payout profiles of forwards

mirror-image of that of a short position. The payoff of the *long* forward position is delivery price minus underlying price, while the payout of the *short* forward position is underlying price minus delivery price.

Forwards have been around for some 3800 years. They can be traced back to Mesopotamia.[5] A Babylonian clay tablet sitting at the British Museum in London documents a typical problem when trading forwards from the year 1750 BC, namely the quality of the deliverable into a forward contract.[6]

7.5 Futures

Futures contracts are similar to forwards, but they are highly standardized, publicly traded and cleared through a clearing house. The futures contracts are standardized so that they are *fungible*—meaning that they are substitutable one for another. This fungibility implies that a trader who bought a futures contract can offset the economic exposure by selling a futures contract. Figure 7.5 contrasts a forward to a futures contract and gives the contract specifications of a specific corn futures contract, listed on the Chicago Mercantile Exchange (CME).

Underlyings to futures contracts include: soft commodities,[7] hard commodities, stocks and stock indices, foreign exchange (FX) rates, interest rates, bonds, real estate indexes, economic events, equity indexes, swaps, energy prices and weather. Some futures allow for physical delivery, in which case it needs to be specified what can be delivered into the futures by the short.

Futures can be used for *speculation* and *hedging* purposes. To illustrate how hedging works in the context of futures, let's take the example of a

Comparing forwards to futures	
Forward	**Futures**
Private contract between two parties ("over the counter")	Contract traded on an exchange
Not standardized	Standardized
Usually one specified delivery date	Range of delivery dates
Settled at end of contract	Settled daily
Delivery or final settlement usual	Usually closed out prior to maturity
Some credit risk	Virtually no credit risk

Example: CME corn futures	
Contract Size	5,000 bushels (127 metric tons)
Deliverable Grade	#2 Yellow at contract Price, #1 Yellow at a 1.5 cent/bushel premium #3 Yellow at a 1.5 cent/bushel discount
Pricing Unit	Cents per bushel
Tick Size (min. fluct.)	1/4 of one cent per bushel ($12.50 per contract)
Contract Months	March, May, July, September & December
Trading Hours	CME Globex (Electronic platform): Sunday – Friday, 7:00 p.m. – 7:45 a.m. CT and Monday – Friday, 8:30 a.m. – 1:20 p.m. CT
Last Trade Date	The business day prior to the 15th calendar day of the contract month.
Settlement Procedure	Physical Delivery
Last Delivery Date	Second business day following the last trading day of the delivery month.

Fig. 7.5 Comparison forwards vs. futures and example of a corn futures contract

beer brewing company.[8] As shown in Fig. 7.6, the brewer turns raw materials, i.e., input factors, into beer. If the prices of those raw materials increase, the brewer could raise the beer price. However, that strategy could easily backfire. The beer industry is very competitive and market share could be lost. Also, beer prices may have been fixed long-term vis-a-vis the distributors. Another way to deal with the risk of increasing raw material prices would involve the use of futures. The beer brewer is what is called a *natural short* in the beer production's input factors. *Natural* indicates that the exposure has not been created artificially through financial instruments, but is the result of engaging in an economic production process. *Short* reflects the requirement to buy the commodity in the future (while "delivering" it into the production process at a price previously assumed when production planning was carried out). Adding a properly weighted position of a long futures contracts to the natural short position helps offset the price exposure to the underlying.

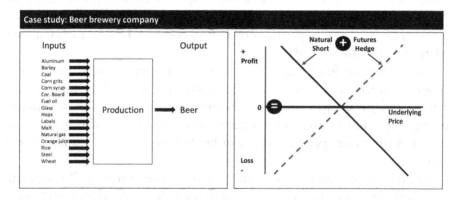

Fig. 7.6 Case study: beer brewing company

One specific property of futures to be discussed here is the margining requirements. There are two types of margins that affect any futures trader: *Initial margin* and *variation margin*. Initial margin is the amount (percentage) of a futures contract value that must be on deposit at the futures exchange at trade inception. The purpose of margin is to avoid contract defaults. Since a futures contract is not an actual sale, one only pays a fraction of the asset value when establishing a futures position.[9] Variation margin is a variable margin payment made to, or received by, the futures exchange on the back of price movements of the futures contracts. Variation margin is paid or received on a daily or intraday basis to bring the mark-to-market value of the futures, adjusted for the already posted margin, back to the initial margin requirement.

7.6   Swaps

Swap contracts, in comparison with forwards, futures and options, are one of the more recent innovations in derivatives contract design. The first currency swap contract, between the World Bank and IBM, dates back to August of 1981.

The basic structure of a swap contract involves two contract partners agreeing to swap two different types of payments (see Fig. 7.7). Each payment is calculated by applying some interest rate, index, exchange rate or the price of some underlying commodity or asset to a notional principal amount. The principal amount is considered to be *notional* because the swap generally does not require the transfer or exchange of principal (except for foreign exchange swaps and some foreign currency swaps). Payments are scheduled at regular intervals throughout the tenor of the swap.

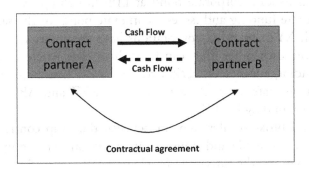

Fig. 7.7   Basic structure of a swap

7.6.1 Fixed-to-Floating Interest Rate Swap

The most plain-vanilla (basic) swap is the fixed-to-floating interest rate swap.[10] Here, one contract partner of the swap agreement pays the other contract partner a *fixed* interest rate on an agreed-upon notional amount for a contractual period of time. In return, the other contract partner pays a variable, or *floating* interest rate based on the same notional and for the same period of time. The floating rate is an interest rate that resets periodically based on an interest rate index. A common floating rate is LIBOR. Sometimes a spread (in basis points) is added to or subtracted from the floating rate. There is no exchange of principal at the beginning or the end of the swap transaction. Figure 7.8 Illustrates the cash flows in an interest rate swap.

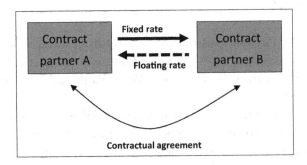

Fig. 7.8 Fixed-to-floating interest rate swap

An example for interest rate swaps is shown in Fig. 7.9. Without a swap market, corporates have to fund themselves in the market according to their funding needs. For example, XYZ corporation needs floating-rate funding and issues a corporate bond at LIBOR + 25 bp; ABC corporation needs fixed-rate funding and issues a corporate bond for the same maturity at 11.5%. If XYZ and ABC corporations have the ability to exchange cash flows between each other, they can fund themselves where they have comparative funding advantages, XYZ fixed and ABC floating, and then enter into an interest rate swap. As a result, both XYZ and ABC corporations improve their funding level.[11]

Typically, a broker-dealer steps in between the swap contract partners[12] and offers a tailor-made and timely swap execution. As a compensation for its liquidity service, the broker/dealer charges a bid/offer (2 bp in the example depicted in Fig. 7.10).

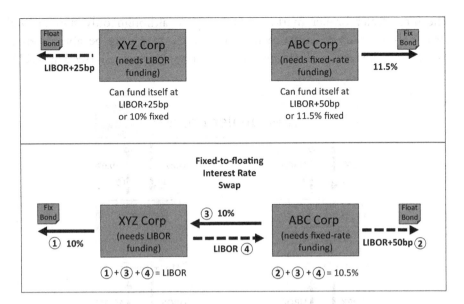

Fig. 7.9 Utilizing comparative funding advantages with an interest rate swap

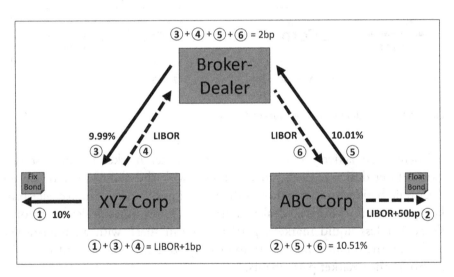

Fig. 7.10 Interest rate swap with broker-dealer as intermediary

Even more realistically, each corporate customer uses its own broker-dealer (house bank, etc.) for their swap transaction. Broker-dealers then turn to inter-dealer brokers, with whom broker-dealers offset their derivative exposure, often at mid-market prices (apart from a broker fee).

The inter-dealer broker market is very liquid, although only standardized structures are traded. Thus, each broker-dealer may only be able to enter into a proxy hedge[13] and will need to keep some residual risk (see Fig. 7.11).

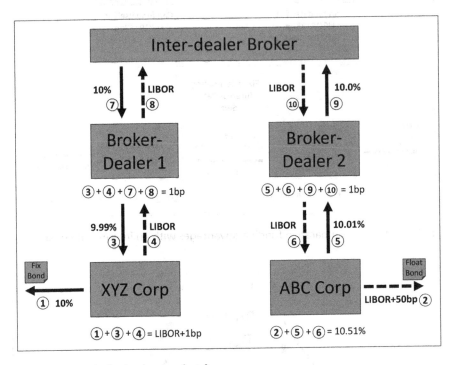

Fig. 7.11 Inter-dealer broker market for swaps

There is an actively traded inter-dealer broker market for interest rate swaps. Inter-dealer brokers provide dealers with the ability to trade on an electronic basis with each other in the most liquid[14] assets. Inter-dealer brokers provide anonymity, so dealers don't get to know other dealers' positions/flows. For less liquid markets, participants can speak with an inter-dealer broker on the phone who will try to identify "trading interest" and availability from other market participants.

7.6.2 Foreign Exchange Swap

A foreign exchange swap (also: FX swap or FOREX swap) differs from an interest rate swap because the principal amount is exchanged both at trade inception (t_0) and at maturity (t_1).

A typical foreign exchange swap begins with a start leg at t_0 that is indistinguishable from a spot transaction in which one currency is exchanged for another at the present spot rate (FX spot). The second leg is a forward transaction at the forward foreign exchange rate (FX fwd) at the time of trade inception. Thus, a foreign exchange swap is essentially the combination of a spot and forward foreign exchange transaction (see Fig. 7.12).

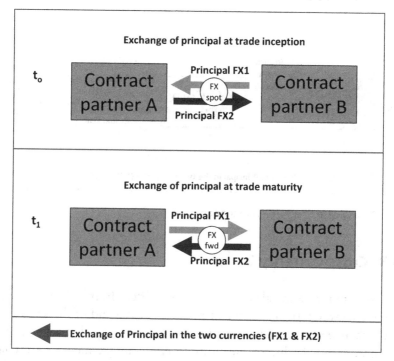

Fig. 7.12   Foreign exchange swap

Foreign exchange swaps are used by both foreign and domestic investors to hedge foreign exchange risk. An example for foreign exchange swaps is shown in Fig. 7.13. An EU-based corporation needs to make a JPY-deposit (which will be returned at a later point in time) with a Japanese trading partner. A foreign exchange swap turns the JPY cash flows into EUR cash flows. Thus, foreign exchange risk is eliminated, while the difference in the EUR-principal payments (due to the differences in exchange rates FX spot vs. FX forward) reflects the cost of making the deposit.

Foreign exchange swaps are also used for speculation in foreign currencies.

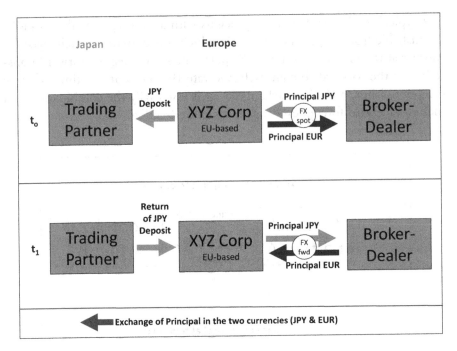

Fig. 7.13   Use case of a foreign exchange swap

7.6.3 Cross-Currency Swap

A cross-currency swap (also: XCCY swap) differs from a foreign exchange swap in two ways: The exchange of principal at the end of the swap is at the same exchange rate, at which the principal was exchanged at trade inception; also, throughout the life of the swap, interest rate payments are exchanged based on the two currencies. Interest rate payments could be set such that they are both fixed for the two currencies, both floating, or one fixed vs. one floating rate. Because the final exchange of principal is based on an exchange rate different from the prevailing forward FX rate at trade inception, cross-currency swaps tend to have significant counterparty risk[15] (see Fig. 7.14).

Cross-currency swaps are often used to monetize comparative advantages, in the capital market. An example for cross-currency swaps is shown in Fig. 7.15. Facebook Inc. is a US dollar-based company that needs funding in dollar for investment projects in the USA (server farms, research facilities in California, etc.). It turns out, however, that there are a lot of European investors looking to buy EUR-denominated Facebook debt (they like exposure to Facebook credit risk for credit risk diversification reasons, but don't

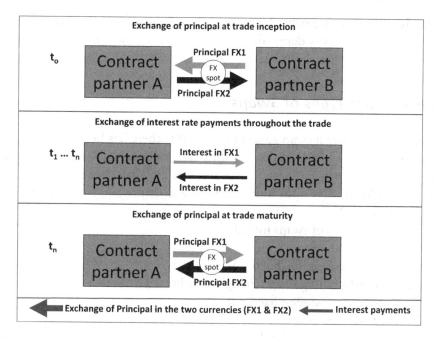

Fig. 7.14 Cross-currency swap

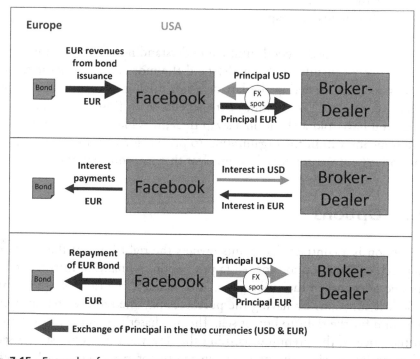

Fig. 7.15 Example of a cross-currency swap

like the exchange rate risk inherent in dollar-denominated Facebook bonds). Because of this excess demand, Facebook could finance itself in the EU at very competitive (i.e., low) interest rate levels.

7.6.4 Other Types of Swaps

Since the first formal swap agreement in 1981, there has been a tremendous amount of market innovation and financial engineering, leading to a wide array of swap variations. Some types of swaps may have been developed primarily to change the "optics" of a derivative structure and to create misleading economics.[16]

Additional types of swaps include:

- Basis swap (floating-for-floating);
- Amortizing/accruing swap (changing notional);
- Step-up swap (changing fixed rate);
- Forward-starting swap;
- Equity, commodity and index swap;
- Credit default swap;
- Total return swap;
- Callable/extendable swap.

Once you developed a good intuitive understanding of plain-vanilla swaps, it is not very difficult to also understand the more exotic structures. More important than mastering the last detail of pricing of a particular swap is being able to clearly communicate its benefits to an (institutional) end-user. Once you have sold a client on a swap trade, it is likely not very difficult to find someone within the organization to price it for you; in contrast, if you have priced a structure, it is far from clear that someone will trade on it.

7.7   Options

An option is a contract that grants owners the right but not the obligation to purchase (a call option) or sell (a put option) a financial instrument for a specific price, called the strike price, at or before[17] the time of option expiration. It functions by having the purchaser pay the seller/writer an option premium for the right to buy or sell. The purchaser's potential loss is limited to the price of the premium, curbing the downside. In contrast, the seller of an option receives the premium in return for risk exposure. An option position consisting of option purchases is also called a *long* position; the seller of an option is said to have a *short* position. Options are traded on organized exchanges and OTC derivatives markets.

7.7.1 Options Payout Profiles

The economic exposure of options at the time of option maturity can be graphically described through payout profiles. Because payout profiles of options resemble the shape of sticks used by hockey players, they are also commonly referred to as *hockey stick* diagrams, or *hockey sticks* for short.

There are two elements to the cash flows generated by options. First, because there is a value to having the right to defer a decision, the buyer of an option has to pay an option premium to the seller of the option. From the perspective of the option buyer, the option premium is a negative cash flow; from the option seller's viewpoint, it is a positive cash flow. Second, depending on whether the option is exercised at option expiration, an additional cash flow is been triggered. This cash flow, if it happens, will always take the direction from the option seller to the option buyer. The cash flow depends on the underlying price at option expiration in relation to the strike price set at the time of trade inception. Figure 7.16 illustrates the cash flows from the perspective of a call option buyer.

There are four distinct option positions that can be discussed in detail: A *long call* (purchase of a call option), a *short call* (sale of a call option), a *long put* (purchase of a put option) and a *short put* (sale of a put option) (see Table 7.1).

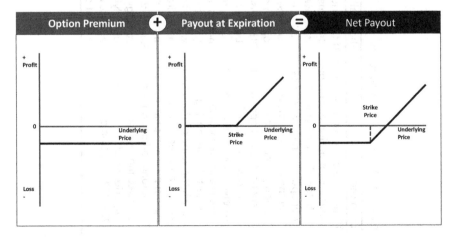

Fig. 7.16 Hockey stick diagram from the perspective of a call option buyer

Table 7.1 Types of option positions

Long call	Short call	Long put	Short put
If the price of the underlying at the time of option expiration is below the strike price, the call option expires worthless and the long loses the entire option premium paid	If the price of the underlying at the time of option expiration is below the strike price, the call option expires worthless and the short keeps the entire option premium received	If the price of the underlying at the time of option expiration is above the strike price, the put option expires worthless and the long loses the entire option premium paid	If the price of the under-lying at the time of option expiration is above the strike price, the put option expires worthless and the short keeps the entire option premium paid
Otherwise, the call option will be exercised and the long receives money upon exercise	Otherwise, the call option will be exercised and the short has to pay money upon exercise	Otherwise, the put option will be exercised and the long receives money upon exercise	Otherwise, the put option will be exercised and the short has to pay money upon exercise
There is a break-even price (BEP) of the underlying, at which the value of the option at expiration equals the option premium paid initially	There is a break-even price (BEP) of the underlying, at which the value of the option at expiration equals the option premium paid initially	There is a break-even price (BEP) of the underlying, at which the value of the option at expiration equals the option premium paid initially	There is a break-even price (BEP) of the underlying, at which the value of the option at expiration equals the option premium paid initially
For the long call option strategy to make money, the underlying price needs to be above the BEP at option expiration	For the short call option strategy to make money, the underlying price needs to be below the BEP at option expiration	For the long put option strategy to make money, the underlying price needs to be below the BEP at option expiration	For the short put option strategy to make money, the underlying price needs to be above the BEP at option expiration

Combining the cash flows from the option purchase and the option cash flows at the time of option expiration in one single cash flow diagram, hockey sticks can be drawn for all four distinct option positions (see Fig. 7.17).

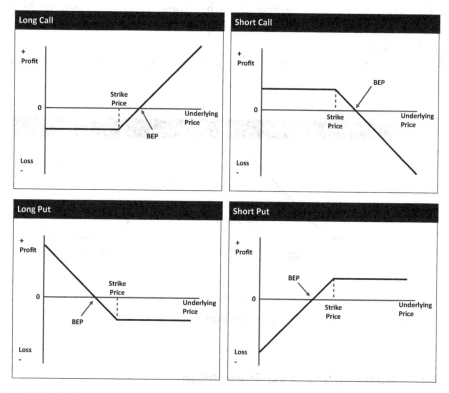

Fig. 7.17 Hockey stick diagrams for long and short positions in calls and puts

7.7.2 In-the-Moneyness

The strike price of an option in relation to the current underlying price determines whether an option is said to be *in-the-money* (ITM), *at-the-money* (ATM) or *out-of-the-money* (OTM).

For call options, if the strike price is less than the current market price of the underlying, the call option is said to be *in-the-money* because the holder of the call has the right to buy the underlying at a price which is less than the price he would have to pay to buy the underlying in the market. The converse of in-the-money is *out-of-the-money*. If the strike price equals the current market price, the call option is said to be *at-the-money*.

For put options, if the strike price is greater than the current market price of the underlying, the put option is said to be *in-the-money* because the holder of the put has the right to sell the underlying at a price which is greater than the price he would receive from selling the underlying in the market. Again, the converse of in-the-money is *out-of-the-money*. If the strike price equals the current market price, the put option is said to be *at-the-money*.

Figure 7.18 illustrates the in-the-moneyness for a call and for a put option.

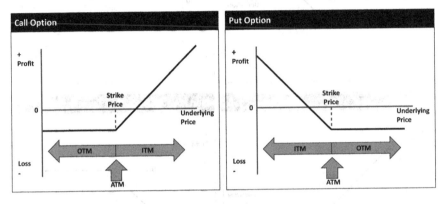

Fig. 7.18   In-the-moneyness for calls and puts

7.7.3 Intrinsic Value vs. Time Value

The amount by which an option, call or put, is in-the-money prior to expiration is called its *intrinsic value*. The intrinsic value equals the value of the option if it were to be executed immediately. Time value is the value from being able to defer option exercise to the exercise date.

By definition, an at-the-money or out-of-the-money option has no intrinsic value; the time value is the total option premium. Nobody would execute an OTM or ATM option, but the option is still valuable because the underlying price is volatile and could, between now and option expiration, move such that the option is ITM on the expiration date.

If the value is known for an ITM option (because the option is quoted in the market), the time value can be calculated by subtracting the intrinsic value from the option value. When the value of an OTM or ATM option is known, this equals the time value of the option.

Figure 7.19 illustrates the relationship between intrinsic value, time value and total value for a call and for a put option.

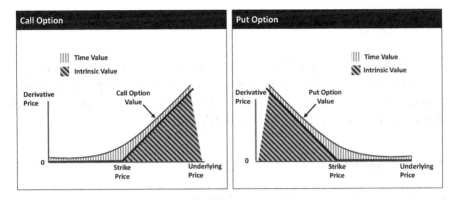

Fig. 7.19 In-the-moneyness for calls and puts

7.7.4 Options Greeks

The so-called *Greeks* measure the various sensitivities of an option's change in price with respect to a small movement in some underlying variable. Each sensitivity is assigned a Greek letter. Every option has a different risk profile with respect to the various risk sensitivities. Knowing these risks allows one to pick the most appropriate (hedging or speculative) position and to manage the risks throughout the life of the trade.

Sensitivities are calculated only for small incremental changes. The four most relevant sensitivities are Delta (δ), Gamma (γ), Theta (θ) and Vega[18] (ν) (see Table 7.2).

Table 7.2 Option Greeks

Greek letter	Name of sensitivity	Explanation
δ	Delta	Price change for an option, relative to the price change in the underlying asset
γ	Gamma	Change in delta, relative to the price change of the asset
θ	Theta	Change in the option price relative to a one-day change in expiration. Also called time decay
ν	Vega	Change in the option price relative to a 1% change in volatility

There are more than four sensitivities calculated for options. However, for an intuitive understanding of options it is usually sufficient to know the main Greeks.

7.7.4.1 Delta

Delta (δ) is the change of the option price with respect to the underlying. It can be viewed as the "hedge ratio" between underlying and derivative, defined as the change in the price of the derivative, ΔP_D, divided by the change in the price of the underlying, ΔP_U.

7.7.4.2 Gamma

Gamma (γ) is the change in delta, relative to the price change of the underlying. It can be viewed as the change of the "hedge ratio" between underlying and derivative, defined as $\delta_2 - \delta_1 = (\Delta P_{D,2}/\Delta P_{U,2}) - (\Delta P_{D,1}/\Delta P_{U,1})$.

7.7.4.3 Theta

Theta (θ) is the change in the option price relative to a one-day change in expiration, also called *time decay*. Generally, the longer the time remaining until an option's expiration, the higher its premium will be. This is because the longer an option's lifetime, the greater the possibility that the underlying share price might move so as to make the option in-the-money. All other factors affecting an option's price remaining the same, the time value portion of an option's premium will typically decay (i.e., decrease) with the passage of time.

7.7.4.4 Vega

Vega (v) is the change in the option price relative to a 1% change in the volatility. The higher the expected (implied) volatility of the underlying, the higher the probability that the option moves (further) into the money, i.e., increasing its intrinsic value. It can be calculated as $P_{D,2} - P_{D,1}$, whereas $P_{D,2}$ is calculated with an implied volatility of one percentage point above that of $P_{D,1}$ (all else being equal).

See Fig. 7.20.

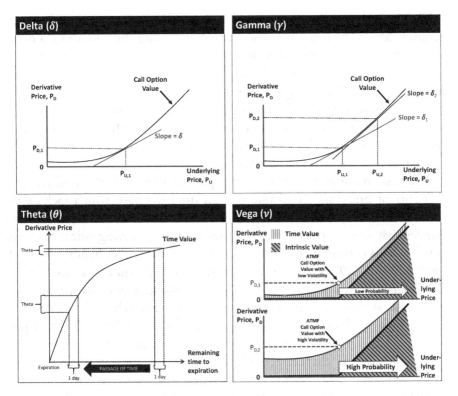

Fig. 7.20 Delta, gamma, theta and vega of a call option

7.7.5 Intuition of Derivative Pricing

Bookshelves in libraries are filled with books about derivative pricing. But that's not necessarily a good thing. Because many people have been scared away from even trying to learn the basics about derivative pricing in general, and options pricing in particular. There is the assumption that advanced skills in math and stochastics would be necessary to develop a general knowledge about it. The truth is that even if you only have a purely intuitive understanding about this topic, you can use it quite frequently in almost any sales, trading or research function. In fact, the derivative pricing experts who speak at derivative conferences are typically not the ones that are put in front of clients. Those who are good at communicating the intuition are the ones talking to clients. My advice would be to get the intuition right and have someone else worry about the detailed math.

The first thing, when it comes to derivative pricing, is to develop a good intuition about the price dynamics of the underlying. By definition, a derivative is based on the price of an underlying; thus, derivative pricing without a thorough understanding of the underlying is impossible. While sounding obvious, this is often enough ignored. For example, the US subprime mortgage crisis that triggered the financial crisis of 2007–2008 was caused primarily by a genuine misunderstanding about the underlying, i.e., subprime mortgages, and less so because of some errors in pricing derivatives (such as residential mortgage backed securities).

The basic premise for modeling the price dynamics of the underlying is that current prices reflect all information from the past, which include the information about how historical prices evolved to the prevailing price. This implies that *future* prices cannot be predicted by analyzing prices from the *past*.[19] This is consistent with the so-called efficient-market hypothesis developed by Fama (1970) . It also reflects what in stochastics is referred to as a Markov property. The price path of the underlying is modeled to be a random walk, starting with the current market price and where the past is irrelevant. Such random walk can be illustrated by imagining a drunk person leaving a bar. The person is so drunk that he/she needs to hold on to the next light post, but then forgets where he/she came from before moving on to the next light post. Because the drunk person has no recollection where he/she came from, the past path is irrelevant. Moving forward, there is also the chance that the drunk person moves back to the previous light post (see Fig. 7.21).

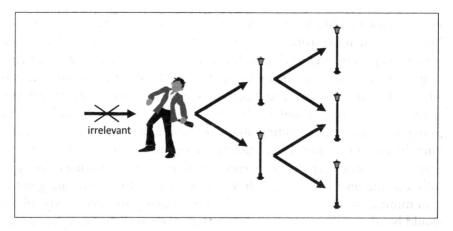

Fig. 7.21   Drunk person representing a random walk

Applying the drunk person-analogy to the modeling of stock prices (as one possible underlying instrument for derivatives), we could construct a random walk with the following features: The past is irrelevant (also referred to a *memory loss*), the expected change in value is zero, and the best predictor of a future value is the current value.[20] Over time, there is increasing potential for the stock price to have moved further away from the starting point, which is reflected in a higher variance[21] (see Fig. 7.22).

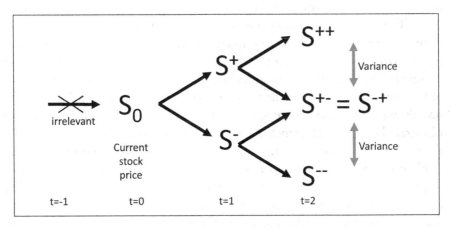

Fig. 7.22   A random walk model for stock prices

Each particular increment of a random walk has variance that is proportional to the time over which the price was moving. This is a very convenient relationship. You will hardly ever find anyone refer to the term *variance* in sales, trading and research. Instead, market participants talk about *volatility*. Volatility is used synonymously for *standard deviation*. Standard deviation, abbreviated by the Greek letter Sigma (σ), is the square root of variance (Var). Thus, $\sigma = \sqrt{Var}$. Because variance is proportional to time, volatility is proportional to the square root of time. To illustrate the relationship between time and volatility, let's look at a specific example. Someone tells you that the *implied annual volatility* of a stock is 40%. *Implied* means that this is not some market participant's estimation or the outcome of some model, but "extracted" from market prices (such as option prices), so that it reflects *market expectations*. *Annual* means that the 40% deviation from current prices relates to a one-year period. A 40% annual volatility means that with a given probability[22] the stock price will not change more than 40% up or down from the current price over a one-year period. Given a 40% annual volatility, how much would be the expected volatility over a three-month period? In other words, with the same probably with which price changes do not exceed 40% over 12 months, what would be the equivalent-probability percentage change over three months? If volatility was proportional to time (like variance is), the answer would be one-quarter of 40%, or 10% (because three months are a quarter of one year). But this is not the case. Volatility is *not* proportional to time, but proportional to the square root of time. This means that the three-month, or quarterly, volatility $\sigma_{quarterly}$ is the square root of ¼ (3 months divided by 12 months) time the annual volatility σ_{annual}. Since the square root of ¼ is ½, the quarterly volatility would be 20%. This is somewhat surprising at first sight. How can it be that over a 3-month period the stock moves up and down 20% with a certain probability, but over a whole year only 40%? The answer can be derived from what we saw in Fig. 7.22: In the second, third and fourth quarter of the year, some of the movements from the first quarter will likely be reversed due to stocks not always moving in the same direction all the time. Like a drunk person (illustrated in Fig. 7.21), stock prices move back and forth, undoing some of their initial price moves by subsequent moves in the opposite direction.

Now that we have developed a basic understanding about the evolution of prices of the underlying, the next step is to derive a price for the derivative. Using a call option as a concrete example, we can develop a framework that for each possible price outcome of the underlying calculates the corresponding price of the call option. Obviously, in a "state" of the world when the underlying price goes up, the value of the call option increases, and vice versa. The current value of the call option then would be approximately[23] the sum of the probability-weighted call option values at option expiration.

7.7.6 Binomial Options Pricing

Binomial pricing models are one type of valuation methods that are based on drawing a binomial tree representing the price path of the underlying, calculating the implied value of the derivative at each modeled state of the world, called node, and then aggregating those values with considering their probabilities of occurrence.

First, we are going to use a binomial model to price an at-the-money (ATM) call option (i.e., a call option where the strike price is set to be equal to the current price of the underlying) in an environment *without* volatility. This is a somewhat unrealistic first assumption, because pretty much all financial assets are subject to potential price changes, but it will be useful to show how option values critically depend on the presence of uncertainty. An example for an underlying that has close to no price volatility would be the US federal funds target rate set by the US central bank, or more precise the Federal Open Market Committee (FOMC) of the US Federal Reserve, during the period between scheduled FOMC meetings. Typically, the target rate is only changed on one of the eight scheduled FOMC meetings, so during the period between one FOMC meeting and the next scheduled one, the target rate remains constant.[24] The binomial pricing of a 1-year call option with a strike price of 100 for a stock trading at a price of 100, where there is zero volatility ($\sigma = 0\%$), is presented in Fig. 7.23. Because there is no volatility, the stock price is expected to remain at 100. The option payoff at expiration of a 100-strike call is zero when the underlying trades at 100. Since the assumed probability (p) of the stock ending at 100 is 100%, the expected option payoff is 100% times zero, or zero.

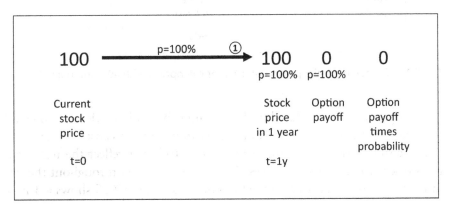

Fig. 7.23 Binomial pricing of a 1-year 100-strike call option without volatility

The binomial model with only one single tree-node illustrates the maybe most important fact about options in general: Without uncertainty, there is no time value to options.[25] As a next step, we are extending the binomial model to allow for some uncertainty in underlying price. Let's assume an annual volatility of 40% (as in Sect. 7.7.5). The one-node model now becomes a two-node model, because the price of the stock does not remain at 100, but can go up or down. For some technical reasons,[26] we assume prices to go up and down by $e^{0.4}$ and $e^{-0.4}$, respectively, with e being the mathematical constant (Euler's number) used to create exponential functions. The probabilities for the up- and down-move (p_u and p_d) are then calculated such that the probability-weighted underlying prices for the up and the down move equal the current underlying price. Figure 7.24 presents the calculation for our call option. A first estimation of the option value is 19.6, resulting from a 40% probability of the call option being worth 49, and a 60% chance of the option expiring worthless.[27]

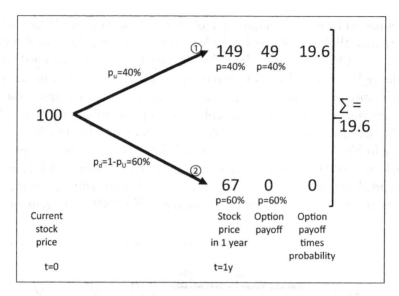

Fig. 7.24 2-node binomial pricing of a 1-year call option with 40% annual volatility

The option price calculated in the two-node binominal pricing framework may be a useful first estimate but suffers from one unrealistic assumption: that the stock price only jumps once a year. To better reflect the realities of the stock market, in which prices changes continuously throughout the day, more nodes are introduced to the binomial tree. Figure 7.25 shows a 3-node

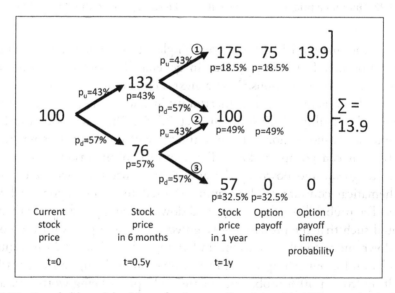

Fig. 7.25 3-node binomial pricing of a 1-year call option with 40% annual volatility

binomial pricing of the same call option, where two stock price moves are possible: one after 6 months and another just prior to option expiration. Constructing the three-node tree requires calculating the underlying price in 6-month intervals; semi-annual volatility $\sigma_{s.a.}$ is calculated according to the square root formula.[28] Price movements up and down, as well as up- and down-probabilities, are calculated as before. The intrinsic option payoffs are calculated for all three nodes, and the sum of all probability-weighted intrinsic option payoff equals the new model option value. Note that the calculated option value in the 3-node binomial model (13.9) differs from the one calculated in the 2-node model (19.6).

The price of an option calculated by the binomial pricing method is significantly impacted by the number of tree nodes used. Figure 7.26 illustrates how with an increasing number of nodes the model prices converges to a value that can be assumed to be a realistic estimate.

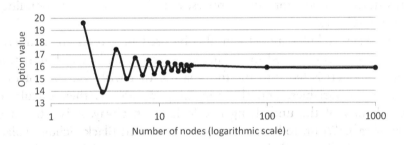

Fig. 7.26   Convergence of call option prices when increasing the number of nodes

7.7.7   Black–Scholes Options Pricing

The Black–Scholes, or Black–Scholes–Merton, option pricing model is a partial differential equation commonly used since the 1970s to estimate the value of European options. The binomial pricing model discussed in the previous section is linked to the Black–Scholes model as far as binomial pricing approached the Black–Scholes price if, under certain technical assumptions, the number of nodes goes to infinity.

The model is derived from the idea of continuous delta hedging and maintaining a risk-free position at all times. The CAPM suggests that such a risk-free position should earn (only) the risk-free rate of interest. Thus, option pricing no longer depends on risk premia. The model is based on a number of assumptions, such as:

- Returns of the underlying are lognormally distributed;
- Continuous trading without transaction costs is possible;
- Flat yield curve (i.e., one interest rate for all maturities).

The beauty about the Black–Scholes model is that it is a closed-form solution that can be calculated with relatively little computational power.[29] Also, there are only five inputs to the calculation, which are:

- The current price of the underlying;
- The strike price of the option;
- The time to option expiration;
- The volatility of the underlying;
- The risk-free rate of interest.

The Black–Scholes option pricing model does not only provide a closed-form solution for option prices, but also for the corresponding risk measures (Greeks).

The Black–Scholes model can also be used in a reversed manner: The option price (as observed in the market or calculated by a different, more realistic model) is fed into the formula together with four out of the five usual input variables, and the remaining variable is then calculated. If the volatility of the underlying is calculated that way, it is referred to as *implied volatility* or, to be more precise, as implied Black–Scholes volatility. Traders typically use their own proprietary option pricing models to calculate the fair value of options. Instead of quoting the price of the option, they then often quote the *implied volatility* that, if entered into a Black–Scholes pricing engine, returns the desired option price. Quoting options in Black–Scholes volatility does not imply that the trader believes that a Black–Scholes model is an appropriate pricing tool, nor that it was used for pricing. Black–Scholes volatility is merely a convenient way to quote options.

While academic literature tends to focus on the Black–Scholes model, a variation of the model, called Black or Black-76 model, is actually much more widely used. In it, the underlying is not the spot price (e.g., the current stock price), but a discounted future price. Here, the forward price is assumed to be log-normally distributed. This model is more suited to price options on futures, bonds, caps, floors and swaps.

You can work an entire career in derivatives without anyone ever asking you to write down the Black–Scholes formula.[30] That's why the formula is not listed here. What is far more important than memorizing the formula is knowing their shortcomings and ways people try to calibrate the simple model to the complexities of the real market. Some of them are listed in the sections below.

7.7.8 Beyond Black–Scholes

The Black–Scholes option pricing formula was merely the starting point for the development of many other, improved option pricing frameworks. Apart from the Black model of 1976 and the binomial pricing model, developed by Cox, Ross and Rubinstein in 1979,[31] which were already mentioned in the previous sections, there is one additional model from the 1970s worth knowing about: The Cox and Ross model developed in 1976, which extended option pricing to allow for a *discontinuous price movement* in the underlying by assuming a jump-diffusion process.[32]

Following the stock market crash of 1987, commonly referred to as Black Monday, the assumption of *constant volatility* came under intense scrutiny. It was widely acknowledged that volatility assumptions suitable for pricing ATM options did not yield meaningful results when applied to OTM or ITM options. The early models from the 1970s and 1980s were simply fed with adjusted volatility inputs to compensate for their shortcomings. When displaying various volatility inputs for different strike levels, the graph looks like a skew or a smile. It turns out that the empirical observation of a volatility skew or smile can be captured by a model through making volatility itself a random process (i.e., assuming volatility of volatility, sometimes called vVol), and various stochastic volatility models have been developed in the 1990s. Two of those should be mentioned here: The first one is the Heston model of 1993. The Heston model can be calibrated against historical prices of the underlying. The second is the so-called SABR model, which stands for Stochastic Alpha, Beta, Rho, developed by Hagan, Kumar, Lesniewski and Woodward, in 2002. This model can be calibrated against observable option prices. The SABR model is very popular among option traders because it allows for a very realistic capturing of real-life effects. For example, the model allows to fine-tune the distribution assumption for the underlying anywhere from normal to lognormal, accounts for volatility of volatility and specifies the *skewness* and *smileness*. However, calibration of the SABR model is not trivial and often trading desks run dedicated programs at the end of a trading day that re-calibrate the SABR parameters.

While few people need a detailed understanding about all details of the most advanced option pricing models, I always found it very useful to have at least enough knowledge about derivative pricing to have a conversation with the option traders on a regular basis. Often, the trading desk's insight about issues when calibrating the bank-used model provides valuable input for client conversations, research topics or trade idea generation. For example, I used to feed observable option prices (for ATM and OTM options) into a mixture of distribution model (such as SABR that allows for various degrees in the mix between normal and lognormal) to extract the market-implied view about the degree of normality of the returns of the underlying. Specifically, I was looking at the implied normality of interest rates. For a while, interest rate options were priced with the implied assumptions of interest rates being lognormally distributed. When interest rates pushed lower and there was a real possibility of them turning negative, the implied distribution assumption became increasingly normal. At some point, even the standard normal distribution would not be able to explain the high premia charged in the market for low-strike options. The model had to be calibrated such that more than 100% of normality had to be assumed and then some lognormality subtracted. This is referred to as super-normality. If you catch such a moment as the first person, you got yourself a very good talking point that sets you apart from other market participants.

7.7.9 Options Hedging

Many textbooks grossly simplify the decision-making process when it comes to option hedging in an institutional context. One may find problem descriptions like this:

> Investment Fund XYZ includes 10,000 stocks of corporation ABC, currently trading at €120. The fund manager wants to protect the fund against a drop of the price of the ABC stock below €100 within one year. If the 1-year €100-strike Put cost €500 and each Put option has 100 ABC shares as the underlying, how many Put options would the portfolio manager have to purchase and what would be the cost of the hedge?

In my entire career, I have never been confronted with a situation like this. In fact, even if problems like this were to exist, the institutional investor would likely not even call a global market professional in a sales, trading or research department, but rather execute the hedge without help. Textbook examples are typically constructed for didactical reasons, not to fit with reality. A more realistic option hedging question one could face is this:

Investment Fund ABC consists of a diversified portfolio of stocks and bonds. The fund manager wants to protect the fund against possible adverse effects from a member of the European Union leaving the EU within the next 5 years. Which option strategy would you suggest when the fund manager is willing to pay an annual option premium of 10 bp?

Approaching any hedge problem typically starts with identifying the universe of hedge instruments your institutional client is able to and willing to consider. Not all investors are allowed to trade derivatives. Of those who do, not all are allowed to trade options. At this stage already, *derivative marketing* becomes critical. A bond investor may find swaps suspicious. Telling the investor to hedge bonds with swaps may not work. Once we marketed tailor-made swaps as "synthetic bonds." Replacing a bond (that traded rich) by a synthetic bond appeared much more familiar to the investor.

When the hedge instrument gets selected, there are many factors being considered. If the textbook tells you that the portfolio manager wants to hedge a position in *ABC* stocks and there are put options on *ABC* stocks and on *DEF* stocks trading in the market, the solution would likely be to use the *ABC* stock put options. In the real world, this may not be the case. Maybe the hedge takes place during trading hours where the market for ABC stock options is closed, while the one for DEF stock options is open. Maybe ABC stock options are illiquid and cannot be traded in the size needed. Maybe transaction costs (fees, commissions, etc.) on ABC stock options are significantly higher than that of DEF stock options.

Once potential hedge instruments are identified, the questions of the proper *hedge ratio* becomes relevant. Even before the question is addressed how much the option price moves when the underlying changes (i.e., the Delta of the option), one has to estimate how much the underlying of the option will move when the to-be-hedged security moves. Again, in the textbook this is not an issue because ABC stocks are hedged with options on ABC stocks. If, however, a 9-year bond is hedged by options on the 10-year swap rate (because swaptions are more liquid than bond options, and because swaptions on 10-year rates are more liquid than swaptions on 9-year rates), one need to calculate (or estimate) the beta between 9-year bond yields and 10-year swap rates. Using a simple DV01-ratio will not suffice because it assumes that for every basis point move in the 9-year bond yield, 10-year swap yield move by exactly one basis point in the same direction.[33] A commonly used hedging strategy is *regression-based hedging*. Here, an empirical analysis is conducted by constructing a regression model between the to-be-hedged and the hedge instrument. This often turns out to be as much art as science because depending on the length of the historical data series, its frequency and whether absolute levels or changes are used, results may vary considerably. Sometimes information from the option market are incorporated in the analysis to create a so-called *volatility-weighted hedge*. There are many approaches[34] and there is no right-or-wrong. It helps to know which hedging strategies your client prefers. If you suggest something too simple, you come across as ignorant; if you suggest something too complicated, your client may view the hedge as too complex. Also, some of the more sophisticated clients (especially hedge funds) may expect from you that you calculate hedge ratios according to different models and using different calibrations. They will typically only transact if the various hedge ratios are somewhat similar. If not, the trade is in fact less of a hedge and more so a *model trade* because the performance of the "hedge" depends on whether one had picked the "right" model to describe the price relationships. Most market participants try to stay away from "model trades."

Once a potential option is identified as a hedge instrument and the proper hedge ratio has been established, client-specific preferences need to be taken into consideration. Some investors are not prepared to pay a net premium. Some others will only consider long gamma positions. Yet others look for positive carry. Each customer is different, so there is hardly a one-fit-all solution.

Last but not least, the question of adjusting the hedge over time needs to be addressed. Some hedges are *static hedges*. A static hedge is a trade in which the hedge ratio between the to-be-hedged security and the hedge product does not change. Thus, no adjustments are necessary throughout the hedge period. For example, if the interest-rate exposure of a fixed-rate bond should be eliminated, a so-called *true* asset swap could be established by overlaying the bond with a swap that has matching cash-flow dates and coupon rates. As the bond and the swap approach maturity, cash flows should remain matched and there is typically no need for adjustments.[35] However, the majority of derivative hedges are so-called *dynamic hedges*. A dynamic hedge is a trade in which the hedge ratio between the to-be-hedged security and the hedge product changes over time, creating the need for occasional re-balancing of the trade. This shall be illustrated in more detail.

Many market participants have to offset negative convexity in their trading portfolio or business model through the purchase of volatility products (i.e., options). Those investors include participants in the US mortgage market, such as mortgage hedge funds, mortgage servicers and GSE's like Fannie Mae or Freddie Mac (because of their mortgage portfolio). Some investors, such as certain foreign central banks or some commercial banks, choose not to hedge out the negative convexity. However, those that do hedge have to concern themselves with the intertemporal optimization of their dynamic hedging activity.

Typically, negative convexity in a portfolio is mitigated by an overlay consisting of positively convex instruments such as swaption straddles and strangles. While it is comparably simple to offset the risk of a short option position through a long position in a similar option, replicating the optionality inherent in a *mortgage* product with swaptions is far from trivial. This is because mortgages are *path-dependent*, while standard swaption products are not. If interest rates decrease, say 100 bp, and then return to initial levels, the value of a swaption will not have changed significantly (ignoring time-decay and a possible change in implied volatility). Mortgage products, however, will likely have suffered because of the pre-payment associated with the decrease in rate.

When the goal is to compensate for the adverse effects of path-dependency in mortgage product, a buy-and-hold strategy of standard options (swaptions, treasury bond options, futures options, etc.) will not do. Instead, investors must frequently *monetize* the hedge overlay. This is done by taking profit after a significant move in rates has occurred and establishing a new hedge at then-prevailing market conditions. Instead of thinking of two transactions, the unwind of an existing option position and the purchase of a new option, one can view this as one adjustment in strike and option maturity. This is what is typically referred to as *rolling strikes*.

Rolling strikes requires an active management of the option hedge. Investors have to make a conscious decision as to when and how often strikes are to be rolled. While rolling strikes at a high frequency ensures that in-the-moneyness is monetized (and does not get lost if interest rates revert to previous levels), this results in higher transaction costs. Not surprisingly, the optimum hedge frequency is higher when no transaction costs are assumed.[36] In the real world, however, transaction costs make a significant difference and less frequent strike rolls produce lower overall costs.

Instead of adjusting the swaption hedge in fixed intervals, investors may wait until after a significant market move before rolling strikes. The argument to be made is that there is little point in rolling a strike when interest rates have hardly changed. However, notice that even if interest rates are unchanged, swaptions are aging and need to be rolled into longer-maturity swaptions at some point. If trigger levels for changes in 10-year swap rates are increased from, say, 25 bp to 30 bp, 35 bp, 40 bp and 45 bp, the frequency of hedging decreases. Requiring larger interest rate moves before strikes are rolled helps reduce transaction costs, but also decreases the amount of intrinsic option value that is monetized. In the extreme, trigger levels are set so wide that swaptions are not re-balanced at all and are held until maturity.

7.7.10 Volatility and Distribution Assumptions

One very common mistake of people starting out their career in Global Markets is to assume that there is *one* single volatility for a product or a product class. What is the volatility for US interest rates? There is no answer to this question. First, volatility of which kind of model are you talking about? Black–Scholes volatility, Black volatility, or from any other pricing model? Then, different instruments are quoted as different volatilities. Swaptions, caps/floors, bond options, stock options all have different volatility levels. Finally, ATM options are priced at a different vol than ITM or OTM options.

Because different market participants use different pricing models, options are quoted as implied volatilities using agreed-upon reference models. In the broker markets, swaptions and cap/floors are quoted in "log vol," corresponding to the Black model. That does not imply that the Black model is the best model to use, only that if those vols are plugged into a Black model, then the resulting prices are the current market prices. Also, basis-point (so-called normalized volatility) quotes are given. Volatility skews are quoted as an indication for how much log vols need to be adjusted for non-ATM options (due to the limitations of the Black model). Table 7.3 shows an overview inter-dealer broker page for interest rate option that directs to further pages on which the actual quotes are being displayed. Not only are there multiple types of volatilities to choose from, but also are some generic structures quoted on a price (i.e., premium) basis.

Table 7.4 shows the format of one of the most important broker screens for derivative pricing in fixed income, the ICAP VCAP1 screen. It displays implied Black volatility (i.e., volatility when using the Black model) for ATM swaption straddles with EONIA discounting. This is already very specific, as those implied volatility levels would have little meaning for, say, caps, bond options, OTM interest rate options, let alone stock or commodity options. On top of that, there is a specific volatility quote for various maturities (i.e., time to swaption expiration) and tenors (i.e., duration of the swap underlying the swaption).

Table 7.3 Example of interest rate option quotes in the inter-dealer broker market[a]

```
                        ICAP EUR Interest Rate Options

                - - - - - Swaptions - - - - -
Swaption Log Vol EONIA discounted                                    <VCAP1>
Shifted Swaption Log Vol EONIA discounted                           <VCAP1A>
Shifted Swaption Log Vol shifted values                             <VCAP1B>
Swaption BP Vol EONIA discounted Calendar Days                       <VCAP6>
Swaption BP Vol EONIA discounted Business Days                      <VCAP6BD>
Swaption BP Vol EONIA discounted Physically settled Calendar Days    <VCAP6P>
Swaption BP Vol EONIA discounted Physically settled Business Days   <VCAP6PBD>
Swaption Spot Premium EONIA discounted Cash settled                  <VCAP2>
Swaption Forward Premium EONIA discounted Cash settled              <VCAP2A>
Swaption Spot Premium EURIBOR discounted Cash settled              <VCAP2B>
Swaption Forward Premium EONIA discounted Physically settled        <VCAP2P>
Swaption Forward Premium Physical/Cash settled spread              <VCAP2PC>
Swaption Forwards (1y - 10y tails)                                   <VCAP8>
Swaption Forwards (15y + tails)                                      <VCAP9>
Swaption Skews (Cash Settled)                                      <ICAPSKEW>


    - - - - - Caps & Floors (all EONIA discounted unless specified) - - - - -
Cap/Floor Log Vols                                                   <VCAP3>
Shifted Cap/Floor Log Vols                                          <VCAP3A>
Cap/Floor Normal Vols                                               <VCAP10>
Cap Spot Premium                                                     <VCAP4>
Cap Spot Premium (EURIBOR discounted)                              <VCAP4A>
Floor Spot Premium                                                  <VCAP5>
Floor Spot Premium (EURIBOR discounted)                            <VCAP5A>
Fwd Start C/F & Wedges composite                                    <VCAP7>
```

[a]Stylized reproduction of a typical display of the inter-dealer broker ICAP

Table 7.4 Swaption Log Vol in the broker market[a]

VCAP1

EUR ATM Swaption Straddles – Black Volatilities (Eonia disc)

	1Y	2Y	3Y	4Y	5Y	6Y	7Y	8Y	9Y	10Y	15Y	20Y	25Y	30Y
1M Opt				136	85.2	62.3	50.6	43.4	38.3	34.6	24.6	21.6	20.6	19.9
2M Opt				145	90.0	66.0	53.5	45.7	40.5	36.5	26.4	23.3	22.6	21.7
3M Opt				145	90.8	68.5	55.6	47.7	41.9	38.0	27.6	24.6	23.7	23.0
6M Opt			287	126	85.9	67.6	56.7	49.2	43.8	39.7	29.3	26.0	25.1	24.5
9M Opt			268	112	81.7	65.2	55.4	49.2	44.3	40.5	30.6	27.4	26.4	26.1
1Y Opt			142	98.9	77.6	63.6	54.7	48.6	44.0	40.5	31.2	28.2	27.3	26.9
18M Opt		161	104	82.1	69.1	59.2	52.2	47.1	43.1	40.0	31.9	29.3	28.6	28.5
2Y Opt		113	88.1	72.4	62.6	55.2	49.4	45.2	42.0	39.5	32.2	30.0	29.4	29.3
3Y Opt	118	80.8	68.6	60.1	54.0	49.0	45.3	42.4	40.1	38.2	32.4	30.8	30.5	30.5
4Y Opt	86.1	64.6	57.5	52.2	47.7	44.5	42.0	40.0	38.4	36.9	32.2	31.1	30.9	31.0
5Y Opt	66.7	54.4	49.5	46.1	43.2	41.0	39.3	37.8	36.6	35.6	31.7	30.8	30.7	30.8
7Y Opt	48.4	42.6	40.1	38.3	37.0	35.9	35.0	34.4	33.9	33.4	30.8	30.3	30.4	30.5
10Y Opt	37.0	35.1	34.2	33.4	33.0	32.7	32.5	32.3	32.2	32.3	30.9	30.5	30.4	30.5
15Y Opt	31.8	31.5	31.6	31.7	32.0	32.2	32.5	32.6	32.9	33.4	31.6	30.9	30.4	30.2
20Y Opt	33.8	34.1	34.6	34.8	35.2	35.5	35.4	35.5	35.6	35.6	33.3	31.4	30.4	29.6
25Y Opt	37.9	37.4	37.8	37.5	37.5	37.3	37.0	36.5	36.5	36.3	33.6	31.1	29.8	28.6
30Y Opt	38.5	38.7	38.1	38.4	38.1	37.7	37.1	36.2	35.8	35.7	33.2	30.3	28.6	27.4

[a]Stylized reproduction of a typical display of the inter-dealer broker ICAP

Once you have found an appropriate vol level for a generic ATM option structure, you likely have to adjust for the fact that the structure you are setting out to price is not exactly ATM. This requires an adjustment depending on your distribution assumptions. If you are using a normal model and assume the returns of the underlying to be strictly normally distributed, then no adjustment is required. However, the real world is seldom as simple as that. When looking at historical distributions of changes in the underlying asset, one typically finds that there is not one single distribution assumption that fits all time periods and market regimes. At times, changes appear to be close to normally or lognormally distributed, giving the illusion that a corresponding pricing model would do a good job in capturing the pricing dynamics. However, at other times the observed market outcome lies far beyond what a classical pricing model would assign any meaningful probability to. This is also referred to as *fat tails*.

Take a look at Fig. 7.27. It shows the results of a strikingly simple study I conducted in the Fall of 2008, right after the financial crisis of 2007–2008 hit. All I did was to count and to plot the frequency with which changes in the US dollar 2-year swap rate occurred for different levels of magnitude, both for the period January–December 2007 and January–September 2008. This is not a particularly sophisticated analysis, but a simple visual inspection of the graphs suggests that the assumption of normally distributed changes in interest rates seemed okay for during first period, while during the financial crisis the market behaved quite differently. Anyone who had used a normal (or lognormal) model to describe the price dynamics of 2-year swap rates (and many did!) would have greatly underestimated the probability of occurrences of large interest rate changes. Put differently, the actual distribution of interest rates had, compared to a normal or lognormal distribution, fat tails during the crisis.

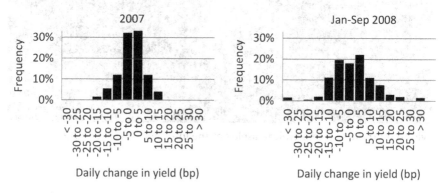

Fig. 7.27 Observed frequency distribution of daily changes in the 2-year swap rate

7.7.11 Correlation and Correlation Assumptions

Correlations play an important role in risk management and derivative pricing. On a portfolio level, diversification benefits are typically measured by the degree of correlation between individual securities.

Correlation, a measurement of the dependence or independence of financial time series and typically estimated quantitatively as the linear correlation coefficient of return, has always known to be plagued by a number of shortcomings. The most prominent one is that correlations between financial assets vary over time. Historical correlation (i.e., correlation estimated from past data) depends on the phase of the economic cycle and the length of the time series, among other things. Implied correlation (i.e., correlation parameters backed out of market prices of instruments) is much harder to observe than, say, implied volatility due to the scarcity of correlation products traded. There are also other issues in the field of correlation, such as directionality (correlation increasing during a crisis) and autocorrelation (trending correlation).

Empirical evidence suggests that correlation between assets (and asset classes) not only varies significantly over time, but also *increases* during times of financial crisis of 2007–2008. This is particularly problematic from a risk management point of view because it suggests that diversification benefits and hedge efficiencies are diminishing precisely when they are needed the most.[37] It is worth noting that there also exist pairs of financial measures for which correlation *decreases* during crisis. For example, short-dated interest rates and short-dated credit spreads tend to be positively correlated during normal (calm) times, but then exhibit a stark decline in correlation during times of crisis (turmoil regimes). Figure 7.28 illustrates this for three-month US Treasury bill yields and three-month TED spreads.[38] It is interesting that the COVID-19 pandemic does not appear to follow the usual pattern of a *financial market* crisis, at least as of May 2020.

It is not difficult to see why correlations between many financial market assets are changing significantly during periods of stress. During calm times, most trading activity is triggered by random events, e.g., a bank entering into an interest-rate swap, a pension fund buying particular types of securities or a corporate customer hedging some currency exposure. When this kind of "noise" orders are directed at broker-dealers, they will use discretion to hedge (i.e., balance their trading book) according to where they see relative value. This causes flow to spread across various financial market products, limiting the knock-on effect of one transaction in a particular product

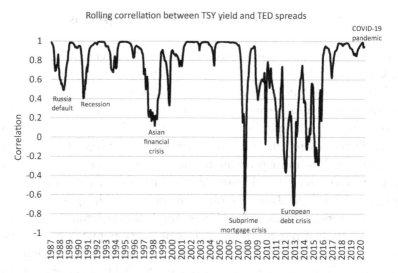

Fig. 7.28 Rolling correlation between 3-month Treasury yields and TED spreads (Rolling one-year correlation calculated from daily data (*Source* Federal Reserve Bank of St. Louis 2020)

on another specific instrument. For example, one broker-dealer may hedge a 9-year interest-rate swap with a corporate customer by entering into an off-setting 10-year swap in the inter-dealer broker market, another may trade in 10-year on-the-run government bonds, yet another may establish a position in 10-year corporate bonds.

However, during times of market stress,[39] market participants are often forced by institutional rules to act in a non-discretionary way. A mutual fund manager facing significant net redemptions must liquidate part of the portfolio in a proportional matter; a broker-dealer forced to scale down risk limits on short notice will likely, as a first step, *proportionally* reduce risk limits to most of its trading books, forcing trading desks of all kind of asset classes to sell off inventory; investor sentiment switching from risk-on to risk-off causes portfolio rebalancing flows from risky assets into what are perceived to be less-risky assets (e.g., stocks into bonds), creating simultaneously executed flows in otherwise hardly correlated markets. A crisis typically limits market participants' ability to postpone trades, to look for proxy hedges or to view the other market participants' behavior as a cause for relative value opportunities that suggest entering into opposite transactions. Instead, heard-like behavior can be observed. Lock-step trade executions then create high correlations between assets that exhibited only little joint-movement prior to the crisis.

In the context of client conversations, you will likely have to defend any implicit or explicit correlation assumption within your analysis or pricing. The client may suspect that there is only an illusion of correlation, created through a careful selection of historical data. The client may fear that correlation is only caused temporarily by current market participants' behavior[40] and that there may be a *regime shift* down the road. Correlation is not just some statistical relationship, but something you are expected to have an explicit view on and a story to tell about.

7.8   Remaining Humble in Derivative Space

Some of the most intelligent, yet humble people I have met throughout my career have been either working in derivative space (i.e., trading or marketing derivative products) or have developed a strong derivative mindset. It is easy to see why. There are so many different ways to model derivative products, to calibrate any given model and to interpret the results from a risk management perspective, that no derivative-savvy person would ever claim to know everything. The more you know about derivatives, the more you realize you don't know, to paraphrase Aristotle's famous saying.

I remember one situation in my early days working as a desk strategist at a derivative sales desk. My job was to ferret out market dislocations that would lead to actionable trade ideas. I had just finished a relative value spreadsheet that compares US government bonds on an asset swap basis.[41] My calculations flagged one bond that traded above par to be cheaper than a neighboring bond that traded below par (on an asset swap basis). I was very excited about this observation and was ready to propose buying the cheap and selling the rich security (in a so-called *bond switch*) to clients. Luckily, one of my colleagues advised be to speak to an experienced derivative trader at our proprietary trading desk first. When I proudly presented my findings to him, he listened patiently, smiled and then asked me a series of questions. Did you account for the fact that one of the two securities is the cheapest-to-deliver instrument into a futures contract? How did you adjust for different funding levels (in repo)? Which stub rates did you use for the swap calculations? Did you consider that some investors are reluctant to buy bond trading above par for tax reasons? How much is the duration difference "worth on the curve"? Which type of asset swap calculations did you perform (true asset swap or yield-yield asset swap[42])? At the time, I was discouraged and disappointed that the experienced trader identified so many potential errors in my analysis. I then tried to incorporate all those aspects in my analysis. Not surprisingly, there was no longer a dislocation between the two bonds.

As a derivative-savvy person, the first reaction to any inconsistency in prices is typically not that there is some sort of market dislocation, rather that there must be something conceptually wrong in the way the relative value model had been set up or how it was calibrated. Put differently, a lot of faith is given in the market's ability to price securities in a non-arbitrage matter, while one's own ability to know something other market participants have been missing is constantly questioned.

How a misplaced trust in models can get you into hot water can be illustrated by the following story:

> A young finance professor was dating a girl that lived in the same city. One day she suggested to him to move into the same apartment. That way, they would save the money for the second apartment. The finance professor applied option theory to the situation and responded: If we move together, we save rent. However, if we were to separate at a later point, one of us would have to find a new apartment, which is time consuming and difficult. Therefore, keeping the second apartment is an option worth paying for in case the relationship would not last. His girlfriend reflected on his answer, then responded: Well, if you don't have enough confidence in our relationship then let's break up now. She then dumped him.

The story illustrates how the girlfriend had apparently applied linear thinking, while the finance professor seemingly developed a richer model for decision making. Only that his model was not rich enough, ignoring completely findings from signaling theory. By assigning a high option value to the keep-the-second-apartment option, the professor revealed having used a high implied volatility. A high implied volatility in terms of a relationship equates to doubts about the outcome of dating. Sending this signal causes a reassessment of the situation by the girlfriend. Ironically, by trying to *hedge* the worst-case scenario (break-up), the professor *caused* it.[43]

What this fictitious story shows is that one should never have full confidence about pricing and risk management of derivatives. What derivatives are teaching us is to remain humble and to keep asking "what am I missing?" Before you know it, you will apply this type of skepticism to financial instruments outside of derivatives, or even everyday life.

Notes

1. *Inflation-linked Bonds* (also called *Inflation Bonds* or *Linkers*) are government bonds designed to offset the capital eroding effects of inflation. The interest rate remains fixed, but the principal is adjusted to match changes in a price index. In the U.S., they are called Treasury Inflation Protected Securities, or TIPS. By comparing the yield of a nominal (regular) bond to the yield of an inflation-linked bond (same issuer and same maturity), the break-even inflation rate can be calculated. It is the inflation rate that equates the expected return of an inflation-linked bond and a comparable nominal bond.
2. Boesler (2012).
3. Some people suspect it has something to do with the church's roughly $200 million sex abuse debt. See Herguth (2019).
4. Examples include: stocks (e.g., option on IBM stock), bonds (e.g., Treasury bond future), commodities (e.g., gold future), indices (e.g., S&P500 futures), interest rates (e.g., LIBOR caps), foreign exchange rates (e.g., Dollar-Yen forward), credit quality (e.g., credit default swap), economic indicators (e.g., consumer price index futures), climate indexes (e.g., heating degree days weather derivative), real estate (e.g., National Council of Real Estate Investment Fiduciaries Property Index swap), other derivatives (e.g., option on futures).
5. Parts of Iraq, Syria, Turkey and Iran in modern days.
6. It is a letter from a man named Nanni to a merchant Ea-nasir complaining that the wrong grade of copper ore has been delivered after a gulf voyage and about misdirection and delay of a further delivery.
7. Soft commodities are agricultural commodities as opposed to those that are mined.
8. For a more detailed analysis of the hedging needs at the US brewer Anheuser-Busch, see Tuckman (2015).
9. For example: If CME margin requirements are 15%, one can "control" $100,000 of assets with only $15,000 (deposited as initial margin).
10. Hull (2018, 156–157).
11. Hull (2018, 158–159).
12. Two corporate customers entering into a bilateral transaction directly with each other creates a number of disadvantages: Transaction needs to occur at precisely the same time; the hedge structure needs to be matching each other (in this case: same maturity of bonds); the transaction volume needs to be identical (i.e., same notional); corporates potentially reveal proprietary information about their business to competitors or business partners.

13. A proxy hedge is a risk-mitigating transaction in which the risk of a specific financial instrument is reduced by establishing an offsetting position in another highly (but not perfectly) correlated financial instrument.

14. Only standardized structures are traded. Thus, for customized structures a broker-dealer may only be able to enter into a proxy hedge and will need to keep some residual risk.

15. Hull (2018, 169–173).

16. Hull (2018, 757–770).

17. Depending on whether the option is a so-called *European option*, or an *American option*. American options allow buyers to exercise the option rights at any time before and including the day of expiration. European options allow execution only on the day of expiration.

18. "Vega" is not really a Greek letter. It is represented by the Greek letter nu (ν).

19. A catchy way to phrase this is to say that it does not pay to read yesterday's newspaper.

20. In random walk theory, those are called Martingale features.

21. Variance is a statistical measure for how widely distributed numbers are. More precisely, it is the expectation of the squared deviation of a random variable from its mean.

22. The probability associated with a 1-standard deviation event is roughly 67% for a normal distribution.

23. This is only an approximation because we are ignoring the concept of time value of money and do not differentiate between actual probabilities and so-called risk-neutral probabilities. The goal here is merely to develop a rough intuition, while leaving the technical details to option-specific books like Hull (2018).

24. However, the FOMC may also hold *unscheduled* meetings as necessary to review economic and financial developments, so even for the Federal funds target rate between scheduled FOMC meetings there is some small volatility.

25. Ignoring the potential intrinsic value of an option at this point.

26. This is to make the trees of the binomial tree re-combining, i.e., an up-move followed by a down-move gives the same value as a down-move followed by an up-move.

27. For simplicity, we ignore the need for discounting the probability-weighted option payoffs (occurring at option expiration) to the present day when calculating the option value as of today.

28. $\sigma_{\text{semi-annual}} = \sigma_{\text{annual}} \times \sqrt{1/2}$.

29. The Black-Scholes formula is simple enough for the first hand-held computers that came out in the 1970s to perform the calculation so that they could be used on the trading floors of major exchanges.

30. I have never ever heard anyone on Wall Street refer to it as Black-Scholes-Merton formula, as it is called in most textbooks to give credit to Robert Merton, who independently developed the model at the

same time as Black and Scholes. There is just not enough time for this kind of political correctness on the trading floor.

31. The model was then refined by Harrison and Kreps in 1979 to use equivalent martingale measures.

32. This is achieved by a Brownian motion à la Bachelier plus a Poisson-like jump process. The model has some other useful features, such as the ability to price options on underlyings that pay dividend or the introduction of risk-neutral valuation.

33. There are two unrealistic assumptions made here: First, that 9- and 10-year yields move in lockstep, i.e. that the yield curve only moves in a parallel manner. Second, that the spread between bond and swap yields (i.e., in case of government bonds the so-called swap spread) does not change.

34. Tuckman (2012, chapter 8).

35. Unfortunately, this is only approximately true. Every time the floating leg of the swap (e.g., linked to EURIBOR) sets, the combination of bond and swap has some duration risk that may require fine-tuning in the hedge. Also, the relationship between bond and swap yield may change over time (as swap spreads have varying degrees of directionality), requiring changes to the hedge ratio between bonds and swaps.

36. In fact, in the absence of transaction costs instantaneous delta-hedging would equate to option replication and should result in an expected P&L of close to zero under certain assumptions (unchanged implied volatility, log-normal distribution of interest rates etc.)

37. See, for example, Chua et al. (2009).

38. The TED (short for "Treasury-Eurodollar") spread is the difference between the tree-month Treasury bill rate and the three-month LIBOR rate. It is widely used as an indicator of credit risk as it can be viewed as a measurement for the difference in credit quality between US Treasury debt and high-grade bank debt. It represents the risk premium associated with uninsured bank liabilities.

39. One form of stress would be a significant deterioration in asset prices, forcing market participants to realize mark-to-market losses and to adjust their leverage according to capital requirements; another form of stress would simply be a higher volatility in the market, resulting calculated Var's to exceed Var limits and causing deleveraging activity.

40. For example, the volatility-based hedge fund Artemis Capital Management opined in a letter to investors that the increase of global correlations may be related to government interventions (money printing, quantitative easing, etc.) as such stimulus triggers buying of assets across the board. See: Unified Risk Theory: Correlation, Vol, M3, and Pineapples, third Quarter 2010 letter to investors from Artemis Capital Management LLP from September 30, 2010.

41. An asset swap is a combination of an asset, here the U.S. government bond, and an interest rate swap that has matching cash flows and cash flow dates.

This eliminates, at least in theory, most interest rate (or duration) risk and makes assets with different maturity dates and coupon rates comparable to each other.

42. In a *true asset swap* (also called *par-par asset swap*), the swap is structured such that the client invests par (100), while the difference to the traded price is received by or subsidized from the swap desk. In the case of an asset trading above par, the client would pay 100 while the swap desk would subsidize the difference. Since an above-par instrument can be assumed to have a higher coupon compared to an otherwise identical par instrument (same credit quality, same maturity, etc.), the upfront payment received from the swap desk is being amortized via higher coupon payments. In a *yield-yield asset swap*, the swap spread is not computed based on a swap that matches all cash flows of the underlying bond. Rather, it is the yield spread between the asset and a market-swap of similar maturity. The asset swap would be executed on a DV01-neutral basis, so that a 1-bp move in yield causes the same dollar amount of price change in both the asset and the swap.

43. Maybe this is alike to the so-called observer effect in Physics, suggesting that a measurement within a system cannot be made without affecting the system. By attempting to measure the break-up probability and communicating this to his girlfriend, the professor actually changed the break-up probability.

References

BIS. 2019. OTC Derivatives Notional Amount Outstanding by Risk Category. https://www.bis.org/statistics/about_derivatives_stats.htm. Accessed on January 20, 2020.

Boesler, Matthew. 2012. CHART OF THE DAY: This Is the Most Powerful Chart We've Seen Yet That Shows the Market Is Afraid of Mitt Romney. Yahoo! News Business Insider, 12 October. https://news.yahoo.com/chart-day-obamas-election-odds-173201032.html. Accessed on January 20, 2020.

Chua, David B., Mark Kritzman, and Sébastien Page. 2009. The Myth of Diversification. *Journal of Portfolio Management* 36 (1): 26–35.

Fama, Eugene F. 1970. Efficient Capital Markets: A Review of Theory and Empirical Work. *Journal of Finance* 25 (2). Papers and Proceedings of the Twenty-Eighth Annual Meeting of the American Finance Association New York, NY December 28–30, 1969 (May 1970), 383–417.

Federal Reserve Bank of St. Louis. 2020. TED Spread. https://fred.stlouisfed.org/series/TEDRATE. Accessed on May 17, 2020.

Herguth, Robert. 2019. Much of $100 Million from Sale of Holy Name Lot to Go to Church Sex-Abuse Debts. *Chicago Sun Times*, 8 February. https://chicago.

suntimes.com/2019/2/8/18317337/much-of-100-million-from-sale-of-holy-name-lot-to-go-to-church-sex-abuse-debts. Accessed on January 20, 2020.

Hull, John C. 2018. *Options, Futures, and Other Derivatives.* Boston, MA: Pearson Prentice Hall.

Tuckman, Bruce. 2012. *Fixed Income Securities: Tools for Today's Markets.* Hoboken, NJ: Wiley.

Tuckman, Bruce. 2015. In Defense of Derivatives: From Beer to the Financial Crisis. CATO Institute, Policy Analysis No. 781, 1–34.

8

Exercises

8.1 Exercises for Chapter 2 (A Taxonomy of the Banking Business)

8.1.1 Section 2.2.1

It appears that global investment banks are increasingly becoming American. Find reasons why the European share of the investment-banking market share is declining.[1]

8.1.2 Section 2.2.2

After the financial crisis of 2007–2008, demand for separating commercial banking from the volatile investment-banking business gained traction in political discussions. However, banks successfully lobbied against legislation that enforces such separation. Discuss benefits and disadvantages of allowing bank to engage in both investment and commercial banking.

© The Author(s) 2020
F. Tata, *Corporate and Investment Banking*,
https://doi.org/10.1007/978-3-030-44341-2_8

8.2   Exercises for Chapter 3 (Fundamentals of the Banking Business)

8.2.1   Section 3.1.1

Can you think of a financial market participant (firm) that has some units considered to belong to the buy-side and other units viewed as sell-side? What are potential problems in such a situation?

8.2.2   Section 3.1.2

Assume a bank with revenues primarily coming from maturity transformation. How is this bank's profitability impacted by an inversion of the yield curve? What could the bank do to mitigate the negative effects?

8.2.3   Section 3.1.3

Access the latest *Global Monitoring Report on Non-Bank Financial Intermediation* published annually by the Financial Stability Board (https://www.fsb.org). Within the group of shadow banks, what is the share of assets held by hedge funds? Do hedge funds have a smaller or larger market impact than what their percentage share of assets suggests? Why?

8.2.4   Section 3.1.4

Research differences and commonalities between the London Stock Exchange and the New York Stock Exchange. Consider aspects like breadth of listed securities, market capitalization and origin of listed corporations, daily trade volume and trading schedule.

8.2.5   Section 3.1.5

America's pension funds fell short of their projected returns in 2019, while already being underfunded by as much as $4.2 trillion.[2] At the same time, they tripled their investments into *alternative* assets (including hedge funds, private equity and real estate funds) since 2005 to almost 27% in 2019.[3] Discuss potential problems arising from this situation.

8.2.6 Section 3.1.8

How would the efficiency of financial markets be impacted if *all* investors would become passive (index) investors or were to invest into index funds only?

8.2.7 Section 3.1.11

It is mid-June, one day prior to a scheduled FOMC meeting. The current Fed funds target rate is 1.5% and there is the perceived risk that the Fed could raise rates. A client calls you and asks what you think the probability is for a Fed hike.

Available information:

- The July Fed funds futures trades at a price of 98.445.
- There is no scheduled FOMC meeting in July.
- The Fed is not expected to *lower* the Fed funds target rate at the June meeting.
- The FOMC is expected move rates in 25 bp increments.
- The convexity adjustment between futures and forwards is neglectable.
- During the months of July, the Fed funds effective rate has historically traded an average of 3 bp above the target rate due to pressure early in the month on the back of quarter-end followed by the July 4th holiday.
- 20 economists have been polled by Bloomberg about what their market expectation for the July FOMC meeting is. All of them are reporting an unchanged target rate as the most likely scenario.

8.2.8 Section 3.2.1

You are a research analyst preparing a publication in May. You would like to get a sense about what the implied probability is for a near-term increase of short-dated interest rates up to, but not exceeding 50 bp, from current (forward) levels. You don't have much time and the calculation can be approximative. The only information you have available are the Eurodollar futures and options quotes provided in Table 8.1.

Eurodollar futures prices are determined by the market's forecast of the 3-month London Interbank Offered Rate (LIBOR). The futures prices are derived by subtracting the implied interest rate from 100. That price reflects the market's expectation of 3-month LIBOR in the future. If interest rates rise, the price of the futures contract falls, and vice versa.

Table 8.1 Eurodollar futures and options quotes

Contract	Price/premium	Delta
June Eurodollar futures	96.00	1.00
June 96.00-strike call	0.29	0.50
June 96.50-strike call	0.11	0.25
June 96.00-strike put	0.29	0.50
June-95.50-strike put	0.11	0.25

8.2.9 Section 3.2.2

You are a derivative trader. A particular call option trades at a price of €10 with a delta of roughly 50%. The underlying trades at €100. According to your own pricing model, the option is worth €8 with a delta of 40%.

You believe the market to inefficient and want to sell one option at €10, hoping to make €2 if the market price converges to your own model price. You also hedge the delta-exposure through the purchase of a delta-equivalent amount of the underlying.

Should you buy €40 worth of the underlying (hedge according to your model) or €50 of underlying (hedge according to market)?

8.2.10 Section 3.2.3

Which of the following transactions are pure (riskless) arbitrage opportunities?

- You are offered a free lottery ticket that has a non-zero probability of a profit (positive cash flow) in the future.
- You are offered to buy a (risk-free) government bond below par (at a price below 100).
- Instead of depositing money at negative interest rates (in a negative interest rate environment) in a bank account, you place your money in a deposit box.

8.2.11 Section 3.2.4

Which of the following cost would you assign to *monitoring expenditures*, *bonding expenditures* and *residual losses* according to the Jensen/Meckling framework?

- Cost of shareholders hiring an auditing firm;
- Cost of annual employee review;

- Cost of salesperson taking client out for dinner;
- Cost of bailing out a failing bank to taxpayers.

8.3   Exercises for Chapter 4 (Sales)

8.3.1   Section 4.1

Why is the clean desk policy also important from a risk management perspective?

8.3.2   Section 4.2.1

The sales departments of second-tier broker-dealers (that are trying to increase market share) are often composed of more senior salespeople compared to those working for highly ranked broker-dealers. From an onboarding perspective, how can this be explained?

8.3.3   Section 4.2.2

The current price of a bond is quoted as "102-16 at 102-16+" by your trading desk. A client asks for an offer for $200 million. As a junior salesperson, you accidentally quote the trader's bid. The trader assumes having bought the bond and hedges accordingly (by selling $200 million worth of the bond in the inter-dealer broker market). When confirming the trade with your client, you notice your mistake.

What is the trading desk's loss if the trader agrees to the execution you just confirmed with the client and now has to adjust the hedge accordingly (i.e., needs to buy back $400 million in the market)? Assume two scenarios:

- The market price has not changed;
- Due to the client's buying in the market, the market price has ticked up to "102-17 at 102-17+."

8.3.4   Section 4.2.3

Think of reasons why salespeople are typically keen to help hedge fund clients to iteratively develop their trade ideas? Why are hedge funds less inclined to work with the sell-side's sales force on trade details?

8.3.5 Section 4.2.4

Try to define the fine line between providing market color and revealing confidential client flow information.

8.3.6 Section 4.2.5

How important do you think are traders' axes in financial markets that are highly competitive and have very tight bid-ask spreads?

8.3.7 Section 4.2.6

Many successful salespeople make regular use of research publications, put out by their own research department. Discuss a few ways how a salesperson can deepen the client relationship by using research.

8.3.8 Section 4.2.7

Why is it in the best interest of buy-side institutions to prevent its own employees from going out with sell-side employees (wine and dine and other forms of client entertainment), even though the sell-side firms are regularly picking up the tab?

8.3.9 Section 4.2.8

Do you see a potential conflict of interest when the sell-side is "educating" the buy-side about complex financial market products (such as mortgage products or derivatives)?

8.3.10 Section 4.3

Looking at the agency relationship between a broker-dealer (principal) and a salesperson (agent), which potential conflict of interest can you identify if the salesperson's long-term career plan is to apply for a job with one of his/her current clients?

8.3.11 Section 4.4

Sell-side firms often put mid-career sales and research people in charge of suggesting new trade ideas (often on a daily basis) to the buy-side. There is a somewhat cynical explanation for this: It makes no sense to put a very *junior* employee in charge of trade idea generation, as that person lacks the market/product knowledge and skill set required to identify trade opportunities; it makes little sense to have a very *experienced* market professional look for trade ideas on a daily basis either, because that person knows too much about potential risks in supposedly good trade ideas and will find good reasons against most suggested trade ideas. In which sense does the sell-side utilize cognitive biases to their advantage here? What are the consequences of this for the buy-side?

8.4   Exercises for Chapter 5 (Trading)

8.4.1   Section 5.1.1

There are situations where market participants that are typically considered market takers start acting like market makers. For example, a pension fund that needs to buy securities could, instead of lifting the offer (buying at the offer price) of a dedicated market maker (broker-dealer, etc.), announce to be a "bid" for the securities. What would be the reason for such behavior? How do you think the dedicated market makers react to the unexpected market making behavior of the former market taker?

8.4.2   Section 5.1.3

A phenomenon observed by most people selling goods on their own stand at a flea market is the following: During the first hour, a lot of transactions take place, creating an optimistic mood. But then, for hours hardly anything sells any more (unless prices are lowered). How can this be explained by adverse selection and order flow toxicity?

How can order flow toxicity help explain why over the counter (OTC) markets often provide more liquidity than anonymous electronic markets? In OTC markets, the client has to identify himself/herself by name, reveal the direction of trade as well as the trading quantity.

8.4.3 Section 5.1.4

The financial market regulation MiFID II includes the following provision:

> Without prejudice to Regulation (EU) No 596/2014, for the purposes of the provisions of this Regulation concerning client order handling, client orders should not be treated as otherwise comparable if they are received by different media and it would not be practicable for them to be treated sequentially. Any use by an investment firm of information relating to a pending client order in order to deal on own account in the financial instruments to which the client order relates, or in related financial instruments, should be considered a misuse of that information. However, the mere fact that market makers or bodies authorised to act as counterparties confine themselves to pursuing their legitimate business of buying and selling financial instruments, or that persons authorised to execute orders on behalf of third parties confine themselves to carrying out an order dutifully, should not in itself be deemed to constitute a misuse of information.[4]

How does this relate to front running and the concept of first to market?

8.4.4 Section 5.1.5

You suspect that stocks perform better on days on which there is an unusually high trading volume. From a particular stock exchange, you obtain a historical data set, showing the opening price, the closing price and the total daily trading volume for each listed stock. You back-test the following trading strategy: "Buy a stock at the open if the daily trading volume is twice the average trading volume of the previous week, and then sell the same stock on the at the closing price." Backtesting suggests superior profits. Identify flaws with this backtesting strategy.

8.4.5 Sections 5.2.1 and 5.2.2

You just assumed the role of a junior swap trader on the derivative desk. You are asked to put a price on a 10-year swap deal. The market price according to an inter-dealer broker screen is 1.2%, while your internal pricing model suggests a model price of 1.3%. Which price should you quote? What should you do?

8.4.6 Section 5.2.4

Conduct a P&L decomp for the following situation: A US dollar-based portfolio manager invests $100 million into (risk-free) UK government bond, denominated in Pound Sterling (GBP) that trades at par (i.e., at a price of 100) with the then-prevailing exchange rate being 0.77 GBP/USD. On the following day, the UK bond price falls to 99 and the exchange rate changes to 0.76 GBP/USD.

8.4.7 Section 5.3

Assume the following situation: You are a flow trader, making markets in a product for two type of clients: mutual funds and hedge funds. One day, all your mutual fund clients tell you that they will stop trading with you because they are going to execute their orders on some electronic trading platform. Now you are stuck with trading exclusively with hedge funds. What is the problem?

8.4.8 Section 5.4

Why do you think clients are not so happy about their broker-dealer's flow traders also engaging in prop trading?

8.4.9 Section 5.5

How do you expect potential principal-agent problems between hedge fund traders and investors into the hedge fund created by hedge funds traders' compensation schemes impact the hedge fund managers' investment behavior?

Find arguments supporting and arguments contradicting the notion that hedge funds engaged in statistical and latency arbitrage are beneficial to the overall market, because they provide liquidity to other market participants and cause market prices to reflect new information more rapid.

8.4.10 Section 5.6

A company with total assets of $100 is financed with $50 of debt and $50 of equity. The interest rate on debt (i.e., r_{debt}) is 10%, so total interest payments are $5. The return on assets (i.e., r_{assets}) is assumed to have the following possibilities:

- 30% return on assets with a probability of 30%;
- 10% return on assets with a probability of 38%;
- 5% return on assets with a probability of 30%;
- −50% return on assets with a probability of 2%.

Calculate the *expected* (average) return on assets. Calculate the return on equity (i.e., r_{equity}) in all four scenarios. Calculate the *expected* (average) return on equity. Discuss the leverage effect.

8.4.11 Section 5.7

Write a code in any programming language you know that executes the following simple trading algorithm: A buy order for 5000 stocks is divided into five sub-orders of 1000 stocks each, to be executed every ten minutes. What are possible advantages of splitting larger orders into smaller child orders? What are possible risks?

8.5   Exercises for Chapter 6 (Research)

8.5.1 Section 6.2.1

You are a sell-side research analyst, and for weeks, you are publishing the opinion that all markets you are supposed to cover are arbitrage-free and security prices are trading at fair value levels. Eventually, the head of sales starts complaining about you to the head of research. What could be the reason for this?

8.5.2 Section 6.3.1

Some attention-seeking research analysts are inclined to issue buy recommendations based on overly optimistic profit projections. What could be the problem with that?

8.5.3 Section 6.3.2

At least one large universal bank has an "Alternative View" research team that promotes ideas that are, more often than not, contrary to the so-called house view published by the regular strategy group. Apart from a potential entertainment value, what is the benefit to clients in receiving conflicting strategy calls from the same bank?

8.5.4 Section 6.3.6

Planes broadcast their position and speed, among other things, through a technology called ADS-B (Automatic Dependent Surveillance-Broadcast).[5] ADS-B receivers can be bought for less than $50. Thus, anyone can now decode and display ADS-B transmissions to track flights in real time. Think of ways to use alternative data extracted from aircraft-tracking in the context of financial market research.

8.5.5 Section 6.4.2

In the years 2002 and 2003, the slope of the 10- to 30-year part of the swap yield curve ("10s30s") was historically unusually steep (some 80–100 bp). During that time, many research analysts pointed out that during the previous 10 years, the difference between the 30-year and the 10-year swap yield was on average 30–35 bp and that the curve inverted in 10s30s only for a very brief period between February and August 2000. One class of products that got heavily promoted at the time was the so-called non-inversion note. A non-inversion note is a structured note that pays an above-market coupon, contingent on the yield curve not being inverted (i.e., upward-sloped). Discuss the risks of non-inversion notes (from an investor's perspective). What kind of economic events could lead to losses?

8.5.6 Section 6.5

Analyze the sample trade idea provided in Box 8.1 with respect to the critical elements of a trade idea (as listen in Table 6.2). Which elements are included? Which are missing?

Box 8.1: Sample trade idea

Trade Idea: Sell August–September FF futures spread

- The front end of the yield curve has re-steepened following today's strong economic data.
- Fed fund futures now imply a roughly 75% chance of a 25 bp Fed hike in August and a chance of additional hiking in September.
- The risk-return profile of positioning against two consecutive 25 bp hikes looks attractive now.

Today's jobs report triggered a bear steepening, as market participants prepared themselves for further tightening. August Fed fund future contracts, closing at an implied Fed fund effective rate of 5.395%, imply a roughly 76.5% probability of another 25 bp hike on the next FOMC meeting in August. September Fed fund futures trade at a 7 bp higher implied rate, suggesting more tightening to come afterwards.

The slope between August and September Fed fund futures contracts appears steep on a risk-return perspective, as this spread should tighten for most of the possible FOMC outcomes on the following two meeting. We recommend that investors consider the following trade to take advantage of this recent re-steepening of the front-end yield curve.

Trade construction

Sell 1000 contracts FFQ6 (August-06)	@ 94.605	
Buy 1000 contracts FFU6 (September-06)	@ 94.535	
	7 bp	7/5/2006 closing levels

Economic motivation

We restrict our analysis to nine distinct scenarios for the outcome of the following two FOMC meeting: No move, 25 bp easing or 25 bp tightening on the August-8 meeting, followed by either one of the three outcomes on the September-20 meeting. We ignore moves of 50 bp or larger as well as intra-FOMC-meeting moves.

The following table summarizes the results. First, we assume potential Fed moves for the following two FOMC meetings. "25" represents a 25 bp tightening, "0" means unchanged and "−25" stands for a 25 bp easing. We also list the last occurrence of each stated scenarios (including the previous Fed move). For the scenario of two consecutive easing moves (−25/−25) we looked for the last time the Fed tightened, then eased on the following two meetings.

Then, we calculate the fair-value implied FF-rate, given the FF target assumptions for each scenario. Finally, we state the resulting August–September FF futures spread and the corresponding P&L of an August–September FF futures spread trade established at 7/5/2006 closing levels.

FF move									
8-August	25	25	25	0	0	0	−25	−25	−25
20-September	25	0	−25	25	0	−25	−25	0	25
Last occurance	6/06	6/00	10/84	11/99	8/00	7/86	4/85	5/81	3/84
FF target									
8-Aug	5.50	5.50	5.50	5.25	5.25	5.25	5.00	5.00	5.00
20-September	5.75	5.50	5.25	5.50	5.25	5.00	4.75	5.00	5.25
FFQ6 rate	5.44	5.44	5.44	5.25	5.25	5.25	5.06	5.06	5.06
FFU6 rate	5.59	5.50	5.41	5.34	5.25	5.16	4.91	5.00	5.09
Spread (bp)	14.8	6.05	−2.7	8.75	0	−8.75	−14.8	−6.05	2.7
P&L (bp)	−7.8	0.95	9.7	−1.75	7.0	15.75	21.8	13.05	4.3

While two consecutive 25 bp tightening moves result in a 7.8 bp loss, seven out of nine scenarios show a positive P&L. Tightening followed by on-hold, and on-hold followed by tightening, two scenarios with a high perceived probability, are close to P&L-neutral. Other combinations result in a significantly positive expected profit.

Risks

The main risk of the trade is a continuing steepening of the front end of the yield curve, i.e. a perceived increasing chance of two consecutive 25 bp tightening moves. Even worse would be a potential 50 bp tightening at the September FOMC.

8.5.7 Section 6.6

It is your very first day in the research department. Your boss is out visiting client and all research analysts appear to be busy preparing for an upcoming quarterly strategy publication. After approaching many strategists, you are finally asked by one of the senior analysts to develop a trade idea all by yourself. "If you can come up with a good one, we'll put it into the quarterly publication," you are told. You suspect that the other analysts just don't feel like dealing with you right now and that this assignment is merely to keep you busy. However, you decide that you need to impress the other strategists by coming up with something good. How could you go about finding a trade idea?

8.5.8 Section 6.7

In 2003, a $1.4 billion settlement between Wall Street securities firms and regulators sought to eradicate conflicts of interest that led analysts to issue overly positive research on companies, a phenomenon designed to help win investment-banking deals. Research the events surrounding this regulatory enforcement action and answer the following questions[6]:

- Which conflicts of interest were discovered?
- Who was harmed by the research practice?
- Which measures are to be taken as part of the settlement to reduce conflicts of interest?
- Are all conflicts of interest eliminated?

8.6 Exercises for Chapter 7 (Derivatives)

8.6.1 Section 7.3

A company would like to hedge its own profitability and inquires with an investment bank whether it could purchase derivatives on its own P&L. Where lies the problem?

8.6.2 Section 7.4

The corporate finance department of a US dollar-based producer expects to receive €10 million in six weeks when their goods are expected to arrive in Europe and the importer makes a payment, as promised. To protect against adverse changes in the EUR/USD exchange rate, the producer enters into an FX forward contract with a bank, essentially locking in the USD-value of €10 million six weeks from now. Has the US-based producer eliminated all FX risk? If not, what could still happen?

8.6.3 Section 7.5

You are long one corn futures contract trading on the Chicago Mercantile Exchange (CME). On the last trade date of the contract, you realize that you are not prepared to take delivery of some 127 metric tons of corn bushels. What should you do?

8.6.4 Section 7.6

Think of reasons why corporate customers tend to do their swap business with banks (acting as intermediaries), as opposed to finding other corporations that look for offsetting exposures and then to trade with them directly?

8.6.5 Section 7.7

What is the fundamental difference between a long forward and a long call option?

8.6.6 Section 7.7.4

You are head of a derivative trading desk. One of your traders tells you that he/she has various derivative positions in his/her trading book, but all risks measured by the Greeks cancel each other out perfectly. He/she asks to go on a 6-week vacation. What problem do you see?

8.6.7 Section 7.7.6

Why going through the trouble of calculating option prices on *binomial trees* when there are alternative closed-form solutions for option prices, such as *Black–Scholes*? Can you think of a reason?

8.6.8 Section 7.7.9

Assume being a manager at corporation XYZ and you have been awarded 1000 stocks as part of your management incentive compensation. You don't want to have any economic exposure to XYZ stocks, but your employment contract prohibits you from selling stock awards within the first three years. However, you are free to create any XYZ exposure synthetically in the derivatives markets.

The derivative type you chose to use for hedging purpose is: XYZ stock at-the-money (ATM) call options (either long or short); each call option gives the right to buy 100 shares. Assume the delta of ATM call options to be roughly 0.5.

Calculate the delta-equivalent position in call options (hedge ratio) that creates an offsetting exposure to the price risk of 1000 XYZ stocks.

8.6.9 Section 7.7.10

During the financial crisis of 2007–2008, some market "dislocations" were quoted with z-scores of 7 or higher in some research analysts' reports. Z-scores indicate how many standard deviations an observation is above or below the mean. With daily data and assuming a standard normal distribution, one would expect a (one-sided) 3-standard deviation event about once every 3 years, a 4-standard deviation event once every 125 years and a 5-standard deviation event once every 14 thousand years. Looking at z-scores above 7 is silly, because statistically those events only happen once every 14 billion years, which is about the age of the universe.

Address the following questions:

- What does it tell us about a chosen distribution assumption if one observes 7-standard deviation moves every 10 years or so?
- What are the consequences to hedge funds and other "relative value" players?
- How could pricing models be adjusted to capture so-called "fat tails"?

Notes

1. Hint: See Goodhart and Schoenmaker (2016).
2. Gillers (2019).
3. Bowen (2019).
4. European Union (2016, Recital 110).
5. Bachman (2019).
6. Hint: See Labaton (2003).

References

Bachman, Justin. 2019. Hedge Funds Are Tracking Private Jets to Find the Next Megadeal. *Bloomberg Businessweek*, 2 July. https://www.bloomberg.com/news/articles/2019-07-02/hedge-funds-are-tracking-private-jets-to-find-the-next-megadeal. Accessed on January 20, 2020.

Bowen, Jay. 2019. Pension Funds Chased Alternative Investments After the Crisis. They Missed the Bull Market. *Barron's*, 26 August. https://www.barrons.com/articles/biotechs-la-jolla-pharma-and-milestone-see-big-stock-purchases-51579089613. Accessed on January 20, 2020.

European Union. 2016. Commission Delegated Regulation (EU) 2017/565 of 25 April 2016 Supplementing Directive 2014/65/EU of the European Parliament and of the Council as Regards Organisational Requirements and Operating Conditions for Investment Firms and Defined Terms for the Purposes of That Directive. *Official Journal of the European Union*, L 87/1, 25 April. https://eur-lex.europa.eu/legal-content/EN/TXT/?uri=CELEX%3A32017R0565. Accessed on January 20, 2020.

Gillers, Heather. 2019. America's Pension Funds Fell Short in 2019. *The Wall Street Journal*, 6 August. https://www.wsj.com/articles/americas-pension-funds-fell-short-in-2019-11565092806. Accessed on January 20, 2020.

Goodhart, Charles, and Dirk Schoenmaker. 2016. The Global Investment Banks Are Now All Becoming American: Does That Matter for Europeans? *Journal of Financial Regulation* 2 (2): 163–181.

Labaton, Stephen. 2003. Wall Street Settlement: The Overview; 10 Wall St. Firms Reach Settlement in Analyst Inquiry. *New York Times*, 29 April. https://www.nytimes.com/2003/04/29/business/wall-street-settlement-overview-10-wall-st-firms-reach-settlement-analyst.html. Accessed on January 20, 2020.

Index